The Sandinista Legacy

Lessons from a Political Economy in Transition

Ilja A. Luciak

University Press of Florida

*Gainesville/Tallahassee/Tampa/Boca Raton
Pensacola/Orlando/Miami/Jacksonville*

Copyright 1995 by the Board of Regents of the State of Florida
Printed in the United States of America on acid-free paper
All rights reserved

00 99 98 97 96 95 6 5 4 3 2 1

Library of Congress Cataloging-in-Publication Data

Luciak, Ilja A.
   The Sandinista legacy: lessons from a political economy in transition / by
Ilja A. Luciak.
      p.   cm.
   Includes bibliographical references and index.
   ISBN 0-8130-1369-0 (alk. paper)
      1. Nicaragua—Economic conditions—1979–   2. Nicaragua—Politics
and government—1979–1990.   3. Nicaragua—Rural conditions.
   4. Agriculture—Economic aspects—Nicaragua.   5. Cooperative
socieites—Nicaragua.   I. Title.
   HC146.L83   1995
   338.97285—dc20   95-6520

The University Press of Florida is the scholarly publishing agency for the State University
System of Florida, comprised of Florida A & M University, Florida Atlantic University,
Florida International University, Florida State University, University of Central Florida,
University of Florida, University of North Florida, University of South Florida, and
University of West Florida.

University Press of Florida
15 Northwest 15th Street
Gainesville, FL 32611

For my mother and father
For Jane and Kurt

Contents

Tables

Preface

The so-called end of history has brought on an era of revisionism. In the case of Sandinista Nicaragua this means that some of the most ardent supporters of the revolution (including high-ranking Sandinistas) have experienced a metamorphosis into critics. They maintain that the Sandinistas were never in touch with the people and that their top-down vanguardist style led to their defeat in the 1990 elections. On the right, analysts and politicians want us to believe that they deserve credit for the democratization of Nicaragua. Opinions on the Sandinista project range from "the threat of the good example" to "a failed experiment in socialism." What is the legacy of the revolution?

The reality of the Nicaraguan revolution was complex and lends itself to conflicting interpretations. I examine the Sandinista record from the perspective of the "popular classes"—the intended beneficiaries of the revolutionary project. I focus on the transformation in the rural sector, analyzing the role of rural women, small and medium farmers, and agricultural workers. An understanding of the Nicaraguan countryside is essential to overcome "the limitations of the prevailing, urban-oriented interpretations of the Sandinista revolution."[1] I reach the conclusion that the Sandinista government did deliver on many promises while it failed the people on others. This mixed record is the subject of my book. I understand my work as centered in the tradition of radical political economy, which "focuses on the social conditions under which all people will be treated equally."[2] The concern for social justice that requires political and economic democracy led me to conduct the research for this manuscript. It is a central thesis of my book that the Sandinistas rightly claim credit for the most significant legacy of the revolution—the institutionalization of representative democracy.[3]

This study analyzes the legacy of the Sandinista revolution in the context of the political economy of transition. I argue that the recent transformations in the world system—from the withering away of "Realsozialismus" in Eastern Europe and the Soviet Union to the transition from authoritarian rule toward more democratic forms of government taking place in Latin America and Africa—share a common problematic. The typical traits of these transitions come into focus if we analyze the mode of production and the hegemonic projects that emerge in these societies. Articulation, i.e., the joining of various modes of production, characterizes societies in transition. Further, the success of reformist governments and revolutionary movements that seek to initiate radical change, depends primarily upon winning the ideological struggle. Thus, governments in transitional societies pursue hegemonic projects in order to establish control over the apparatuses of state power. Although the content of these hegemonic projects differs across societies, they all share the need for the building of class coalitions. The resulting policy of national unity tends to be in conflict with the fundamental goals of the hegemonic project. In the Nicaraguan case this contradiction was manifest in the policy goals of national unity and popular hegemony.[4]

These two policies complemented and contradicted each other. Popular hegemony was supposed to transform the inherited political system to benefit the previously marginalized majority, yet success in this revolutionary goal required the cooperation of the capitalist class within a framework of national unity, i.e., attainment of the second goal. The main contradiction arising from the two policies was the probability that national unity would entail the perpetuation and even the creation of socioeconomic and political structures that were likely to be in conflict with popular hegemony. In the Nicaraguan context the course of the dialectic relationship of popular hegemony and national unity would be determined by the respective strengths of the bourgeoisie and the popular classes.

In the first chapter I discuss the political economy of transition and provide the theoretical framework for the study. I argue that social formations, from Eastern Europe and the Soviet Union to developing countries such as Nicaragua or Angola, are characterized by an "articulated" mode of production. This mode represents the combination of a pre-

dominant capitalist or communist mode (in the case of developing countries there are also remnants of a feudal mode) with new forms of production that are being introduced by the new government. The articulation of various forms of production corresponds to a political project
based on the incorporation of all sectors of society into the process of
transformation. The political forces seeking to transform society need to
establish their hegemony. Thus, a crucial question concerns the authoritarian or democratic practice of this hegemony.

In chapter two I analyze the Sandinista hegemonic project. I discuss the
Sandinista concept of democracy, examining its participatory and representative aspects. My focus is on the attempt of the Sandinistas to combine representative and participatory forms of democracy into a model
that would guarantee political democracy and at the same time ensure
popular hegemony in order to further the social transformation of
Nicaraguan society. Through an examination of the formal political
structures instituted by the revolutionary government, I establish the
extent to which the policies of national unity and popular hegemony
shaped their composition. I argue that popular hegemony was mediated
by the Frente Sandinista de Liberación Nacional's (Sandinista National
Liberation Front, FSLN) control of power.

In chapters three and four I analyze the institutionalization of new
social relations. I discuss the evolution of the two main rural grassroots
movements, the Asociación de Trabajadores del Campo (Association of
Rural Workers, ATC) and the Unión Nacional de Agricultores y
Ganaderos (National Union of Farmers and Ranchers, UNAG). It was
the main function of ATC and UNAG to represent the interests of the
rural sector in Nicaragua's political system and to transform the traditional relations of production. The rural mass organizations experienced
success and failure in confronting this important task. I am particularly
interested in determining to what degree these grassroots movements
were representative and democratic and to what extent they enjoyed
autonomy from the Sandinista party and the state.

In chapter five I evaluate the impact of the Empresa Cooperativa de
Productores Agropecuarios (Cooperative Enterprise of Agricultural Producers, ECODEPA) on the emergence of grassroots democracy in
Nicaragua. The ECODEPA project, which entailed the creation of a network of cooperative peasant stores throughout the country, is an important example for the viability of a democratic, participatory development
strategy. I focus on the quality of democratic participation by the

peasantry in the stores and the extent to which the farmers gained control over their economic future.

No study of Nicaragua's rural sector can be complete without an examination of the role of rural women, the focus of chapter six. For most of the 1980s, the Sandinista government focused on the survival of the revolution rather than lending its support to the struggle for women's rights. My discussion of female participation in the rural grassroots movements establishes that progress was made in the area of practical gender interests. Women benefited as members of the peasant and worker classes from the fundamental restructuring of productive relations. The realization of a feminist agenda, however, was never given priority.

I conclude this book with an assessment of the revolution's legacy. The greatest achievement of the Sandinistas was the consolidation of formal, representative democracy. The revolutionary government sought to construct a democratic framework that would balance the pursuit of national unity with the transformation of the political system in benefit of the popular classes. The Sandinista experiment entails valuable lessons for the political elites and the people of Eastern Europe and the successor states of the Soviet Union.

This book would not have been possible without the support and encouragement of a great number of people, only a few of whom I can recognize here. For their advice early on and their continued support I thank Peter Snow and Gerhard Loewenberg. Rose Spalding played the most important role in strengthening the arguments in this manuscript, offering kind words and constructive criticism in two reviews. Nola Reinhardt and several other anonymous reviewers made many useful suggestions to improve the final product. My discussions with Dennis Gilbert helped me to clarify many arguments. Chapter 2 was greatly improved by the sharp pen of George Herring and Kenneth Coleman. I want to express my gratitude to my brother Mikael and his wife, Claudia, as well as to Ursula and Helmut Reischer, for their interest in my work and their special kindness. Roz Frank introduced me to the farmers' movement and was a challenging companion during my initial stay in Nicaragua. Special thanks go to Maxine Riley, Kim Hedge, and Terry Kingrea for assistance in typing the manuscript at various stages.

This manuscript is based on field research conducted in Nicaragua from October 1984 to July 1985, December 1985 to February 1986, November to December 1989, and during the summers of 1988, 1989, 1992, and 1993. Research support came from a variety of sources. I am particularly grateful to the Society of the Humanities at Cornell University. A postdoctoral fellowship for the academic year 1989—1990 gave me time to reflect, conduct field research, and write a substantial part of this manuscript. I also acknowledge the support of Virginia Polytechnic Institute and State University. Several grants, among them two Humanities Summer Stipends and a grant from the Women's Research Institute and Women in World Development Program, provided support for several summers of field research. A consultancy for the Swedish International Development Authority (SIDA) allowed me to study the development of the ECODEPA project. Chapter 5 is partially based on the report I submitted to SIDA. I am particularly grateful to Daniel Asplund and Bengt Kjeller for their support and interest.

Finally, I had the opportunity to teach at the Universidad Centroamericana (UCA) in Managua during 1984—85. Jaime Whitford, UCA's dean of humanities, offered invaluable help in gaining access to government and Sandinista party officials. It was during this time that I came to admire the Nicaraguan people. Their continuing struggle for peace and justice inspired me to write this book. I am particularly grateful to Daniel Núñez, Gladys Bolt, Juan Tijerino, "Chico" Javier Saenz, Mario Pérez, Francisco "Chico" Gutierrez, and the many other people associated with the National Union of Farmers and Ranchers who have taught me that a revolution can indeed create "the new human being." Edgardo García and Denis Chavarría from the Association of Rural Workers were also very helpful. No one, however, touched my heart like Flora Abreu and Luis Enríque Ñurinda.

Excerpts from chapters 2 and 4 originally appeared in "Popular Democracy in the New Nicaragua: The Case of a Rural Mass Organization," *Comparative Politics* 20, no. 1 (October 1987): 35—55. Parts of chapters 3 and 4 appeared in "Democracy in the Nicaraguan Countryside: A Comparative Analysis of Sandinista Grassroots Movements," *Latin American Perspectives* 17, no. 3 (Summer 1990): 55—75. An earlier version of chapter 2 was included as my contribution to an edited book: Kenneth M. Coleman and George C. Herring, eds., *Understanding the Central American Crisis: Sources of Conflict, U.S. Policy, and Options for Peace* (Wilmington, Del.: Scholarly Resources, 1991). This material is protected by copyright and is used here with permission from the publishers.

Abbreviations

AMNLAE   Asociación de Mujeres Nicaragüenses, Luisa Amanda
          Espinoza (Association of Nicaraguan Women, Luisa
          Amanda Espinoza)
AMPRONAC Asociación de Mujeres ante la Problemática Nacional
          (Association of Women Confronting the National
          Problematic)
ANAP   Asociación Nacional de Agricultores Pequeños (Small
          Farmers' Association)
APP   Área de Propriedad del Pueblo (State Sector)
APT   Área de Propriedad de Trabajadores (Area of Workers'
          Property)
ASGANIC   Asociación de Ganaderos de Nicaragua (Association of
          Nicaraguan Ranchers)
ASOGAES   Asociación de Ganaderos de Estelí (Association of
          Ranchers of Estelí)
ATC   Asociación de Trabajadores del Campo (Association of
          Rural Workers)
BIR   Batallones de Infantería de Reserva (Reserve Infantry
          Battalions)
BND   Banco Nacional de Desarrollo (National Development
          Bank)
CA   comisión de abastecimiento (provisions committee)
CAAN   Confederación de Asociaciones de Algodoneros de
          Nicaragua (Confederation of Nicaraguan Cotton-
          growers)

CAD   comisión de abastecimiento departamental (departmental provisions committee)

CAN   comisión de abastecimiento nacional (national provisions committee)

CAS   Cooperativas Agrícolas Sandinistas (Sandinista Production Cooperatives)

CC   Consejos Consultivos (Consulting Councils)

CCS   Cooperativas de Crédito y Servicio (Credit and Service Cooperatives)

CD   Coordinadora Democrática (Democratic Coordinator)

CDC   Centros de Desarrollo Cooperativo (Centers for Cooperative Development)

CDS   Comités de Defensa Sandinista (Sandinista Defense Committees)

CIA   Central Intelligence Agency

COSEP   Consejo Superior de la Empresa Privada (Superior Council of Private Enterprise)

CSM   Cooperativas de "Surcos Muertos" ("Dead Fence" Cooperatives)

CST   Central Sandinista de Trabajadores (Sandinista Workers Central)

CT   Colectivos de Trabajo (Work Collectives)

CUS   Confederación de Unificación Social (Confederation for Labor Unification)

CV   comité de vigilancia (oversight committee)

CZPT   Comités Zonales de Trabajadores Permanentes (Zonal Committees of Permanent Workers)

EAP   economically active population

ECLA   United Nations Economic Commission for Latin America

ECODEPA   Empresa Cooperativa de Productores Agropecuarios (Cooperative Enterprise of Agricultural Workers)

ED   ECODEPA Departamental (Departmental ECODEPA)

EN   ECODEPA Nacional (National ECODEPA)

FAGANIC   Federación de Asociaciones Ganaderas de Nicaragua (Federation of Cattlemen Associations of Nicaragua)

FENACOOP   Federación Nacional de Cooperativas Agropecuarias (National Federation of Agricultural Cooperatives)

FO   Frente Obrero (Workers' Front)

FONDILAC   Fondo de Desarrollo de la Industria Lactea (Development Fund for the Milk Industry)

FSLN   Frente Sandinista de Liberación Nacional (Sandinista
National Liberation Front)

FSM   Federación de Sindicatos Mundiales (World Federation
of Unions)

GN   Guardia Nacional (National Guard)

GPP   Tendencia Guerra Popular Prolongada (Prolonged Popular War Tendency)

I-ADB   Inter-American Development Bank

INIES   Instituto Nicaragüense de Investigaciones Económicas y
Sociales (Nicaraguan Institute for Economic and
Social Research)

JS-19   Juventud Sandinista, 19 de Julio (July 19th Sandinista
Youth)

MAP-ML   Movimiento de Acción Popular Marxista-Leninista
(Movement of Popular Action, Marxist-Leninist)

MDN   Movimiento Democrático Nicaragüense (Nicaraguan
Democratic Movement)

MICOIN   Ministerio de Comercio Interior (Ministry of Internal
Commerce)

MIDINRA   Ministerio de Desarrollo Agropecuario y Reforma
Agraria (Ministry of Agricultural Development and
Agrarian Reform)

MILPAS   Militias Populares Antisomocistas (Popular Anti-
Somocista Militia)

MPU   Movimiento Pueblo Unido (United People's Movement)

OAS   Organization of American States

ORIT   Organización Regional Interamericano de Trabajadores
(Interamerican Regional Organization of Workers)

SCC   Swedish Cooperative Center

SEV   Sindicatos de Empresas Varias (Union of Several Enterprises)

SUE   Sindicatos Únicos de Empresa (Unions Executive Boards)

TC   Tienda Campesina (Peasant Store)

TP   Tendencia Proletaria (Proletarian Tendency)

UCA   Universidad Centroamericana (Central American University)

UNAG   Unión Nacional de Agricultores y Ganaderos (National
        Union of Farmers and Ranchers)
UNO   Unión Nacional Oppositora (National Opposition
        Union)
UPANIC Unión de Productores Agropecuarios de Nicaragua
        (Union of Nicaraguan Agricultural Producers)
USAID   United States Agency for International Development

Chapter 1

The Political Economy of Transition

The 1980s have witnessed remarkable transformations in the world system. Most important were the withering away of "Realsozialismus" in Eastern Europe and the transition from authoritarian rule toward more democratic forms of government that characterized developments throughout Latin America and Africa.[1] In 1991 the most significant event in recent history galvanized world attention—the breakup of the Soviet Union. Few, if any, students of politics had predicted these changes. If we are not to remain equally in the dark about the direction these societies will take in the future, we need to understand the dynamics of these transformations.

When we study the transition from authoritarian rule toward more democratic forms of government in Latin America and Africa or the collapse of communism in Eastern Europe and the Soviet Union, it becomes evident that these societies face a problematic that shares many features.[2] On the surface, these transitions appear to go in different, at times even diametrically opposed directions. In the case of Nicaragua or Angola, for example, revolutionary regimes posited the construction of socialism as the objective of the transition, while reformers in Eastern Europe and the Soviet Union abandoned "Realsozialismus" in an effort to move from planned toward market economies. Nevertheless, these regime changes share a common dialectic. Its characteristics come into focus if we analyze the mode of production and the hegemonic projects that emerge in these societies.

Martha Harnecker has emphasized that the concept of "transition" needs to be defined clearly if its use is not to be devoid of meaning, since

1

one could argue that "everything is in transition because everything is historical."[3] I employ the concept to describe the initial phase of a mode of production when the structures inherited from the past continue to shape the new system. Thus I discuss a stage when social relations and productive forces, following a radical change in the political sphere, are still in contradiction. Karl Marx recognized that an emerging new system always bears the "birthmarks" of its past. Discussing the case of a communist society, he affirmed: "What we have to deal with here is a communist society, not as it has *developed* on its own foundations, but, on the contrary, just as it *emerges* from capitalist society; which is thus in every respect, economically, morally and intellectually still stamped with the birthmarks of the old society from whose womb it emerges."[4] Carlos Vilas, in his discussion of Third World transitions, has stated bluntly that a revolutionary transformation constitutes "a much lengthier process than is generally believed. The image of a revolution as an instantaneous break with everything old and the accelerated construction of the new [system] is infantile. The building of new economic structures, of a new political system, of new attitudes, values and behaviour, is a long process."[5]

This reality leads to the inevitable contradictions that prevail in transitional societies. The dialectic relationship between productive forces and social relations in an emerging mode of production determines the course of the society's development. This relationship needs to be examined within the larger, societal context. Since classes are the protagonists of the economic and political struggle, a thorough understanding of class relations is essential if we are to understand the evolution of a transitional society. In the Nicaraguan case, Orlando Núñez has argued that transition can be understood as "the process that mediates between the political revolution (new relations of power vis-à-vis the dictatorship, the counterrevolution and imperialism) and the social revolution (new relations of production or economic struggle vis-à-vis decapitalization, speculative commercialization and greater social differentiation produced by the market). The change in the social relations of production begins with the political revolution, but cannot advance without having finished it."[6]

In a transitional society, it is the task of the new regime to confer legitimacy to the relations of production that are being introduced while delegitimizing the ones that are to be superseded. This task becomes even more complex when certain relations that are in conflict with a government's pronounced goals need to be preserved in the short run. For example, Mikhail Gorbachev, hoping to avoid the complete disintegration of Soviet society and the consequences this would inevitably entail for the welfare of the people, sought to defend social relations (e.g., the monopoly on political power of the Communist party) that were no longer viable. Similarly, the Sandinistas had to legitimize capitalist relations of production, realizing that they were necessary for the development of Nicaragua's economy, despite the fact that this impeded the construction of socialism. Contradictions and an ensuing ideological struggle were the outcome of these dilemmas.

The "Articulated" Mode of Production

Jürgen Habermas, the critical theorist, argues that societies often combine elements of several different modes, since "there are only a few instances in which the economic structure of a specific society coincides with a single mode of production; both intercultural diffusion and temporal overlay permit complex structures to arise that have to be deciphered as a combination of several modes of production."[7] Thus, societies are not characterized by the existence of one uniform structure; rather, every social formation consists of a variety of economic and social structures.[8] This is particularly evident in societies that undergo radical change.

Societies in transition are not characterized by a "pure" mode of production. Instead we find the articulation of several different modes. The emerging mode is characterized by the articulation, i.e., the combination, of various modes of production. An analysis that focuses on a society's economic base in terms of this articulation provides insights into the dynamics that characterize transitional societies. Articulation in this context is conceived as "any practice establishing a relation among elements such that their identity is modified as a result of the articulatory practice."[9] Ronald Chilcote affirmed that the notion of articulation of modes of production was given prominence by the writings of French Marxists.[10] In the Latin American context, it was Ernesto Laclau who emphasized the importance of mode of production analysis.

In transitional societies we encounter a combination of productive relations, essentially based upon three modes of production: the capitalist mode, the statist mode (this mode characterized the "communist" systems of the Eastern European countries and the Soviet Union), and the socialist mode.

Capitalism may be defined as an economic system in which one class of individuals ("capitalists") owns the means of production ("capital" goods, such as factories and machinery), hires another class of individuals who own nothing productive but their power to labor ("workers"), and engages in production and sales in order to make private profit.

Statism is a set of productive relations (and productive forces) characterized by control by a small, self-selected group through the political apparatus, while there is a very large class of controlled and exploited workers.

Socialism is defined here as a set of productive relations (and productive forces) that are democratically run by workers or by all citizens, so that it is impossible to have a class of exploiters and a class of exploited.[11]

Although no country can claim a fully developed socialist mode of production as its own, the construction of socialism has been and still is (although these days with an emphasis on social democracy) the stated goal of many political elites. Indeed, whereas communism has been discredited, Western European countries with strong social democratic traditions (Sweden, for example) have strengthened their appeal from Eastern Europe to Latin America and Africa. A free-market economy, but with the state assuring a just distribution of the produced surplus, is the model the former communist countries seek to emulate. This institutional setup is also attractive to revolutionary societies in the Third World that have abandoned old models of class warfare for more pragmatic solutions.

It was the stated objective of the Sandinista leadership to transform Nicaraguan society from a dependent capitalist country into a socialist society. The revolutionary leadership was convinced that this would be the proper strategy to guarantee the provision of basic needs to the poor majority, which had been marginalized during the reign of the Somoza family. Carlos Fonseca, a cofounder of the Sandinista Front, affirmed in 1970 that "socialism is the only perspective which the people have in order to bring about radical change in their living conditions."[12] In order to determine whether the normative goals advocated by the revolutionary regime, such as the building of a society that functions according to the "logic of the majority," were indeed realized, I focus on the introduction of new relations of production. Particularly, I evaluate the extent to which domestic structures were modified to allow for political participation by the rural proletariat and agricultural producers. Although the primary focus of this book is on the domestic dynamics of the Sandinista transition, it is important to realize that external factors constituted the ultimate constraints for Nicaragua's development. In particular, economic and military aggression sponsored by the United States had considerable impact on the course of the revolution.[13]

Revolutionary Nicaragua was neither capitalist, statist, nor socialist. Instead it had a mixed economy, characterized by the combination of a predominant capitalist mode, remnants of precapitalist (i.e., feudal) relations, and new productive relations introduced by the Sandinista government. The dominant mode of production continued to be capitalist, if we consider the main characteristic of the capitalist mode to be that the "ownership of the means of production is severed from the ownership of labour-power."[14] The Sandinistas supported the capitalist sector that was mainly engaged in agro-export production through a generous credit and pricing policy in the realization that the success of the revolution was inextricably linked to the performance of the agro-export sector.[15]

I discuss the mode of production emerging in Nicaragua in the context of the rural sector where the articulation of various forms of production was manifest. Precapitalist relations, in the form of *mediería, aparcería, colonato,* and *precarismo* could be found throughout the country. These relations of production involved sharecropping and other kinds of arrangements whose main characteristic was the exploitation of the peasantry by a feudal aristocracy that appropriated the surplus produced by the peasant class. New relations of production were introduced in the countryside in the form of the *area de propriedad del pueblo* (state sector, or APP) and the Sandinista cooperatives, whose members held the means of production in common. Examining the emerging productive relations in the Nicaraguan countryside, I focus on a particularly interesting experiment—the creation of cooperative peasant stores.

Although the bourgeoisie held considerable economic power, the Sandinistas determined the basic rules of the economic system. The revolutionary government nationalized the banking system and controlled external and internal trade in an effort to dominate the capitalist sector and establish its hegemony. Sandinista policies in dealing with the bourgeoisie followed the Gramscian prescription:

> Undoubtedly the fact of hegemony presupposes that account be taken of the interests and the tendencies of the groups over which hegemony is to be exercised, and that a certain compromise equilibrium should be formed—in other words, that the leading group should make sacrifices of an economic-corporate kind. But there is also no doubt that such sacrifices and such a

compromise cannot touch the essential; for though hegemony is ethical-political, it must also be economic, must necessarily be based on the decisive function exercised by the leading group in the decisive nucleus of economic activity.[16]

The concept of articulation refers not only to "combining different modes of production, but it also implies the dialectical relationship between the economic base and political superstructure."[17] The latter point is essential since emphasis on the connection between a country's mode(s) of production and its prevailing superstructure brings into focus the determining characteristics of the political struggle in a transitional society. The success of reformist governments and revolutionary movements that seek to initiate societal transitions (i.e., radical change) depends initially upon winning the ideological struggle.

The Struggle for Hegemony

Governments in transitional societies pursue hegemonic projects. They need to firmly establish control over the ideological apparatuses of state power[18] in order to implement their agenda successfully. The transformations that these societies seek to undertake are so profound, affecting every sector of society, that a basic societal consensus is required if the changes are to be carried out under conditions of relative peace. There are of course other ways to achieve hegemony, primarily the establishment of a dictatorship. Peaceful transitions, however, require as a *sine qua non* the consent of the people. Thus, I focus on *ideological hegemony,* in line with Gramsci, who conceived of hegemony as "politics-as-consent."[19]

The struggle for hegemony is designed to either replace the hegemonic project of a regime in power or to fill a power vacuum after a successful revolution. In essence, the task is to establish "consensual legitimacy or counter-hegemonic presence in both civil society and the state."[20] Whereas Gramsci insisted that "there must always be a *single* unifying principle in every hegemonic formation" and located this principle in the working class,[21] transitional societies are characterized by hegemonic coalitions that cannot be reduced to one fundamental class. The Nicaraguan experience, in particular, emphasized the necessity of multi-class coalitions.

The content of hegemonic projects differs across societies. In the case of the Soviet Union's successor states and the emerging societies of Eastern Europe, the substance of the project concerns democratization and the introduction of a free market economy. The establishment of "popular" hegemony, on the other hand, was the goal of Sandinista Nicaragua. The revolutionary government sought to impose a "logic of the majority" against an entrenched elite. The popular classes in developing countries and the promarket forces in Eastern Europe and the Soviet Union face the same dilemma: they represent the majority in their respective societies but are nevertheless too weak to carry out their projects based on their own strength. Thus, they are forced to follow a policy of national unity, i.e., they need to establish alliances with their antagonists. It is for this reason that we observed a class alliance between the capitalist sector and the worker and peasant classes in Nicaragua or coalitions between communists and democratic forces in Eastern Europe.

In order to achieve ideological hegemony, the building of class coalitions is essential. The protagonists of a hegemonic project differ according to the particular goals they want to achieve. What unites the different groups in the alliance is basic support for the hegemonic vision of the society's future. By contrast, the goal of national unity requires coalitions among opposing sectors. These antagonistic forces are included in the alliance in the recognition that the realization of the hegemonic project requires the cooperation (at least in the short term) of sectors of society that pursue different objectives. For example, Nicaragua's agrarian bourgeoisie whose class interests were in conflict with the Sandinista project, was nevertheless courted by the revolutionary government. As stated earlier, this happened because the capitalist producers controlled the main source of hard currency—the agro-export economy.

Hegemony: Authoritarian versus Democratic Practice

Several decades before the Sandinistas took power, Gramsci described the complex task facing any revolutionary leadership when he theorized about the role of political leaders before and after attaining governmental power. In establishing its hegemony, the Sandinista Front needed to dominate its enemies and lead its supporters. In Gramsci's words: "A class is dominant in two ways, i.e., 'leading' and 'dominant.' It leads the classes which are its allies, and dominates those which are its enemies. Therefore, even before attaining power a class can (and must) 'lead'; when it is in power it becomes dominant, but continues to 'lead' as well

. . . there can and must be a 'political hegemony' even before the attainment of governmental power, and one should not count solely on the power and material force which such a position gives in order to exercise political leadership or hegemony."[22]

In the discussion on Sandinista democracy, I hold the view that the foundations for the Sandinista hegemonic vision were laid during the insurrection and corresponded to the reality of prerevolutionary Nicaragua. The hegemonic project was multiclass in nature. It united workers, peasants, a large percentage of the population employed in the informal sector of the economy, small merchants, and professionals. Vilas has affirmed that "the revolution is made with what is available, and in Central America, as in the greater part of the Third World, more of those sectors of the working and impoverished masses exist than of the proletariat in a strict sense. Thus, what is important here is not the participation in itself of these *intermediate* forces but the character of the political class project that incorporates this participation. And in this, the physical dimension of the proletariat is, in *principle,* of secondary relevance."[23]

In Nicaragua, these popular forces, "led" by the Sandinista Front, sought to "dominate" the bourgeoisie. It was the participation of the bourgeoisie in the overthrow of the Somoza dictatorship that determined the features of this "domination." Domination emerged in the form of the policy goal of national unity. Under this policy the bourgeoisie initially participated in governing Nicaragua and received economic incentives to engage in production. Yet the limits of bourgeois participation were clearly defined by the hegemonic project that subordinated the interests of the bourgeoisie to the needs of the "poor majority." The Sandinistas acknowledged the complexity of the country's economic and political reality. Instead of following an orthodox Marxist strategy, the leadership sought to initiate a transformation based on a pluralist political system, a mixed economy, and nonalignment. In pursuing its objectives, the new government succeeded in establishing the legitimacy of its hegemonic project. The Sandinistas dominated the political/ideological discourse but were not equally successful in gaining control over the economy.

The Sandinista attempt to transform profoundly the political economy of the Nicaraguan countryside is clearly evident in the case of the rural grassroots movements that are the focus of this book. Susan Eckstein has emphasized that the concerns of members of the agricultural community differ according to property and labor relations: "Rural wage laborers are preoccupied with wage and work conditions, proper-tied peasants with the price of products they market and the goods and services they consume, and tenant farmers and sharecroppers with the demands on their labor."[24] Thus, in order to get a complete picture of the transformation taking place in the countryside, I discuss all significant rural sectors. The analysis of the challenges facing agricultural workers reveals the difficulty that the government experienced in benefiting its core supporters. On the other hand, the dialectics of national unity and popular hegemony can best be observed in the case of the farmers' move-ment, which embodied both policy goals.

The relationship between the Sandinista Front and the grassroots movements raises a fundamental question concerning the democratic or authoritarian practice of Sandinista hegemony. Whereas the bourgeoisie was to be "dominated" within the framework of national unity, the pop-ular classes were supposed to enjoy full democracy under the policy of popular hegemony. The grassroots movements were the guarantors of this "popular" hegemony. This task would have required representative, democratic organizations that enjoyed autonomy. With the possible exception of the farmers' movement, however, the Sandinista mass orga-nizations did not exhibit these characteristics. The Sandinista Front con-trolled these movements closely from the top down. In a typical corpo-ratist fashion, the leadership of the mass organizations was selected by the party. Equally significant, the grassroots movements showed defi-ciencies in their internal democracy. They failed to institutionalize formal democratic procedures, essential to keep the leadership accountable to the base.

The Sandinista hegemonic project suffered from a central short-coming. The Sandinista party viewed itself as the "vanguard" of the rev-olution, a conception that easily leads to a manipulative relationship between "vanguard" and "masses."[25] This authoritarian potential was in turn replicated within the mass organizations. Thus, Sandinista Nicar-agua experienced a constant tension between the vanguardist style of politics (authoritarian practice) and the stated goal to strengthen grass-roots democracy (democratic practice).

In the Nicaraguan case, the political struggle enjoyed relative autonomy starting with the insurrection. This was evidenced by the fact that "the revolution emerged triumphant before the economic crisis in the agroexport economic model ruptured."[26] The predominance of the political sphere continued once the Sandinistas were in power. Yet the hegemonic project ultimately disintegrated because the government failed in bringing the economy under control. Although I postulate the primacy of the political struggle for societies in transition, changes initiated in the political sphere can ultimately only be sustained if they are reflected and supported in the economic base. In the final analysis, success in the political sphere is necessary but not sufficient to stay in power. José Luis Coraggio predicted the demise of the Sandinista revolution in the mid-1980s when he maintained that "political will cannot endlessly substitute for the material conditions of human existence, and at a certain point, the crisis of economic reproduction can begin to have ideological and eventually political effects contrary to the consolidation of the revolution."[27] By 1990 the economy had deteriorated to a point that the commitment of the Nicaraguan people to the revolution could no longer be sustained. Faced with severe economic deprivation and continued military aggression, the people voted for change.

The Challenge of Transition: Recent Studies

Many of the ideas expressed in this manuscript have been validated by the findings of other studies on revolutionary transformations. Starting in the 1970s, researchers focused on the role of the peasantry in Third World revolutions.[28] Jeff Goodwin and Theda Skocpol point out the work of Scott, Migdal, Popkin, Paige, and Wolf, for having "enriched our understanding of agrarian socioeconomic relations and peasant political behavior," maintaining, at the same time, that "these debates have focused insufficient analytic attention on two other issues—themselves closely related—which can take us further toward an understanding of revolutionary movements and transfers of power in the contemporary Third World. The first issue is the formation of revolutionary coalitions that invariably extend well beyond peasants alone. The second issue is the relative vulnerability of different sorts of political regimes to the formation of broad revolutionary coalitions and, perhaps, to actual overthrow by revolutionary forces."[29] I would add a third issue, namely, the need to understand better the record of revolutionary regimes once they have attained power.

Timothy Wickham-Crowley's excellent comparative study on guerrillas and revolutions in Latin America makes an important contribution in helping us to understand the relative vulnerability of regimes. He argues that Somoza's Nicaragua and Batista's Cuba were particularly

vulnerable to insurrectional forces because the two regimes are characterized as "mafiacracies." In his words, "Patrimonial praetorian regimes,
or mafiacracies, have shown themselves to be strikingly vulnerable to
revolutionary overthrows because of their peculiar lack of supports in
civil society, and because of their corresponding tendency to elicit cross-
class opposition to the patrimonial ruler."[30] Goodwin and Skocpol reach
a similar conclusion, affirming that "revolutionaries in the contemporary
Third World are most likely to succeed when civil society as a whole can
be politically mobilized to oppose an autonomous and narrowly based
direct colonial regime or a Sultanistic neo-patrimonial regime."[31] In the
Nicaraguan case, the forging of a cross-class opposition to Somoza's rule
during the insurrection led to the emergence of the Sandinista policy of
national unity.

Excellent work has been done on the conditions necessary for guerrilla
movements to succeed in their struggle. The emphasis of my analysis,
however, is on the postinsurrectional phase. How do revolutionary
regimes hold their multiclass coalition together, once the objective that
constituted the glue binding the coalition together has been realized?
And, equally important, how does the new regime maintain its support
from the popular classes?

Núñez emphasizes the crucial role the party plays during this phase of
the revolution: "The class struggle does not express itself directly in
terms of the two fundamental classes of the social formation (bourgeoisie
and proletariat) but in terms of two contradictory and antagonistic projects, in whose ranks, for or against, the societal forces align themselves.
What is crucial in this alignment is the capacity of the vanguard [i.e., the
party] to unite all existing classes and forces, independent of class origin
or situation, above all as it concerns the peasantry and the urban petty
bourgeoisie who are the majority forces of this society."[32] Multiclass
alliances can be found in a number of revolutionary settings. What sets
the Sandinista project apart from other socialist revolutions in the Third
World (the Cuban experiment, for example) is the fact that the policy of
national unity was maintained *after* the taking of power and embodied
itself in a mixed economy, political pluralism, and nonalignment.[33]

Philip Williams has argued that "alternative conceptions of democracy are not seriously considered . . . in the literature on transitions."[34]
This makes it imperative to examine the Sandinista attempt to construct
revolutionary, democratic Marxism in Nicaragua. On its path toward an
alternative democratic model, the Sandinista party faced two critical

challenges: (1) the former dominant class sought to maintain or regain economic and political power, which led to conflict with the revolutionary forces, and (2) the multiclass alliance of the hegemonic forces eventually faced the reality that the advancement of its sectoral interests was frequently a zero-sum game. This double contradiction, manifest in the policies of national unity and popular hegemony, determined the course of the Nicaraguan revolution. It shaped the Sandinista hegemonic vision and will be the lens through which I will explore the revolution's legacy in the following chapters.

Chapter 2

The Sandinista Hegemonic
Vision: Democracy and Revolution

Nicaragua was once considered the "country in the world with the greatest opportunity to arrive at revolutionary democratic Marxism."[1] On July 19, 1988, the Sandinista leadership officially confirmed the socialist orientation of the Nicaraguan revolution. Speaking on the ninth anniversary of the revolution, President Daniel Ortega elaborated on its character: "This July 19, a certain expectation has been created . . . that the Sandinistas will declare themselves socialist. It appears that they [the Nicaraguan bourgeoisie and the United States] still have not understood that the Sandinistas are socialists, that socialism prevails in Nicaragua since July 19, 1979."[2] Until 1988, the leadership went to great lengths to explain the nature of socialism in Nicaragua in terms of a multifaceted revolutionary project that incorporated many characteristics, socialism just being one of them. Explicit emphasis on socialism raised questions about the foundations and the direction of the Sandinista regime. If socialist, could it be democratic and pluralist?

In North America, democracy and socialism are generally considered mutually exclusive concepts. Yet the reality of the Nicaraguan revolution frequently challenged conventional wisdom. The Reagan and Bush administrations' view of the Sandinistas that informed the popular media portrayed developments in Nicaragua from an ethnocentric, ideological perspective that precluded any possibility for comprehending the complex nature of this revolutionary transformation. Once the Sandinista government had successfully been labeled a "totalitarian communist dictatorship," confrontation with Managua was the logical outcome. Latin American and Western European governments (including main NATO allies) held a different view of the Nicaraguan revolution, a development that isolated the United States within the world community. The support given by these nations to the Sandinistas was in contrast to the 1981–1990 counterrevolution financed and directed by the United States, the objective of which was the overthrow of the Sandinista government. Beginning in 1981, counterrevolutionary forces, financed by the U.S. government and directed by the Central Intelligence Agency (CIA), conducted a campaign of terror against civilians and military operations against the Sandinista army in order to bring down the revolutionary government. In 1987, the International Court of Justice declared U.S. aggression against Nicaragua illegal and ordered the Reagan administration to pay reparations. Despite this judgment, the U.S. government continued the illegal war.

Historic Roots of Sandinista Democracy

Sandinista democracy can be understood as the synthesis of two policy goals: popular hegemony and national unity.[3] These two goals complemented and contradicted each other. Popular hegemony was supposed to transform the inherited political system to benefit the previously marginalized majority, yet success in this revolutionary goal required the cooperation of the capitalist class within a framework of national unity, i.e., attainment of the second goal. The main contradiction arising from the two desired ends was the probability that national unity would entail the perpetuation and even the creation of socioeconomic and political structures that were likely to be in conflict with popular hegemony. Thus, the Sandinistas set out to pursue a revolutionary transformation of society implying a redistribution of benefits toward the poor through an institutional framework in which the rich were to be represented.

The goal of national unity, intended as an incentive for the bourgeoisie to join the revolutionary effort, had precise limits. The interests and demands of the bourgeoisie were to be subordinated to the central objective of the Sandinista revolution—transformation of the political and economic structures to benefit the impoverished worker and peasant classes. This subordination, however, did not preclude the bourgeoisie's "pursuit of profit and personal enrichment."[4]

Carlos Vilas has argued that in neocolonial formations such as

Nicaragua, the subject of the revolutionary transformation is broader than the peasant and worker classes. It includes also intermediate sectors, such as "the non-salaried workers, small merchants, and professional, technical, and intellectual petty bourgeoisie."[5] These "popular classes," which were to benefit from the revolution, did not include the bourgeoisie, although at times agreements were to be concluded with it. Thus, popular hegemony in itself was a policy of alliance. The common denominator for all groups incorporated in the alliance was support for some portion of the Sandinista vision of Nicaragua's future. By contrast, the goal of national unity permitted coalitions among opposing sectors of Nicaraguan society. The dialectic relationship between popular hegemony and national unity would be determined by the respective strengths of the popular classes and the bourgeoisie. Hence, the task facing the Sandinistas was Herculean—to transform society in ways that elicited the cooperation of the bourgeois class while presupposing its domination.

Three main historical factors influenced the Sandinistas' efforts to create their own variant of democracy: (1) the splitting and reunification of the FSLN, (2) the role of the masses in the insurrection of 1977–1979, and (3) the weakness of the worker and peasant classes. The conditions of the guerrilla struggle, especially the difficulty of communication, impeded the development of a common strategy among the various sectors of the Sandinista Front. The principal leaders of the FSLN could not meet between 1970 and 1975 to discuss the lessons learned since the inception of revolutionary struggle in the early 1960s, and they were not able to resolve internal differences on the crucial questions of class alliances and insurrectional strategy.[6] These disagreements developed into an open rift in 1975, when Carlos Fonseca, an eminent leader, expelled several high-ranking members.

Several factions emerged. One group embraced Che Guevara's ideas on the importance of armed struggle in the mountains that would eventually become generalized.[7] The guerrilla fighters would constitute a "vanguard" that would lead the peasants toward victory. Other Sandinistas held that the "war of the guerrilla" eventually would be eclipsed by insurrectional fighting. The latter groups formed the Proletarian and the Insurrectional tendencies, and the former became known as the Tendencia Guerra Popular Prolongada (Prolonged Popular War Tendency, or GPP) faction. The Tendencia Proletaria (Proletarian Tendency, or TP) advocated clandestine organizing among workers, peasants, and progressive youth as a precondition for a successful insurrection. The Sandinista fighters needed to end their isolation from the proletariat and take advantage of this growing, militant sector.[8] The Insurrectional Tendency (commonly known as Terceristas) favored broad class alliances and believed that a progressive accumulation of different social forces would bring down Anastasio (Tachito) Somoza. The Terceristas were convinced that conditions for a successful uprising already existed, whereas the Prolonged Popular War faction urged mobilizing the peasantry for long-term conflict.[9]

Each group attempted to dominate the guerrilla movement, and relations between them were tense until a spontaneous September 1978 uprising led to a reassessment of FSLN strategy. The Sandinistas realized that the guerrillas would have to support the masses rather than the reverse. In March 1979 increased mass participation and the growing crisis of the Somoza dictatorship reunified the Sandinista Front.[10] The leadership was flexible enough to acknowledge that the popular forces had advanced more rapidly than the vanguard. Comandante Humberto Ortega, member of the FSLN's National Directorate and minister of defense under the Sandinistas (and President Violeta Chamorro), summarized the lesson the masses taught the guerrillas: "The uprising of the masses in the aftermath of the assassination of [publisher Pedro Joaquín] Chamorro was not led exclusively by the FSLN. It was a spontaneous reaction on the part of the masses, which, in the end, the Sandinista Front began to direct through its activists and a number of military units. *It was not a mass movement responding to the call of the Sandinistas.*"[11]

This experience demonstrated the importance of a strategy of alliance. The united movement was headed by a nine-member National Directorate composed of Daniel Ortega, Humberto Ortega, and Victor Tirado of the Insurrectional Tendency; Tomás Borge, Bayardo Arce, and Henry Ruíz of the Prolonged Popular War faction; and Carlos Núñez, Luis Carrión, and Jaime Wheelock of the Proletarian Tendency. The directorate agreed to a common platform whose essence indicated the increased importance of the Terceristas. The main element of the program was recognition of the insurrectional character of the struggle, the need for a flexible alliance, and the need for a broad, pragmatic program.[12]

FSLN's evolution toward greater pragmatism was not entirely the work of the Terceristas. Marxist-Leninist ideology predominated in the Sandinista movement until the mid-1970s, when increased resistance to the dictatorship led to the incorporation of many non-Marxists.[13] In particular, many radicalized Christians joined the Sandinistas, thus making the movement less doctrinaire and broadening its ideological appeal.[14] The conditions of Nicaragua's proletariat also shaped the Sandinista vision. Urban and rural workers did not constitute a significant political force under Somoza.[15] Salaried rural workers numbered between 107,000 and 130,000, whereas the urban working class was estimated at between 80,000 and 113,000 workers, about 20 percent of the nonagricultural economically active population (EAP). The revolutionary movement counted also with substantial support from poor peasants who did not have enough land to support their families. This semiproletariat, numbering about 165,000, or 40 percent of the agricultural EAP, was forced to sell its labor power to make ends meet.[16]

The combined numbers of these sectors were significant, and their revolutionary potential was evident. Economically, however, they were at the margins of Nicaraguan society. Thus, the Sandinistas realized that a revolutionary strategy based exclusively on the proletariat and poor peasants would fail. This led them to recruit nonsalaried workers, small merchants, and professionals. The final elements in the anti-Somoza coalition were members of the bourgeoisie, who joined the insurrectional forces out of political convictions (they considered the regime illegitimate) or were motivated by the perceived need to reshuffle the economic cards (Somoza's greed had created a state of affairs in which it was almost impossible for the capitalists to make a profit). Structural weaknesses in the Nicaraguan worker and peasant classes, along with Somoza's ouster by a broad coalition, led the revolutionary authorities to envision an order of political pluralism. The Sandinistas sought the support of all sectors of Nicaraguan society that had suffered under the Somoza dynasty.

Representative and Participatory Concepts of Democracy

To understand the evolution of Sandinista democracy it is necessary to distinguish between the concepts of formal and substantive democracy. *Formal democracy* consists of rules governing the election of leaders and popular participation in decision making. *Substantive democracy* refers to the ways in which public policy reflects popular interests. Representative democracy and participatory democracy are two subcategories of formal democracy. The former emphasizes the electoral process, whereas the latter considers mass participation essential. Substantive democracy also has subcategories representing socialist and capitalist visions of how public policy can be presumed to reflect societal interests. These categories are not mutually exclusive. The form of decision making frequently can condition the substance of the decision.[17] The substance of the Sandinista political system was socialist, yet the country's economy was dominated by a capitalist mode of production, with even some precapitalist relations persisting. Thus, contradictions were inherent in the Sandinista model.

From a formal perspective, the Sandinistas sought to combine elements of representative and participatory democracy. It was their aspiration to attain a new model of revolutionary, democratic Marxism. The participatory element was central to the Sandinista notion of popular hegemony, whereas representative features were necessary for a successful policy of national unity. Participation by the masses would set the priorities of a proposed socioeconomic transition according to "the logic of the majority," i.e., to the benefit of the masses. Yet this transformation was to occur within a kind of national unity that required a mixed economy and political pluralism.

In the 1980s, political theorists across the ideological spectrum started to praise the values of participatory democracy and criticized representative democracy. In the North American context, Benjamin Barber argued "that an excess of liberalism has undone democratic institutions" and advocated a return to participatory politics.[18] Until the Sandinista experiment, revolutionary movements rejected formal democracy, as represented by periodic elections. The views of many revolutionaries had been formed by the experience of "demonstration elections."[19] These meaningless exercises were designed to generate the appearance of legitimacy for a regime, rather than provide the electorate with a vote to determine the makeup of the government. In this context, it is not surprising that the institutions of representative democracy were considered of little value in a social revolution.[20] Revolutionary leaders generally regarded the substance of their revolutionary projects as more important than adherence to the rules of formal democracy. The justified questioning of formal rules, however, has historically not translated into the creation of political systems, distinguished by full participation of the citizenry. Whereas revolutionary governments have demonstrated their capacity to construct social and economic democracy, meaningful political participation has often been restricted.[21]

The Sandinistas chose a road that set them apart from previous revolutionary movements. They began to promote popular participation during the insurrection. For postinsurrectional tasks, they were influenced by the Cuban experience of mass mobilization. The Sandinista Front even enjoyed an advantage over the Cuban guerrillas. Mass participation was limited in the Cuban revolution, but the Nicaraguan insurrection involved thousands of civilians, giving the peasants and workers confidence in their ability to better their living conditions and providing the foundation for mobilizing the masses for reconstruction. Comandante Tomás Borge, member of the National Directorate and minister of interior (1979–1990), emphasized that "it is impossible to build up your revolutionary power without both the quantitative and the qualitative development of the popular organizations . . . the masses themselves must always—now and in the future—speak up in a loud, clear voice on their own behalf. They must develop ways of participating and taking initiatives."[22]

Participatory Democracy and Popular Hegemony

The initial political structures in revolutionary Nicaragua emphasized participatory democracy. At the national level, the Council of State, a corporatist, colegislative body was to guarantee the participation of every major social movement in the political system. Virtually all significant social, economic, and political forces were allocated seats. Originally, the Sandinista leadership doubted the virtue of electoral democracy, although elections had been promised. Structured according to Leninist principles of party-building, the FSLN conceived itself the vanguard of the revolution. Having led the successful insurrection, it was not prepared to have its leadership challenged in elections. Further, the immediate concern of the Sandinista leadership was to improve the socioeconomic conditions of the poor majority, not to provide a political forum for the bourgeoisie.[23]

Nicaragua's history played an important role in the evolution of Sandinista thinking. When General Augusto C. Sandino succeeded in 1932 in raising the cost of U.S. occupation to the point that the Marines were finally withdrawn, his forces disarmed, believing that their task was accomplished. After Sandino's assassination, however, the oligarchy resumed control, and the possibility of restructuring Nicaraguan society was lost.[24] Thus, the Sandinistas did not want to squander their opportunity. Finally, electoral democracy had been thoroughly discredited by the fraudulent elections held during the forty-three years of the Somoza dynasty.

Some FSLN radicals argued that electoral structures were irrelevant to the institutionalization of a participatory model, based on "true popular democracy." In 1980, Julio López, FSLN's secretary for propaganda and political education, argued that "the purpose of elections is not to determine who will have power in Nicaragua. This question has been determined by history and the people affirm this fact on a daily basis."[25] Comandante Humberto Ortega, elaborating the National Directorate's view on elections, presented a similar position: "As everyone will have understood, the elections we speak of are very different from the elections desired by the oligarchs and traitors, conservatives and liberals, reactionaries and imperialists. . . . Never forget that *our elections will be to perfect revolutionary power, not to hold a raffle among those who seek to hold power, because the people hold power through their vanguard— the FSLN and its National Directorate.*"[26]

The bourgeois opposition vehemently rejected this view.[27] While the bourgeoisie advocated the institutionalization of representative features that would have benefited its class interests, the Sandinistas initially implemented their revolutionary views that emphasized participatory democracy.[28] According to Humberto Ortega, power was to be "exercised by Sandinismo, which means the people, through a higher form of organization and their own form of mass organization; here other sectors that are not Sandinistas subsist, but they do so inasmuch as this power permits them to and inasmuch as they really do not affect the revolutionary project."[29] This statement indicates the leadership's intent to establish hegemony over sectors of Nicaraguan society that held opposing views regarding the future of the revolution. The official view of democracy was outlined by the National Directorate of the Sandinista National Liberation Front in 1980:

> For the Frente Sandinista democracy is not measured solely in the political sphere, and cannot be reduced only to the participation of the people in elections. Democracy is not simply elections. It is something more, much more. For a revolutionary, for a Sandinista, it means participation by the people in political, social and cultural affairs. The more people participate in such matters, the more democratic they will be. And it must be said once and for all: democracy neither begins nor ends with elections. It is a myth to want to reduce democracy to that status. Democracy begins in the economic order,

when social inequalities begin to diminish, when the workers and peasants improve their standard of living. That is when true democracy begins, not before. . . . In a more advanced phase, democracy means the participation of the workers in the running of factories, farms, cooperatives and cultural centers. To sum up, democracy is the intervention of the masses in all aspects of social life. We point out all this to establish on a principled basis what the FSLN understands by democracy.[30]

Several conclusions regarding the early characteristics of Nicaragua's popular revolution can be drawn from this statement. Sandinista democracy incorporated representative features, but it emphasized the participatory element. Popular democracy began in the economic order, rather than being restricted to the political sphere, and direct participation by the people in all sectors of socioeconomic life was crucial. Although the leadership did not reject electoral democracy, elections were not to play an important part in the original Nicaraguan model. From a pluralist perspective, the problem with this view of democracy was the limited importance given to representative features: The ruling elite determines whether there is democracy and judges whether policies serve the poor. Without elections, how are workers and peasants to express their opinion and change the government if they so choose? Further, the emphasis given to the participation by the masses in the political process entails a potential problem. It does not necessarily follow that if more people participate in the political system it will be more democratic. The fascist experience in Europe in the 1930s demonstrated that mass participation cannot be equated with increased democracy. Participation by the masses in the political decision-making process is a necessary condition for democratic rule. Yet by no means is it sufficient. The quality of participation that the system offers is the issue, not the mere fact that the masses are mobilized.

Formal State Power and Participatory Structures

Formal political power in the early days of the Sandinista revolution was invested in the Governing Junta and the Council of State.[31] The first Junta, composed of the broad forces that overthrew Somoza, included Daniel Ortega, a member of the National Directorate of the Sandinista Front; Sergio Ramírez of the Group of Twelve; Moisés Hassan of the Movimiento Pueblo Unido (United People's Movement, or MPU); Violeta

Barrios de Chamorro, widow of Pedro Joaquín Chamorro and co-owner of the newspaper *La Prensa;* and Alfonso Robelo, a businessman and head of the Movimiento Democrático Nicaragüense (Nicaraguan Democratic Movement, or MDN).

Although the Junta was nominally the highest decision-making authority in revolutionary Nicaragua, real power was vested in the Sandinista party and its National Directorate. The ideological preferences of the Junta members ensured Sandinista hegemony, since Ortega, Ramírez, and Hassan were all part of the FSLN. The authority of the FSLN, as the final arbiter of all major decisions was officially recognized in September 1980. Within the Sandinista party, in turn, the nine-member directorate's supremacy was uncontested.[32] According to Hassan, it not only determined major policies but also frequently interfered in their execution. The authority of the FSLN and its directorate had moral and practical foundations. It was based on its role as the revolutionary vanguard during the years of struggle against the Somoza dynasty, as well as Sandinista control over the army and police.

The composition of the Junta changed between 1979 and 1981. In April 1980, Chamorro resigned for "personal" reasons, although she later criticized the Sandinista revolutionary agenda.[33] A few days later, Robelo resigned over the changed membership of the Council of State. FSLN immediately replaced them with two other representatives of the bourgeoisie, Rafael Cordova Rivas and Arturo Cruz. By 1981 the Junta consisted of only three members; Cruz had left to become Nicaragua's ambassador to the United States, and Hassan had joined the cabinet.[34]

During the first year of the revolution, the Governing Junta had sole legislative authority, since a legislative assembly representing the interests of the Nicaraguan people at the national level had yet to be established. Thus, from a formal democratic perspective, the new political system showed important limitations. There were no representative political structures, and even a participatory framework emerged slowly. Popular participation was limited to the role of the emerging Sandinista mass organizations in representing their constituents' interests.

This improved with the inauguration of the Council of State, Nicaragua's corporatist, colegislative assembly, in May 1980. It consisted of forty-seven delegates from twenty-nine political, professional, and grassroots organizations and shared legislative functions with the Governing Junta. Originally, it was composed of thirty-three members, only twelve of whom represented the Sandinistas.[35] The majority of the membership was ideologically close to the bourgeois allies of the FSLN during the insurrection. The initial composition of the Council of State reflected the importance of the bourgeoisie in the anti-Somoza coalition. Predominant on the battlefield, the FSLN could not establish hegemony in the anti-Somoza political coalition without losing bourgeois support. Thus, participation by the bourgeoisie in the insurrection and the policy of national unity led to strong representation of bourgeois interests in the original government.

The balance of forces shifted rapidly when the revolutionary coalition took power. In October 1979 the Sandinistas postponed the constitution of the Council of State until May 1980. Changing its original plans, the FSLN added delegates from fourteen new groups to the proposed Council of State, altering the voting in favor of the peasant and worker classes and establishing popular hegemony. Twelve of the fourteen new organizations supported the FSLN, which had an obvious interest in adding them to the council. As represented by Ramiro Gúrdian, the bourgeois opposition argued that this addition violated a central agreement concluded prior to Somoza's fall, but the Sandinistas held that the original composition of the council did not take into account important changes in Nicaraguan society since 1979. For example, not a single grassroots movement was included. Several of these emerging organizations had demonstrated explosive growth and demanded representation for their constituents in the new political structures. The Association of Rural Workers (ATC), for example, had organized more than 100,000 rural workers and agricultural producers by mid-1980, and some of the council's original organizations, such as the Group of Twelve, had been dissolved.[36] The Sandinista mass organizations, together with FSLN and the armed forces, controlled twenty-four of the forty-seven seats in the assembly. The absolute majority held by the popular forces and FSLN made clear the latter's determination to ensure popular hegemony and establish the limits of national unity. The importance of the grassroots movements in the legislature further confirmed the Sandinista emphasis on participatory democracy.

As shown in table 2.1, over its four years, the Council of State's composition changed several times, reflecting the evolution of the Nicaraguan political system. Membership was expanded to fifty-one in the assembly's second session to accommodate the incorporation of new members. Most significantly, the newly founded National Union of Farmers and Ranchers (UNAG) obtained two seats in 1981. The final

Table 2.1. Membership and voting strength in the Council of State, 1981–1984

Organization	No. of Seats
Political parties	
Sandinista National Liberation Front (FSLN)	6
Independent Liberal Party (PLI)	1
Nicaraguan Socialist Party (PSN)[a]	1
Popular Social Christian Party (PPSC)[a]	1
Nicaraguan Democratic Movement (MDN)	1
Democratic Conservative Party (PCD)	1
Social Christian Party (PSC)	1
Liberal Constitutionalist Movement (MLC)	1[b]
Popular organizations	
Sandinista Defense Committees (CDSs)[a]	9
July 19th Sandinista Youth (JS-19)	1
Nicaraguan Women's Association (AMNLAE)	1
Labor organizations	
Sandinista Workers' Central (CST)[a]	3
Rural Workers Association (ATC)[a]	2
Independent General Workers' Confederation (CGTI)	2
Nicaraguan Workers Confederation (CTN)	1
Council for Labor Unification (CUS)	1
Center for Union Action and Unity (CAUS)	2[b]
Federation of Health Workers (FETSALUD)[a]	1
Guilds and other social organizations	
Sandinista Armed Forces (EPS)[a]	1
National Association of Clergy (ACLEN)	1
National Council of Higher Education (CNES)[a]	1
Association of Educators of Nicaragua (ANDEN)[a]	1
National Journalists Union (UPN)[a]	1
Unity of the Miskitu, Sumu, Rama, and Sandinistas (MISURASATA)	1
National Confederation of Professional Associations (CONAPRO)[a]	1
National Union of Farmers and Ranchers (UNAG)[a]	2[c]
Ecumenical Axis (MEC-CELADEC)	1[b]
Private sector organizations	
Nicaraguan Development Institute (INDE)	1
Nicaraguan Chamber of Industries (CADIN)	1
Confederation of Chambers of Commerce (CCCN)	1
Nicaraguan Chamber of Construction (CNC)	1
Union of Nicaraguan Agricultural Producers (UPANIC)	1
Total	51

Sources: Booth, *End and Beginning,* 193; Lozano, *De Sandino al triunfo de la revolución,* 302–3.

[a]Normally voted with FSLN.

[b]One seat added in 1981.

[c]New as of 1981; one of these seats formerly belonged to ATC.

change took place August 6, 1984, when the Movimiento de Acción Popular Marxista-Leninista (Movement of Popular Action Marxist-Leninist, or MAP-ML) and their labor union, the Frente Obrero (Workers' Front, or FO) entered the council. These ultraleft sectors had been excluded in 1980 because the Sandinistas considered their radical criticism counter-revolutionary.[37] The private sector, represented by the Consejo Superior de la Empresa Privada (Superior Council of Private Enterprise, or COSEP) and several right-wing parties left the council in November 1980 when COSEP's vice-president, Jorge Salazar, was killed in a confrontation with the Sandinista police. The bourgeoisie's representatives returned, however, in May 1983.

From the perspective of Sandinista democracy, the Council of State was the first attempt to create a representative structure with a strong participatory component, thus embodying two central features of the revolutionary project. By 1981 the six main Sandinista mass organizations controlled eighteen seats, compared with thirteen for all political parties represented, including FSLN. The popular, corporatist character of the council was to give all sectors of Nicaraguan society the opportunity to participate in national decision making. The grassroots organizations ensured that the poor majority finally had political representation. The Council of State enabled the Sandinista grassroots movements to participate in the decision-making process at the national level and gave them a forum in which to voice their concerns. The six main organizations were the Central Sandinista de Trabajadores (Sandinista Workers Central, or CST), ATC, UNAG, the Asociación de Mujeres Nicaragüenes Luisa Amanda Espinoza (Association of Nicaraguan Women, or AMNLAE), the Comités de Defensa Sandinista (Sandinista Defense Committees, or CDS), and the Juventud Sandinista, 19 de Julio (July 19th Sandinista Youth, or JS-19).[38] They introduced several important laws and constituted 44 percent of the council's membership.[39] Nevertheless, considering their important role in Sandinista democracy, their participation in the council was rather limited. (See table 2.2 for legislative projects introduced by the mass organizations.) Comandante Carlos Núñez, president of the Council of State, criticized them on several occasions for not representing their constituents' interests more forcefully.

When the Sandinistas took power in 1979, Nicaragua had only 138 unions with fewer than 30,000 members.[40] During the revolution, several organizations representing the urban proletariat united into the Sandinista Workers Central. By 1989 this group claimed 600 affiliated

Table 2.2. Legislation introduced by Sandinista mass organizations in the Council of State, 1980–1983

			Organization		
Year	CST	ATC	CDS	JS19J	AMNLAE
1980	Reforms of the work code		Regulation of housing acquired by the state	(1) Law to protect brigadistas[a] (2) Law to constitute consulting councils in high schools	Law of adoption
1981	Reforms of the work code		(1) Reforms of the rent law (2) Law about replacement of birth certificates	Law to promote sports and culture	Law about relations between fathers, mothers, and children
1982			Law to protect the revolutionary vigilants	Law to protect the national artistic, cultural, and historic heritage	Law of food supply
1983		Law to protect the work brigades[b]			

Source: Pensamiento Propio 3, no. 24 (1985).

Note: UNAG did not present a single legislative project during the entire period. This is explained in part by the fact that UNAG is the youngest mass organization and was not represented on the council before 1981.

[a]Law designed to protect the participants in the literacy campaign.

[b]Law designed to protect volunteers participating in harvests.

unions with 150,000 members. It promoted economic policies based on raising productivity and expanding social services rather than on increasing salaries. This created problems for CST, which had to compete with right-wing and ultraleft organizations, whose demands for immediate improvements, although more in tune with working-class wishes, were impossible to satisfy.[41] According to Lucío Jiménez, once government programs for the workers started to improve general living conditions, CST began to gain the trust of the working class.

The Association of Rural Workers was formed in March 1978, as the result of efforts by the Catholic church and the Sandinistas to organize committees of agricultural workers to protest the exploitation of the peasantry.[42] The National Union of Farmers and Ranchers, on the other hand, was established on April 25, 1981, and thus was the youngest of the grassroots organizations. Both rural grassroots movements, ATC and UNAG, made substantial contributions to the development of the Nicaraguan countryside.

In the 1970s, the Asociación de Mujeres ante la Problemática Nacional (Association of Women Confronting the National Problematic, or AMPRONAC) promoted the participation of women in the insurrection and spoke out against human rights abuses by the Somoza regime. After the successful insurrection, the movement honored one of its martyrs by renaming itself the Luisa Amanda Espinoza Association of Nicaraguan Women and started to organize women from all social sectors. Its "Plan of Struggle" sought to integrate women into society on equal terms with men and to overcome injustices and inequalities confronting women in Nicaraguan society.[43]

The Sandinista Defense Committees grew out of neighborhood organizations that provided logistical support for the FSLN during the insurrection. Loosely modeled on the Cuban Committees for the Defense of the Revolution, these groups were organized throughout the country and had more than half a million members by 1984.[44] Although open to all citizens over the age of fourteen, they sought to mobilize people behind the revolution and to assist the state to implement various health, education, and food-distribution programs. Participation in CDSs declined precipitously after the mid-1980s. They were partially revived in 1988 as nonpartisan community organizations.

The July 19th Sandinista Youth originated in the student movement, which played an important part in the insurrection. Comandante Carlos Núñez, the late member of FSLN's National Directorate, considered it the youth organization of the Sandinista party rather than an independent mass organization. Although the organization was not as selective and demanding as FSLN in choosing its members and purported to represent all Nicaraguan young people, its close association with the Sandinista Front distinguished it from the other mass organizations. Its greatest accomplishments were the mobilization of tens of thousands of young people in the literacy campaign of 1980, the coffee and cotton harvest brigades, and, most significantly, the war against the counterrevolution.

According to Núñez, the mass organizations were guided by two principles: "Under the leadership of the Sandinista Front of National Liberation, the mass organizations are guided, we could say, by two important policies. In the first place our mass organizations should guard and work to strengthen the political project of the Revolution; and in the second place they should be true instruments for expressing, channeling and receiving the most urgent demands of the masses."[45] These mass organizations were formed to facilitate effective participation by the people in all areas of their lives. The involvement of the grassroots movements in improving basic needs was an essential goal of Sandinista democracy, which advocated "the intervention of the masses in all aspects of social life."[46] The grassroots movements were particularly active in the literacy and health campaigns. According to Sergio Ramírez, no revolutionary program could have been accomplished without them.[47] At their height, they incorporated more than half of the adult population.[48]

Whereas the Sandinista party represented a vanguard of the most dedicated revolutionaries, the mass organizations were to mobilize broad popular sectors around their own interests.[49] The close relationship between the masses and the FSLN started to develop only two years before the insurrection.[50] Although the Sandinista Front obviously sought hegemony in these organizations, Carlos Núñez maintained that moderate Sandinista leaders also encouraged pluralism and favored their autonomy from the party. These high-ranking officials opposed sectors within the FSLN that wanted to see the mass organizations evolve into important political movements only if they remained under the party's strict control. This position was expressed by radical Sandinista leaders such as Bayardo Arce.[51] Though the radicals supported the development of grassroots movements because they facilitated mobilization of the masses, they feared a threat to their hegemony by independent mass movements and showed little interest in allowing unfettered popular participation.

Other Sandinistas realized that the autonomy of the grassroots movements was of central importance to Sandinista democracy. Only militant, independent organizations could participate in the development of a democratic political system, represent the interests of their constituents before the state and ensure the democratic practice of Sandinista hegemony. These Sandinistas conceived of the party, the state, and the mass organizations as three pillars of the revolutionary project, tied together by a common goal but enjoying relative autonomy.[52] All mass organizations recognized the FSLN as their legitimate vanguard, but they demonstrated various degrees of independence from the party. The degree of autonomy of any mass organization ultimately depended on its strength and its willingness to challenge the government.

The FSLN and the mass organizations have on several occasions fought publicly. In particular, the farmers' movement demonstrated its militancy vis-à-vis the revolutionary authorities. One example of effective grassroots militancy occurred in 1988 when UNAG, over government opposition, obtained debt relief for cattle producers. On other occasions the grassroots organizations changed the government's positions and enlarged their own autonomy. In terms of relative autonomy, the movements ranged from the Sandinista Youth—which, as the youth organization of the FSLN, had little autonomy—to UNAG, the militant farmers' movement, which successfully pursued its interests. In general, the grassroots movements have started to exhibit greater autonomy in the post-FSLN era.

Another problem in the development of strong mass organizations was the lack of their own internal democracy. These organizations failed to institutionalize elections at all levels. In general, elections were held only at the base level, with regional and national leaders appointed by the national leadership upon consultation with the Sandinista Front. Elections in the agricultural workers' organization during the mid-1980s illustrate this point. According to Comandante Bayardo Arce, in the case of ATC, FSLN presented thirty candidates for national leadership positions from which the ATC delegates chose ten.[53] This lack of democracy made it difficult to hold leaders accountable to the base. Nevertheless, efforts to strengthen the internal democracy of the grassroots movements were evident, and some leaders were removed by base pressure. The CDSs, in particular, experienced abuses by local leaders and a general lack of internal democracy.[54] After a critical reevaluation in 1985, elections were held at every level of the neighborhood committees. At times, the Sandinistas sought to strengthen the grassroots movements by imposing new leadership. In 1988 two high-ranking Sandinista officials, Omar Cabezas and Lea Guido, were named to head the CDSs and AMNLAE, respectively. Though Cabezas had some success in restructuring the neighborhood committees, such top-down measures are counterproductive to autonomous, democratic organizational growth.

The dialectic between the grassroots movements and the FSLN has been described as follows: "At times led by, at times ahead of and autonomous from the leadership of the FSLN, in general without a neat definition of the relationship between the revolutionary party and the mass organizations."[55] The necessity of organizing the masses while ensuring the autonomy of their organizations posed a crucial dilemma for the FSLN and the grassroots movements. The mass organizations could play an effective part in transforming society only if they capably represented their members' interests. A high degree of autonomy was essential in order for these interests to be advanced with vigor. The popular movements seemed to grow in autonomy during the Sandinista era of governance, but this did not lead to gratitude at the polls, with the FSLN losing the 1990 elections.

From Revolutionary to Electoral Legitimacy

Despite their initial doubts about electoral democracy, the dominant group within the FSLN—pragmatists such as President Daniel Ortega, Vice-President Sergio Ramírez, and National Assembly president Carlos Núñez—soon recognized the importance of representative features. The pragmatic Insurrectional Tendency once again seems to have modified an ideologically based position. As noted, during the insurrection the Terceristas convinced the two other Sandinista factions to create a broad-based alliance, which became a cornerstone of the policy of national unity. Similarly, the pragmatists argued that representative features would strengthen rather than weaken the regime. Revolutionary legitimacy would be transformed and further strengthened by an electoral legitimacy. Moreover, the FSLN was under pressure, both from the internal opposition and from Western European governments, to strengthen representative democracy. Sectors of the middle class and the business community had been demanding elections ever since 1979. If national unity was to be attained, these demands needed to be taken into account. Also, support by Western European governments, particularly

Sweden, France, and Holland, would be strengthened by assurances that the Sandinista revolution was following the direction of European social democracy. As a result, the government began to reconstruct its vision of national transformation, now emphasizing a combination of representative elements, such as elections of a president and a legislature, with elements of popular participation.[56]

The first significant evidence that the Sandinista leadership was prepared to institutionalize representative features was the electoral process of 1984. When the Front came to power in 1979, it promised to hold elections. Elections were not new to Sandinista ideology; they had been contemplated in the 1977 FSLN program and the June 1979 Governing Junta of National Reconstruction Program.[57] Nevertheless, many observers expressed doubts that the revolutionary government would permit them. These doubts were put to rest on February 21, 1984, when the FSLN set the election date for November 4.

Members of the Sandinista Front vigorously debated the meaning of the elections within the context of Nicaragua's model of popular democracy. The majority of the National Directorate recognized the importance of institutionalizing the revolution through elections, following the reasoning entailed in the concept of representative democracy. The views of the nine members of the FSLN Directorate were diverse, yet the moderates prevailed over the radical Marxist perspective formulated by Comandante Arce.[58] During the election campaign, Arce secretly explained to the political committee of the Nicaraguan Socialist party that the central reason for the holding of elections was to satisfy the demands of the bourgeois opposition and international opinion rather than to decide who would govern Nicaragua. Since the Sandinistas were under attack from both left and right, some obervers interpreted Arce's speech as an FSLN tactic of adapting its position to the perceived interest of the audience. Yet, an analysis of Sandinista statements reveals important differences among the leadership.

Whatever the internal deliberations of the National Directorate, the outcome is evident: elections were held, and the moderates prevailed. According to Carlos Núñez, the directorate discussed the possibility of strengthening participatory democracy through direct representation of the mass organizations in one chamber of a two-chamber assembly. Such a design would have emphasized the priority Sandinista thought assigned to participatory structures, but this proposal was not approved. The advocates of a traditional Western-style model carried the day.

A new law determined that the electorate would comprise all Nicaraguans aged sixteen and older. Voting was voluntary, and the elections were for president, vice-president, and the National Assembly, consisting of ninety members. The president, vice-president, and legislators were elected to six-year terms, the presidency being won by the candidate with a plurality of the votes.[59] To ensure pluralism in the National Assembly, the electoral system provided for proportional representation, and each losing presidential candidate was assured a seat in the National Assembly.

The counterrevolutionary forces, or contras, operating in several regions of Nicaragua constituted a permanent threat to the electoral process and at times disrupted it. More than one hundred voter registration centers could not be opened because of the military situation in the zones where the centers were located.[60] Nonetheless, 93 percent of the estimated voting-age population was registered.[61] Despite Sandinista efforts to ensure a favorable climate for the electoral campaign (most important, the state of emergency was lifted), the bourgeoisie regarded the electoral process with ambivalence. Having insisted on elections since 1979, it denounced the decision to set the election date for November 4, saying it was "too soon," and threatened to abstain.[62]

The opposition candidate who received the most attention was Arturo Cruz, a former member of the Sandinista government and presidential candidate of the Coordinadora Democrática (Democratic Coordinator, or CD). CD represented a broad spectrum of the opposition, including several parties, five private-sector groups, and two unions. CD announced a set of conditions, including separation of party and state, autonomy of judicial power, and the inclusion of contra leaders in a "national dialogue," which had to be met by the government before the opposition would permit its candidate to participate in the contest.[63] CD opted not to register by the established deadline, using the government's refusal to talk with the contra leadership as a pretext.[64] The government and CD continued to negotiate, with several leaders of the Socialist International serving as mediators. The negotiations finally broke down in mid-October, as each side charged bad faith. Thus, Cruz did not participate. It has since become known that the main forces within the opposition alliance never intended to take part, fearing they would help legitimize the revolutionary process.[65]

The Reagan administration sought to discredit the electoral process as soon as the election date was announced and advised the opposition parties to abstain. U.S. diplomats urged the presidential candidates of several conservative opposition parties to pull out of the election, a campaign that succeeded in the case of Virgilio Godoy, minister of labor until 1984 and head of the Independent Liberal party.[66] Despite the Reagan administration's attempt to disrupt the electoral process and discredit the FSLN victory, independent U.S. observers and numerous international delegations confirmed that the elections were the freest and cleanest in Nicaragua's history.[67]

In light of the difficult economic conditions and the toll of the counterrevolutionary aggression, the margin of the Sandinista victory was impressive. Daniel Ortega received 63 percent of the presidential vote (see table 2.3 for complete information) and FSLN candidates won sixty-one of the ninety-six seats in the National Assembly. It seems significant that had the Sandinistas favored the U.S. system of majority vote, the FSLN would have carried every single seat in 1984.[68] The three parties to the left of the Sandinistas got only their presidential candidates into the legislature, and the three parties to the right obtained a total of twenty-nine mandates. From a pluralist perspective, it is important to emphasize that 40 percent of FSLN's slate of candidates were not members of the party. The Sandinistas believed that the delegates' authority and influence among the populace was more important than their membership in the FSLN.[69]

The elections were held, although the government was the victim of military aggression and ideological attack by counterrevolutionary forces and an economic boycott by the United States. The simple fact that FSLN submitted to a popular referendum under such conditions seems further evidence of its commitment to combining social revolution and democracy, for either the boycott or the U.S.-sponsored contra attacks could have been used as a pretext for canceling the elections. The large voter turnout and the substantial majority of ballots cast for FSLN added legitimacy to the Sandinista political leadership and deepened the commitment of many Western European and Latin American governments and solidarity movements to aiding the government. Yet the elections failed to end United States' efforts to destroy the Sandinista revolution. Washington's hostility finally ended with the 1990 elections, although the Sandinistas paid an exceedingly high price: they had to relinquish power.

When Sandinista Nicaragua celebrated its tenth anniversary, it was a state seeking to institutionalize a form of revolutionary democratic Marxism based on a combination of more direct elements of participatory democracy (e.g., the Sandinista mass organizations) and representative democracy through elections. Sandinista democracy was distinct from

Table 2.3. The Nicaraguan elections, 1984

	No.	% of votes registered	deposited	valid
A. Results for president and vice-president				
Registered voters	1,555,597			
Votes deposited	1,170,142	75.4		
Abstentions	381,455	24.6		
Valid votes	1,098,933	70.8		
Invalid votes	71,209	4.6		
FSLN	735,967	47.4	62.9	67.0
PCD	154,327	10.0	13.0	14.0
PLI	105,560	6.8	9.0	9.6
PPSC	61,199	3.9	5.2	5.6
PC de N	16,034	1.0	1.4	1.5
PSN	14,494	0.9	1.2	1.3
MAP-ML	11,352	0.7	1.0	1.0
B. Results for National Assembly				
Votes deposited	1,170,102	75.4		
Abstentions	381,495	24.6		
Valid votes	1,091,878	70.4		
Invalid votes	78,224	5.0		
FSLN	729,195	47.0	62.3	66.8
PCD	152,883	9.9	13.0	14.0
PLI	105,497	6.8	9.0	9.7
PPSC	61,525	4.0	5.3	5.6
PC de N	16,165	1.0	1.4	1.5
PSN	15,306	1.0	1.3	1.4
MAP-ML	11,343	0.7	1.0	1.0

Source: Supreme Election Council (CSE).

Note: FSLN: Sandinista National Liberation Front.

MAP-ML: Popular Action Movement—Marxist-Leninist.

PCD: Democratic Conservative Party.

PC de N: Communist Party of Nicaragua.

PLI: Independent Liberal Party.

PPSC: Popular Christian Party.

PSN: Nicaraguan Socialist Party.

the "popular democracy" of the former one-party states of Eastern Europe, since it allowed for political pluralism. Or, to note another contrasting case, the representation of seven parties in Nicaragua's National Assembly from 1984 through 1990 compared favorably with Cuba, where, in the early 1980s, 96.7 percent of the 441 delegates were affiliated with the Communist party.[70]

The contribution of the Sandinistas to socialist governance consists of

the realization that to assure political democracy, representative structures must allow for pluralist elections that hold existing programs
accountable and encourage consideration of alternate political and social
visions. The goal was to overcome the limits of representative democracy
and integrate it into a much more profound structure that would allow
participation by the previously marginalized majority. Some analysts
have attributed the Sandinista Front's commitment to pluralism and an
electoral process to pressure by the domestic opposition and international opinion. This view appears to be based on the public and private
statements by several Sandinista leaders (for example, Bayardo Arce)
who expressed doubts regarding the value of elections to the revolutionary project. Yet, the elections of 1984 and 1990 make clear that the
Sandinistas took their commitment to elections seriously, despite the misgivings voiced by some members of the National Directorate. In the
words of former vice-president Sergio Ramírez (1984–1990): "Pluralism
is a concept essential to the revolution, maintained not merely by the
recognition of certain right-wing parties so that they can function within
the country, but also to make possible the political and democratic participation of different sectors of the population that never before in our
history had access to that participation."[71]

Thus, political pluralism is not a concession to the bourgeoisie but a
precondition for authentic political life, a real confrontation of views,
which allows the masses decision-making power regarding the essential
questions of the socioeconomic and political life of the country. The institutionalization of political pluralism in Nicaragua can be considered a
legacy of the Sandinista revolution. Important sectors in the Front
reached the same conviction that Rosa Luxemburg expressed in her critique of Lenin and the Russian revolution. Luxemburg understood that
socialism could not be introduced without the widest possible democracy
and freedom. Emphasizing the importance of pluralism for a true democracy, she held: "Freedom only for the supporters of the government, only
for the members of one party—however numerous they may be—is not
freedom at all. Freedom is always and exclusively freedom for the one
who thinks differently."[72]

National Unity: The Bourgeoisie, the Left, and the Sandinistas

One of the most important aspects of Sandinista democracy was the
inclusion of the bourgeoisie in the revolutionary vision.[73] This resulted
from the policy of national unity, based on the FSLN's commitment to

political pluralism and a mixed economy. Although the Sandinistas controlled Nicaragua from 1979 to 1990, the power structure was far from monolithic. The business community, the church, and active political opposition groups were also important contenders. My analysis of the opposition's role in the Sandinista period focuses on the private sector and the left-wing opposition, which illustrate the dialectic inherent in Sandinista national unity.

From July to December of 1979, when initial readjustments of the new political structures took place, the bourgeoisie's share of important political positions in the new political order was astonishing. Only two members of FSLN's National Directorate occupied cabinet positions, while the bourgeoisie held important ministries and a majority on the Council of State. The private sector felt particularly reassured of the Sandinista commitment to a mixed economy, since central positions in the revolutionary government (planning, finance, and the central bank) were held by individuals with excellent reputations in the domestic and international business community.[74] A drastic reorganization of the government in December 1979, however, increased the power of the Sandinistas, displaced several bourgeois members, and reduced the political power of the bourgeoisie considerably. The bourgeoisie saw this advance of Sandinista control as a betrayal of the original program of the revolution. Relations with the FSLN were bound to deteriorate because of fundamentally different conceptions of the future development of Nicaraguan society. Cordial relations ended when the bourgeoisie realized that implementation of the Sandinista design would threaten its privileged position.

Those bourgeois forces who opposed the Sandinistas coalesced around COSEP because of its economic power base. Opposition political parties were weak, several having lost legitimacy because of their previous collaboration with the Somoza dictatorship.[75] COSEP was considered the most effective representative of bourgeois interests. Thus, the FSLN directed its dialogue with the opposition toward the business community represented by COSEP, rather than toward the political parties.[76]

The Sandinista Front realized from the outset that cooperation from the business community was essential to reconstruction, and the policy of national unity was an incentive for the bourgeoisie to cooperate. Though the political power of the bourgeoisie was restricted under this policy, the business community retained substantial economic power within Nicaragua's mixed economy. The mixed economy was established as a consequence of the social compromise implied by the policy of national unity, yet the advance of Sandinista hegemony over the political system was eventually accompanied by the consolidation of economic power. The economic base centered around business enterprises confiscated from Somoza and his associates. These holdings, mostly agricultural in nature, were integrated into the APP and managed by the state. The Sandinistas soon gained control over other key areas of the economy. Indeed, Article 99 of the 1987 Nicaraguan constitution affirmed: "The state directs and plans the national economy in order to guarantee and defend the interests of the majority and to guide it in accordance with the goals of socio-economic progress. The Central Bank, the National Financial System, Insurances and Reinsurances and External Trade, which are [all] instruments to direct the economy, are irrevocably a part of the state sector."[77] Comandante Jaime Wheelock, a member of FSLN's National Directorate, clearly affirmed Sandinista control over the economy. He maintained that "the hegemony of the economic development process is in the new relations of production created by the revolution. It is a hegemony achieved by the nationalization of foreign commerce, of natural resources and of strategic industrial sectors, and with the nationalization of banks. With these measures we have created a system of production and of management which predominates, which is hegemonic, which coexists with forms one could call capitalist to an appreciable degree, and with others that are backward or precapitalist."[78]

In the eyes of COSEP leaders, the bourgeoisie had lost economic power. Ramiro Gúrdian, for example, complained that the government had eliminated the private sector's ability to make important decisions. Despite this weakened position, the business community retained substantial economic power and forced the Sandinistas to cooperate. Relations between the Sandinistas and the bourgeoisie were complex. The revolutionary authorities needed to control the destructive efforts of some right-wing members of the private sector without losing the trust of the bourgeoisie. They also had to restrain zealots within the Sandinista party who considered all capitalists enemies and could not see the need to consolidate the revolution slowly.

The expanding state sector and continuing invasions of private property during the first months of the revolution provoked dissent in the business community. Anxiety in the private sector increased dramatically when private property seemed to be threatened by a March 1980 law.[79] This anti-"decapitalization" law was directed against members of the business community whose distrust in Sandinista policies and insecurity about their economic future led them to halt further investments and allow their plants to run down. The capitalists showed imagination in undermining the economy: "1. refusing to cultivate land; 2. reducing the productive capacity of factories; 3. transporting productive machinery out of the country; 4. refusing to reinvest profits," and depleting Nicaragua's foreign currency reserves.[80] These responses contributed to the country's economic problems, and strengthened popular pressure on the government to take action against the private sector. The Sandinistas responded by seeking to increase the control of the work force over management. They instituted regular assemblies of workers and administrators to discuss the production process of each enterprise.[81] At the same time, the FSLN responded to the private sector's insecurity by legitimizing private ownership of the means of production and by promising to end invasions of private properties by Sandinista mass organizations.

After a short truce, business and government were at odds again. COSEP withdrew from the Council of State in November to protest, among other things, the postponement of the elections.

Relations deteriorated sharply when Jorge Salazar, the vice-president of COSEP, was killed in a confrontation with Sandinista police. According to government accounts, Salazar was part of a conspiracy to overthrow the Sandinistas, but leaders in the business community believed him a victim of government entrapment.[82] This incident considerably damaged relations between the private sector and government, and the business community continued its decapitalization. Rhetorical attacks from both sides increased.

The Sandinistas repeatedly stressed the class character of the revolution and referred to the bourgeoisie as "our internal class enemies."[83] In this climate, COSEP leaders wrote a letter to Daniel Ortega in October 1981, charging the Sandinista Front with betraying the original program of the revolution. It made clear that the right-wing business sector would "in no way support the project to transform this revolution into a new Marxist-Leninist adventure which will only bring more blood and suffering for our own people."[84] It also accused the Sandinistas of attacking the mixed economy, which was being "set back under the advance of the nationalization of property, signaling a project drawn up behind the backs of the people."[85] Perceiving the letter as part of a coordinated initiative to destroy the revolution,[86] the government sentenced the authors to several months in prison. Ramiro Gúrdian, one of the six COSEP leaders who had signed the document, managed to escape to Venezuela before any government action was taken. According to Gúrdian, mediation by President José López Portillo of Mexico was essential to get the COSEP leaders released in February 1982 and allow his own return from exile.

The war contributed to the tense political climate. One of the fundamental problems between the private sector and the Sandinista Front was the conviction of important groups in COSEP that the government would be overthrown by the U.S.-sponsored counterrevolutionary forces. Thus, the bourgeoisie had no incentive to cooperate. In 1988, after the contras ceased to constitute a military threat, the bourgeoisie continued to resist. With the disappearance of the military option, the fight moved into the political arena. The Nandaime incident of July 10, 1988—an antigovernment demonstration that resulted in clashes between police and demonstrators and led to the arrest of several business leaders—indicated the private sector's intention to create a climate of popular unrest to bring down the government. In the same month, the private-sector opposition, led by COSEP and with the active participation of U.S. ambassador Richard Melton, formed a "government of national salvation" and demanded the dissolution of the Sandinista government.[87] These measures sought "to provoke a government crackdown, create martyrs, isolate Nicaragua internationally and derail the Esquipulas peace process."[88] The situation deteriorated further when the Sandinista leadership used the occasion of the ninth anniversary of the revolution to announce the expropriation of the most important private enterprise, a sugar refinery owned by the Pellas family.

Challenges to FSLN hegemony were not limited to the bourgeoisie. The Sandinistas also had to contend with opposition from the other side of the ideological spectrum, in particular from the ultra-left MAP-ML and its affiliated union, FO. Antagonism between the Sandinistas and the Workers' Front dates back to 1972, when a group of Sandinista guerrillas was accused of planning to assassinate the entire Sandinista leadership.[89] These dissidents formed the Workers' Front and participated in the insurrection through their military organization, the Militias Populares Antisomocistas (Popular Anti-Somocista Militia, or MILPAS), which enjoyed substantial working-class support. Its contribution to the overthrow of Somoza was recognized when it received a seat on the original Council of State. Early on, the Marxist-Leninists were considered a challenge to the Sandinista project. A secret 1979 FSLN document described the movement as an "enemy of the revolution." The document states: "The position of the FSLN regarding the parties of the Left is based on the view these parties have of the revolutionary process. If this position entails an actual danger, these parties will be treated as enemies of the revolution. Such is the case of groups which from an ultra-left perspective have taken sabotaging and counterrevolutionary positions. The MAP with its organizations and the Trotskyites; these groups in opposition to the process have to be destroyed."[90]

Contrary to popular belief, the Marxist-Leninists, not the bourgeoisie, can claim the dubious honor of being the first jailed opponents of the Sandinistas. Also, the radical left joined the bourgeoisie in having its political representation restricted. The Sandinista Front eliminated the seat of the Workers' Front when they changed the original makeup of the Council of State. According to Fernando Maletin, the Marxist-Leninists were not allowed to participate in this colegislative body until mid-1984. The Sandinistas repressed the Marxist-Leninists, apparently threatened by their ultra-left critique of the revolution. Carlos Cuadra, the MAP-ML vice-president, denounced the policy of national unity as a capitulation to the bourgeoisie and demanded a dictatorship of the proletariat, accompanied by the nationalization of all means of production. Further, members of the Workers' Front tried to obtain support among the working class by demanding immediate substantial pay increases and the confiscation of factories during a time when the Sandinistas told the workers that the reconstruction of the country had priority over demands for higher salaries. This populist rhetoric challenged the FSLN, which sought to follow a more pragmatic course under the policy of national unity. The Sandinista government was in the unenviable position of being attacked simultaneously from both left and right. Although these sectors were ideologically bitter enemies, they were united in their opposition to the Sandinistas. This opposition was evidently strong enough to provide a common ground for communists and socialists to unite in 1989 with right-wing parties into the Unión Nacional Oppositora (National Opposition Union, or UNO).

During the first years of the revolution, the FSLN overreacted to challenges to its authority. As the institutionalization of the revolution progressed, the Sandinista Front matured in the handling of the opposition and in providing political space for positions representing the full extent of the ideological spectrum. The Nicaraguan voters endorsed the pragmatism of the Front in the 1984 elections. Sandinista candidates gained more than 60 percent of the vote, the radical Marxist-Leninists obtained only 1 percent, and the COSEP affiliates abstained. Nevertheless, the policy of national unity proved only partially successful in gaining bourgeois cooperation for the reconstruction of the economy. Though the so-called patriotic producers—sectors of the rural bourgeoisie who joined the Sandinistas in reconstruction—demonstrated the feasibility of a revolutionary aspiration to national unity, the majority of the capitalist class was not prepared to contribute in the economic arena without sharing political power. In the eyes of leading industrialists, such as Ramiro Gúrdian, the policy of national unity, if it ever existed, ended six months into the revolution when most representatives of the private sector left the government.

At this juncture the revolutionary leadership firmly established the hegemony of the popular classes. The bourgeoisie was not prepared to subordinate its class interests to a development strategy designed to benefit the impoverished majority. The Sandinistas, while attempting to incorporate the opposition into reconstruction, were always clear on the limits of national unity. According to President Ortega:

> Our socialism is a socialism that defends, in the first place, the workers and the peasants as the fundamental forces of the nation. Our socialism also provides all economic and social sectors which exist in Nicaragua with the opportunity to produce and to contribute to the progress of the country. . . . Thus, our socialism defends the institution of a mixed economy and defends political pluralism but within the institutional and constitutional framework, not to deny the power of the people but to work with the government and to work with popular power.[91]

The bourgeoisie had little incentive to participate under Sandinista hegemony as long as it considered the overthrow of the government a viable option. In this regard, the policies of the Reagan administration impeded economic recovery and contributed decisively to the Sandinista defeat in the 1990 elections.

Sandinista versus Popular Hegemony

The hegemonic project of the Sandinistas was based on the reality that the coalition of popular forces that overthrew Somoza was not confined to workers and peasants. Thus, the establishment of a "dictatorship of the proletariat" would have imposed a narrow class vision on a broad anti-Somoza coalition. Instead of following the doctrine of orthodox Marxism, the Sandinistas relied on their own political understanding, which was closer to the theoretical tradition of Antonio Gramsci, whose theory of hegemony "accepts social complexity as the very condition of political struggle and . . . sets the basis for a democratic practice of politics, compatible with a plurality of historical subjects."[92] The Sandinista hegemonic strategy is appealing from a pluralist perspective, since it attempted to enlist all sectors of society in support of the revolution instead of excluding certain sectors from the outset. Indeed, the Sandinista project provides an interesting example of a revolutionary society's effort to combine representative and participatory forms of democracy while seeking to benefit the impoverished majority. However, serious questions must be raised as to the "popular" content of the Sandinista experiment and its democratic or authoritarian practice.

One of the central problems of Sandinista democracy is the concept of popular hegemony. The Sandinistas favored a participatory, direct model of democracy based on grassroots movements. Yet, with the exception of the National Union of Farmers and Ranchers, the mass organizations never achieved the autonomy necessary to assume their intended role. Without strong and independent mass organizations to guarantee popular hegemony, the Front became the guarantor of the "revolutionary" substance of the experience. This raises the question of whether the content of the hegemonic project was actually "popular" or merely "Sandinista." Hegemony was guaranteed through the FSLN's control over the armed forces and the police. All significant lines of power converged on the nine-member National Directorate of FSLN, which controlled the presidency, the National Assembly, and all important ministries.

Popular hegemony thus was mediated by the FSLN's control of power. This constitutes a problem since the Sandinista Front does not necessarily represent the interest of the poor majority. Indeed, the Sandinista leadership became increasingly detached from the popular classes, which contributed to its electoral defeat.[93] The self-conception of the FSLN as representing the vanguard is part of this dilemma.[94] The Sandinista party was instrumental in overthrowing Somoza and constituted the vanguard during the insurrection. For one sector within the FSLN, however, the conception of vanguard implies that the Sandinista leadership knows best the interests of the people. History shows that this view perpetuates in power an elite that becomes detached from the people. The Leninist principles, according to which the Sandinista movement was built, proved very effective during the insurrection. Though they were essential for the survival of a clandestine movement, they were detrimental to the building of revolutionary democratic Marxism in Nicaragua. Rosa Luxemburg's criticism of Lenin and the Russian revolution provides an important lesson for the Sandinista leadership.

This Sandinista conception of vanguard, together with the lack of internal democracy, deserves further scrutiny. FSLN was a vanguard party that had only twelve thousand members in 1985.[95] Since the leadership was not elected, the nine-member National Directorate had absolute control over FSLN policies. In the opinion of Moisés Hassan, a member of Nicaragua's original Governing Junta in 1979, the Front could not be considered a traditional party. FSLN maintained its military structure from the days of the insurrection and had yet to implement the principles of democratic centralism envisioned by V. I. Lenin as the path to follow upon taking power.

The lack of internal democracy was evident in the case of the Sandinista Assembly, the highest decision-making body below the National Directorate. Its one hundred members, appointed by the directorate, had no decision-making power but served as a ratifying body for decisions taken by the directorate. Thus, the National Directorate decided the course of the revolution. Its predominance was bound to change following the Sandinista Front's electoral defeat. In May of 1990, during a critical self-evaluation to find the proper strategy to defend revolutionary achievements and prepare for the long, difficult road toward regaining power, Tomás Borge, former minister of the interior and member of the Sandinista Directorate, argued: "There are no longer, nor can there be, vertical lines and silent assent that, in practice, asphyxiate criticism. . . . It is crucial to regroup forces without sectarianism but with agreement on basic criteria. This requires a definition, or a redefinition if you like, of the content of our Sandinista revolutionary projects. Keeping the essence intact, we must look with a critical spirit at our programmatic platform."[96] "To emerge victorious," Borge continued, it is necessary "to regroup and consolidate our forces through democratic discussion and within the framework of party discipline. To initiate an open democratization of the organization through which the base can elect zonal, regional and national leaders directly, secretly and by making use of con-structive criticism of their leaders."[97] The Sandinistas thus recognized the need to democratize their movement and rethink their program in order to regain popular support.

Conclusion

The revolutionary government's defeat in the 1990 elections stunned friends and foes alike. In light of the overwhelming majority of polls predicting a Sandinista victory, the fourteen-point defeat by the UNO coalition led by Violeta Barrios de Chamorro was a humiliating upset. In addition to gaining the presidency, the UNO alliance secured fifty-one seats in the National Assembly. The Sandinistas obtained thirty-eight, and one went to the Social Christian Party. Daniel Ortega and Moisés Hassan, two of the losing presidential candidates, also received seats since they had obtained more than one percent of the vote. Considering the economic crisis at the time, the Sandinista loss at the polls should have been expected. A harsh austerity program had brought inflation down from 33,000 percent in 1988 to 1,700 percent in 1989, but unemployment was rampant and the loss in buying power (real wages were less than 10 percent of what they were in 1980) had drastically reduced popular consumption.[98] If one adds the threat of continued U.S. aggression in case of a FSLN victory, it is rather aston-ishing that 40 percent of the electorate voted for the Sandinistas. Table 2.4 shows the distribution of votes in the elections for president and the legislature.

Although UNO controlled an absolute majority in the Nicaraguan legislature, it fell short of the 60 percent of votes needed to implement partial changes in the constitution. This left the Sandinista party in a position of considerable influence over future developments in Nica-ragua. The Chamorro regime could effectively govern only if the Sandin-istas would be prepared to play the role of loyal opposition.

It is one of the many ironies of history that the bourgeoisie needed to continue the Sandinista policy goal of national unity, albeit the roles had been reversed. The Sandinista Front declared its willingness to co-operate with the new government while establishing clear boundaries. It would "support the government's positive steps without intransigent opposition at all times and under all circumstances, without impairing a firm and unwavering opposition to any measure intended to destroy [revolutionary] achievements and all that affects popular interests."[99]

Table 2.4. The Nicaraguan elections, 1990

Results for President

Party	No. of Votes	%
FSLN	579,886	40.8
UNO	777,552	54.7
PSOC	5,843	0.4
PLIUN	3,151	0.2
PRT	8,590	0.6
MAP-ML	8,110	0.6
PSC	11,136	0.8
PUCA	5,065	0.4
PCDN	4,500	0.3
MUR	16,751	1.2

Turnout: 86%

Total registered voters: 1,752,088

Total vote: 1,510,838

Total valid vote: 1,420,584

Results for National Assembly

Party	No. of votes	% of votes	No. of seats
FSLN	579,673	40.9	39[a]
UNO	764,748	53.9	51
PSOC	6,308	0.4	—
PLIUN	3,515	0.2	—
PRT	10,586	0.7	—
MAP-ML	7,643	0.5	—
PSC	22,218	1.6	1
PUCA	5,565	0.4	—
PCDN	4,683	0.3	—
MUR	13,995	1.0	1[a]

Source: Supreme Election Council (CSE). Data reported in Latin American Studies Association, "Electoral Democracy under International Pressure: The Report of the Latin American Studies Association Commission to Observe the 1990 Nicaraguan Election" (March 1990): 34–37.

Note: FSLN: Frente Sandinista de Liberación Nacional

MAP-ML: Movimiento de Acción Popular—Marxista-Leninista

MUR: Movimiento de Unidad Revolucionaria

PCDN: Partido Conservador Democratico de Nicaragua

PLIUN: Partido Liberal Independiente de Unidad Nacional

PRT: Partido Revolucionario de Trabajadores

PSC: Partido Social Christiano

PSOC: Partido Social Conservatismo

PUCA: Partido Unionista de Centro America

UNO: Unión Nacional Opositora

[a]Total includes seat given to a losing presidential candidate who obtained more than 1 percent of the vote.

The Sandinistas demonstrated their commitment to defend popular interests during the summer of 1990, mobilizing the grassroots movements to oppose the new government. Several major strikes brought the country to a halt and exposed the government's weakness. This was "governing from below," anticipated in a speech by President Daniel Ortega two days after the election. Many wondered, however, whether the future would prove the FSLN prediction that "the change of government in no way means the end of the revolution."[100]

Chapter 3

The Rural Proletariat:
Beneficiary of Popular Hegemony?

"Only the workers and the peasants will go to the end." This statement, coined in the 1930s by the Nicaraguan patriot General Augusto César Sandino, was omnipresent on billboards throughout revolutionary Nicaragua. It captured the significance that the Sandinistas assigned to the worker and peasant classes in their attempt to build a society based on fundamentally new relations of production. Sandinista democracy conceived the "worker-peasant alliance" as the driving force of the revolutionary project. These previously marginalized classes were the intended beneficiaries of the popular hegemony policy.

In 1980 the rural proletariat and the agricultural producers together represented more than 50 percent of Nicaragua's EAP.[1] Within an estimated agrarian EAP of 428,000, farmers were the predominant sector. Permanent agricultural workers numbered about 100,000. In an interesting reversal of traditional roles, the rural workers produced most of the country's basic food products (rice, sorghum, sugar, and cooking oil), while the peasant producers, in addition to producing crops for domestic consumption, generated the hard currency necessary to fuel industrial expansion through the planting and harvesting of export crops, particularly coffee, cotton, and sugar.[2] The agrarian bourgeoisie, on the other hand, was almost exclusively engaged in agro-export production.[3]

The Historical Struggle of the Peasantry

The history of Nicaragua's peasantry is closely linked to the introduction of export crops.[4] The development of coffee production around 1850 displaced hundreds of small farmers who were primarily engaged in the production of basic grains. A century later, the cotton boom once again resulted in the forced expulsion of peasants from their land. This time, however, the peasants were affected to a lesser degree since the increased need for land dedicated to cotton cultivation was satisfied by converting pastures that had been used for cattle grazing.[5] When cotton prices declined sharply in the 1960s, the rural bourgeoisie began the third cycle of the agro-export economy by moving into the production of beef.[6] Since land and other resources were allocated to the development of export agriculture, the production of basic grains was limited and eventually stagnated.[7] Marginalized peasant producers, who found their access to basic staples curtailed, encountered great difficulties in organizing resistance to this situation, which threatened their traditional way of life. The introduction of labor-intensive crops such as cotton and coffee also accelerated the proletarianization of the peasantry.[8]

During the dictatorship of the Somoza family (1936–1979), the Nicaraguan labor movement, weak even by Central American standards, managed to organize less than 10 percent of the workforce.[9] The absence of strong unions was even more evident in the rural sector. During the 1950s, a total of twenty-five peasant and worker unions formed, with a combined membership of 1,015. The Socialist party and its affiliated labor movement, the Confederación General de Trabajo, were the main forces behind the organizational efforts in the rural sector.[10] As shown in table 3.1, a decade later, sixty-one unions had emerged, incorporating 2,685 members. The incipient worker and peasant movement suffered setbacks because of repressive actions by the Somocista state and the 1967 split of the Socialist party, which deprived it of its main sponsor.[11] In 1975, only forty-eight unions with 2,003 members were left.[12]

A central limitation in the peasantry's struggle to organize itself was widespread urban and rural migration.[13] Poor farmers, displaced by the expansion of agro-export production, frequently chose to migrate to the agricultural frontier in order to continue farming, or they sought employment in the cities rather than continue to face the harsh realities of the countryside. This situation functioned like an escape valve and made it difficult for organized resistance to emerge. For a long time the peasantry chose "everyday forms of resistance"[14] rather than open challenge. This indirect resistance took the form of "migrating to the agricultural frontier, to the cities, seeking shelter under the protection of progressive/paternalistic priests, or resorting to cattle rustling and theft."[15] Dur-

Table 3.1. Rural unions, 1950–1959, 1960–1969

	No. of unions		Members	
Category	1950–59	1960–69	1950–59	1960–69
Unions of agricultural workers	14	33	567	1,307
Peasant Unions	5	14	249	532
Mixed Unions	6	14	199	846
Total	25	61	1,015	2,685

Source: Chavarría y Fernandez, *Apuntes para la historia del movimiento campesino en Nicaragua.* Managua: Monografía de Licenciatura en Sociología, UCA, 1986. Table reported in Serra, *El movimiento campesino,* 52.

ing the 1920s, however, Nicaraguan peasants united under the leadership of Augusto C. Sandino to engage in open warfare.

At the turn of the century, the United States, driven by geopolitical and economic interests, determined the country's politics.[16] The United States intervened several times, starting in 1912. The second U.S. occupation (1926–1933) was vigorously opposed by Sandino, a Liberal army officer, who conducted a successful guerrilla campaign against the U.S. Marines. Sandino's forces consisted of agricultural workers, peasants who had been expropriated during the expansion of export-crop production, and workers from the mines of northern Nicaragua.[17] The desire of the popular classes to defeat the occupying forces was shared by some sectors of the bourgeoisie. Sandino, seeking to construct an effective military alliance, incorporated them into his guerrilla force. As a result of this policy, he was criticized by the Communist International (Comintern), which at the time espoused an "ultra-left line, characterized by a revolutionary puritanism which refused to collaborate with any bourgeois elements."[18] Sandino's pragmatic position represented the historic precedent for the strategy of the Sandinista Front to incorporate broad sectors of Nicaraguan society into an anti-Somoza coalition, regardless of their class identity. Sandino was not content with limiting his struggle to the guerrilla war against the U.S. Marines and their Nicaraguan allies. He also pursued an aggressive social agenda, denouncing the prevailing socioeconomic conditions and demanding an end to the exploitation in the countryside. His social program attracted support from the peasant and worker classes. Starting with a base in the mountains of northern Nicaragua, Sandino's army grew to six thousand men by 1932 and challenged government forces in three-fourths of the country.[19] In a war of attrition, characterized by a series of small battles, the insurgents inflicted heavy casualties on the U.S. forces. The U.S. Marines finally withdrew in January 1933, when the incoming administration of Franklin D. Roosevelt ushered in the era of the "Good Neighbor" policy. With his main objective realized (the expulsion of the *Yanquis*), Sandino signed a peace treaty with President Juan Batista Sacasa. Yet relations between Sandino's forces and the Guardia Nacional (National Guard or GN), which had been established by the United States as a caretaker force, remained tense. On February 21, 1934, Sandino was assassinated by the Guardia, which acted upon direct orders from its commander, Anastasio Somoza García.[20] Somoza then proceeded to eliminate the threat posed by Sandino's forces to his aspiration of assuming complete control over Nicaragua. In a military operation, Sandinista cooperatives in northern Nicaragua were attacked and destroyed. In the town of Wiwilí alone, more than three hundred Sandinistas were slaughtered.[21] Despite all of Somoza's efforts, several important Sandinistas, including General Santos López, survived. Most significantly, Sandino's legacy—his nationalist, anti-imperialist struggle against the oppressors of the poor—was passed on through oral traditions to a new generation of Nicaraguans, willing to continue the fight for justice.

The Sandinista Front and the Emergence of ATC

In July 1961, Carlos Fonseca, Tomás Borge, Sílvio Mayorga, and Santos López founded a new revolutionary movement, the National Liberation Front. In 1963, at the insistence of Carlos Fonseca, the organization renamed itself the Frente Sandinista de Liberación Nacional (Sandinista National Liberation Front), thus establishing the historic link between the anti-imperialist ideology of Sandino and the new struggle for liberation.[22] Fonseca, the eminent Sandinista leader, deserves the credit for having recognized the importance of Sandino. He emphasized that the FSLN needed "to deepen the study of the Sandinista experience and of the documents of the great hero which will serve as a sure guide in the patriotic struggle."[23] Humberto Ortega, one of the key Sandinista military strategists, recognized that "Sandino gave us all the important anti-imperialist and social concepts, as well as the strategies for revolutionary transformation and armed struggle which led to the creation of the Sandinista Front in the 1960s."[24] The Sandinistas, successful in claiming Sandino's legacy, were able to transfer the mystique and admiration that his name elicited among peasants and workers to their own movement.

Sandinista ideology united Nicaraguan society against the Somoza dictatorship and provided the foundation for FSLN's hegemony. Without it, the Sandinista Front would in all likelihood have suffered the same fate as the thirty-two armed movements in Nicaragua's history that had unsuccessfully fought against the local oligarchy and imperialist forces.[25]

From the very beginning, the Sandinista Front proposed a strategy of armed struggle in order to end the rule of the Somoza family. The Sandinista struggle differed from prior insurgencies, however, because FSLN did not constitute itself primarily as a guerrilla movement but as a political-military organization. According to its 1969 program, "FSLN is a political-military organization whose strategic objective is the taking of political power through the destruction of the dictatorship's military and bureaucratic apparatus and the establishment of a revolutionary government based on the worker-peasant alliance and the cooperation of all patriotic, anti-imperialist and anti-oligarchical forces of the country."[26]

The Sandinista leadership espoused Marxist ideology, modified and adapted to Nicaraguan reality by the thought of Latin American revolutionary leaders. Carlos Fonseca summarized the ideological position of the FSLN in 1970:

> To describe us proceeding in the revolutionary struggle, we will be guided by the most advanced principles, by Marxist ideology, by Comandante Ernesto "Che" Guevara [and] by Augusto César Sandino. . . . We are conscious that socialism is the only perspective which the people have in order to bring about radical change in their living conditions. This does not mean that we exclude people who do not think as we do, and although we think that the principles of scientific socialism have to be the fundamental guide, we are prepared to march together with people of the most diverse convictions, interested in the downfall of the tyranny and in the liberation of our country.[27]

In the early 1960s, the FSLN guerrillas suffered several defeats by the National Guard. The surviving Sandinistas realized that their military failures were owing to the lack of effective logistics, too little knowledge of the territory, and not enough support from the local peasantry.[28] Rethinking their strategy, the Sandinistas increased their efforts to politicize the peasantry and established the first clandestine labor unions and cooperatives.

Initially, the peasants started to organize with the help of the Jesuits and some sectors of the Catholic hierarchy.[29] Liberation theology, which by then had profoundly influenced the attitude of the Catholic church toward the poor, was a crucial catalyst for change. The emerging peasant movement was centered in the Pacific region where most of Nicaragua's capital intensive farming is located. Forced expropriation was more widespread in the Pacific region than in the country in general because of the scarcity of fertile land and the expansion of capitalist farming.[30] Consequently, the first important efforts in organizing were centered around Managua, Masaya, and Carazo, towns in a region on the Pacific coast with high population density.[31] The FSLN, together with various progressive religious sectors that included laypeople trained in liberation theology (so-called "Delegates of the Word"), constituted the essential forces behind the emergence of the first committees of agricultural workers.[32] In addition to the Pacific region, unions also emerged in the agricultural frontier, set up by rural workers and poor farmers engaged in coffee production.[33]

According to Wilberto Lara, one of the initial organizers, these early organizational efforts were brutally repressed by the National Guard. Yet this repression did not contain the further development of the incipient peasant movement, which started to extend into the departments of Rívas and Chinandega.[34] At a clandestine meeting in 1977, the peasants discussed the future direction of their struggle for justice. In order to escape detection from the National Guard, the meeting was held at *La Palmera,* a convent of the Catholic church. The participants effectively took advantage of the religious cover and carried bibles.[35] The peasants emerged from this meeting confident of their strength and eager to implement an agenda of reform. The increased activity of the recently formed committees of agricultural workers culminated in a national assembly on March 25, 1978 in Diriamba. On this occasion, "following the instructions of the Sandinista National Liberation Front," the workers formed ATC.[36] Edgardo García, whose background as a Delegate of the Word was the central factor in his decision to join the struggle, was elected as the association's president. Relations between the Sandinistas and the peasants were based on the realization "that their mutual survival depended on a close alliance."[37] The Sandinista Front "needed food, logistic support, and an active mass movement from which to draw recruits" and the peasants "needed the force necessary to overthrow the Somoza regime, which would enable it to implement its own agrarian reform."[38]

The Sandinista Front played an important role in the emergence of

ATC, despite initial difficulties in taking full advantage of the peasantry's revolutionary potential. Early FSLN policy focused on recruiting primarily agroindustrial workers. Thus, it was not surprising that the majority of rural workers and peasants stayed largely aloof from the revolutionary movement. By 1974–1975, however, the FSLN changed its strategy and started successfully to incorporate the peasantry into the guerrilla movement, changing its status from observer to active participant.[39] Some guerrilla forces, operating in northern Nicaragua, even came to consist almost entirely of members from the rural community.[40] Support for the Sandinista cause was particularly strong "in the key agro-export departments of Chinandega, León, and Matagalpa, [where] a twenty-year-old agrarian movement created the conditions for a campesino-FSLN alliance, thus providing a large political and military base for the revolutionaries."[41]

Once the Sandinistas gained the peasantry's support, they had ensured their survival. The creation of "an extensive territorial network of collaborators . . . allowed the rural guerrilla to survive until the triumph."[42] In the insurrection itself, semiproletarians and the urban population played the central role in the fight to liberate Nicaragua's cities.[43] Although the peasantry's participation was not a major factor in the final phase of the struggle, it was crucial in the key northern agro-export departments.[44] Further, it provided the basis for peasant-state relations following the insurrection. The Sandinistas had gained the trust of the peasantry, and their experience during the years in the mountains strengthened the commitment of Sandinista leaders to end the exploitation of the rural sector.[45]

ATC played a political and military role in the insurrection. Jeffrey Gould has argued that ATC's main contribution to the revolutionary struggle was not "union organization but instead its formation of revolutionaries in the field."[46] For example, rural guerrillas, inspired by ATC organizing, supported the Sandinistas in an insurrection in Chinandega province. In some instances, the fighters represented the second generation of peasants who had been involved in the struggle for land in the 1960s.[47] Apart from direct military involvement, ATC denounced the repressive Somoza regime in public demonstrations, organized land invasions in Chinandega province, and set up centers for the training of Sandinista fighters.[48] In an effort to publicize the repression prevailing in Nicaragua's rural sector to the international community, the workers conducted "hunger marches" and occupied the diplomatic mission of the Organization of American States (OAS).[49] These public denunciations of the dictatorship increased ATC's credibility among the rural proletariat.

The leaders of the rural workers' movement paid a heavy price for their participation in the struggle against Somoza. Of the initial group who founded ATC, Edgardo García, the current secretary general, is the only survivor.[50] ATC was not only active in the struggle to defeat the Somoza regime but also played a crucial role immediately after the insurrection of July 1979. García affirmed that ATC members produced food crops on the emerging state farms and maintained the properties of private producers who had fled the country.[51] ATC's efforts were essential since the country was in a state of chaos, with old relations of production being abolished while new ones had not yet emerged. The rural workers' movement, in addition to its activities in maintaining agricultural production, pursued an aggressive recruitment drive among the rural proletariat and small farmers. On December 20, 1979, ATC celebrated its second National Assembly, this time as an officially recognized Sandinista mass organization.

Main Policies and Social Base

In 1978, ATC announced its first *Plan de Lucha,* a program representing the main objectives of the new movement. In this document, the peasants demanded higher salaries, an end to the cheating and exploitative practices of their employers, better working conditions (in particular protection when having to handle toxic materials), an end to child labor, equal salaries for female workers and a stop to sexual exploitation, the right to organize, and a halt to the brutal repression of all rural workers.[52] ATC further argued that "only an integral agrarian reform which would provide us with sufficient land, establish limits for the properties of the landowners, [and] return to the peasants usurped land, could guarantee us true well being."[53]

In the period immediately after the insurrection, the main goals of ATC were to assist the revolutionary government in designing an agrarian reform in order to restructure the old relations of production in the rural sector and to build a strong peasant movement based on the principles of Sandinismo.[54] At that juncture, ATC competed with the Sandinista Neighborhood Committees for the rank of most important grassroots organization in Nicaragua. ATC held three seats on the newly established Council of State, indicating its weight in the new political structures. Of all Sandinista mass organizations, only CDS had more representatives in this colegislative body. ATC's representatives contributed to the formulation of several important laws. The most important ones were the agrarian reform law and the law of the cooperatives. They also introduced a legislative project designed to protect rural workers participating in the coffee and cotton harvest in areas where the counterrevolution was a threat. Following the 1984 elections, ATC had two full representatives and three substitutes in Nicaragua's National Assembly. All five legislators represented FSLN. Finally, the organization held seats on several important policymaking bodies at the national level, which made decisions affecting the lives of the rural proletariat. For example, ATC had representatives on the National and Regional Councils of the Agrarian Reform and the Ministerio de Comercio Interior (Ministry of Internal Commerce, or MICOIN).

The rural workers' movement demonstrated explosive growth in its first years. Representing 12,000 workers in July 1979, ATC had almost 50,000 members by the end of that year and reached more than 100,000 in 1980.[55] The rapidly expanding organization started to incorporate sectors of the rural community with sometimes conflicting class interests. Initially, ATC focused on the needs of the rural proletariat. By 1980, however, the movement responded to the needs of the unfolding revolutionary project and started to organize the peasantry into production cooperatives.[56] Thus, it became a main responsibility of ATC to direct and advise the incipient cooperative movement. Until 1981 ATC defended the interests of three main groups: permanent and seasonal agricultural workers on state and private farms, small farmers, and semiproletarians.[57] Even some medium producers formed part of the movement.

In its early years, the organization was the embodiment of the worker-peasant alliance that constituted the basis of the revolutionary project. The inclusion of small farmers into ATC added to the political importance of the organization and gave ATC increased leverage with the revolutionary authorities. Yet this alliance was not without problems. One of the first challenges facing the organization was to avoid potential conflicts among its diverse constituents. Many agricultural producers felt threatened by landless workers who had started to occupy farms and demanded land under the agrarian reform. "Chico" Javier Saenz affirmed that ATC chose a path different from the Honduran experience, where right-wing groups managed to create conflict between landless workers and small farmers. The rural proletariat who had fought side by side with small farmers in the insurrection had come to respect the small agricultural producers. This understanding found its expression in ATC-supported provisions in the agrarian reform law, which protected the rights of small and medium producers. The organization's relationship with the agrarian bourgeoisie, however, was not equally constructive, because of the strongly developed class consciousness of the ATC leadership. Many ATC leaders had endured great injustices from members of the rural bourgeoisie during the Somoza era and considered all large landowners their enemies. Even the work with small farmers became increasingly difficult for ATC. The organization lacked the capacity to resolve the conflicting demands of agricultural producers and rural workers. Further, Roberto Laguna, an agricultural producer who joined ATC early on, maintained that many farmers were left completely without representation because they resented the antiproducer rhetoric of some ATC leaders and were not interested in joining the existing producer organizations controlled by the rural bourgeoisie. This situation encouraged a group of farmers, most of them Sandinistas, to start the organizational drive for a revolutionary farmers' movement. In 1981 this effort led to the emergence of UNAG.

UNAG's existence resulted in severe setbacks for the rural workers' organization, the most serious ones being the loss of qualified cadres who joined UNAG and the decline in membership. For example, Wilberto Lara, ATC cofounder and a member of its executive committee, left the organization and subsequently became UNAG's second president. The impressive growth of the rural workers' movement came to a grinding halt when the small farmers left to join UNAG. The substantial drop in membership from more than one hundred thousand in 1980 to about 44,000 in 1983 reduced ATC's political significance and leverage considerably. This was manifest, for example, when ATC lost one of its two seats on the Council of State to the newly established farmers' movement. Nevertheless, it can also be argued that the splitting apart of ATC had positive side effects. Most significant, it allowed the organization to concentrate its energies fully on representing the interests of the rural proletariat.[58]

In 1979, ATC was still predominantly an organization of the rural proletariat. At that time it had organized 37,449 workers into unions, and 10,402 small farmers into cooperatives.[59] A year later, the cooperative sector expanded to 48,712 members, and the number of agricultural laborers who had joined ATC increased to 52,396.[60] In terms of absolute numbers, 1980 represented the high point of ATC's organizational development. After that, ATC's growth was either negative or stagnated. According to ATC data, the organization had only 44,413 members in 1983, a total that declined to 41,000 in 1985.[61] Thus, the union lost 11,000 affiliated workers between 1980 and 1985.

Edgardo García, secretary general of ATC, argued that the loss in membership during 1981–1985 was the result of several factors. In his view, the primary reason was lack of interest on the part of the organization itself in the recruitment of more members. Following the trauma of losing two-thirds of the membership to UNAG, ATC leaders considered it more essential to consolidate the remaining base than to recruit new members. Also, the agrarian reform program, while benefiting landless peasants and agricultural workers, reduced the size of the rural proletariat—the potential recruitment pool of ATC. Equally significant was the considerable reduction of the state farms, from 24 percent of the arable land in 1982 to 11.7 percent in 1988,[62] since most of the ATC constituency was employed in the state sector. Although the reduction of the size of the state sector did not always translate into a shrinking labor force, the absolute number of workers employed on the state farms did decline when the Sandinista government implemented austerity measures in the late 1980s. Although these reasons are valid explanations for the difficulties ATC experienced in its organizational growth, they do not provide the full picture.

Membership figures throughout the 1980s indicate that ATC was not completely successful in organizing the agricultural workforce in the state sector and experienced difficulties when seeking to recruit workers on private farms. Considering the distribution of the ATC membership according to state and private sector, we see the following picture. In 1980 the organization represented 30,844 workers on state farms, or 58.9 percent of the rural proletariat affiliated with the union.[63] By 1989 this number had slightly increased to 34,866. Private sector membership, however, declined from 21,552 workers in 1980 (41.1 percent of total) to 14,563 in 1989 (see table 3.2).[64] In 1983 there were 97 state enterprises (each enterprise consisted of several state farms), which employed 64,855 workers.[65] In that year, ATC had a total membership of 44,413 workers, employed in the state and private sector. Although the distribution of ATC members by sector is not available for that year, it is evident that ATC had limited success in organizing the workforce in the state

Table 3.2. Distribution of ATC members employed in
the state and private sectors, 1989

	State sector	Private sector	Total
Region I	5,385	96	5,481
Region II	8,715	3,226	11,941
Region III	2,451	500	2,951
Region IV	4,118	2,600	6,718
Region V	4,300	2,500	6,800
Region VI	9,057	5,581	14,638
Zone III[a]	840	60	900
Total	34,866	14,563	49,429

Source: Association of Rural Workers (ATC).

[a]ATC has no union chapters in Zones I and II.

sector. Based on the figures for 1980 and 1989 it appears that on the
average the union succeeded in organizing about 50 percent of the state
sector. Since ATC was the officially recognized Sandinista union, one
would have expected a higher degree of unionization on the state farms.

No data are available regarding the total number of agricultural
workers who were employed in the private sector. However, since ATC
was stronger in the state than in the private sector, it is clear that the
union's relative weight on private farms was less than on state farms. In
1989, for example, more than two-thirds of the rural proletariat affiliated with ATC was employed in the state sector. In 1980 the figure had
been less than 60 percent. In that year, in terms of overall strength, ATC
succeeded in organizing about 50 percent of the permanent agricultural
labor force, which was estimated at 107,000 people in 1979.[66] For the
rest of the decade, ATC represented between 20 and 30 percent of the
rural proletariat.

The increase in membership between 1985 and 1988, from 41,000 to
52,000, was to a large extent the result of a 1985 policy under which
administrative workers (office workers and management personnel) were
welcomed to join the union.[67] The new policy reflected a revised division
of labor among Sandinista unions. Starting in the mid-1980s, employees
of a particular worksite were supposed to be represented by only one
organization.[68]

From 1988 to 1989, the total number of ATC-affiliated unions increased from 92 to 111, whereas the membership decreased from 52,095
to 48,340 (see tables 3.3 and 3.4). The increase in union chapters

Table 3.3. Permanent workers affiliated with ATC, 1988–1989

A. Number of Members by Crop, 1988

Regions/Zones	Coffee	Cotton	Tobacco	Cattle	Rice[a]	Bananas	Total
Region I	740	—	2,025	600	—	—	3,365
Region II	80	11,000	100	1,611	600	3,760	17,151
Region III	1,800	—	200	1,465	420	—	3,885
Region IV	4,149	120	60	3,205	785	—	8,319
Region V	—	—	—	3,488	600	—	4,088
Region VI	9,676	—	—	3,591	900	—	14,167
Zone III[b]	—	—	—	320	800	—	1,120
Total	16,445	11,120	2,385	14,280	4,105	3,760	52,095

B. Number of Members by Crop, 1989

Regions/Zones	Coffee	Cotton	Tobacco	Cattle	Basic Grains[a]	Bananas	Total
Region I	1,000	—	2,800	600	—	—	4,400
Region II	—	5,795	—	1,022	990	4,200	12,007
Region III	1,262	—	—	1,099	585	—	2,946
Region IV	2,987	—	—	2,088	1,643	—	6,718
Region V	—	—	—	5,800	1,000	—	6,800
Region VI	12,198	—	—	1,945	496	—	14,639
Zone III[b]	—	—	—	460	370	—	830
Total	17,447	5,795	2,800	13,014	5,084	4,200	48,340

Source: Association of Rural Workers (ATC).

[a] In 1989 the rice sector was enlarged to incorporate all basic grains.

[b] ATC had no representation in Zones I and II.

Table 3.4. Base structure of ATC, 1988–1989

A. Number of Unions According to Crop and State or Private Sector Affiliation, 1988

Regions/zones	Coffee S[a]	P[b]	Cotton S	P	Tobacco S	P	Cattle S	P	Rice[d] S	P	Bananas S	P	Total S	P
Region I	2	—	—	—	6	—	2	2	—	—	—	—	10	2
Region II	—	—	5	7	—	—	2	2	1	—	1	—	9	9
Region III	1	1	—	—	1	—	2	—	—	1	—	—	4	2
Region IV	1	7	—	—	—	—	3	—	—	1	—	—	4	8
Region V	—	—	—	—	—	—	9	4	1	1	—	—	10	5
Region VI	7	9	—	—	—	—	3	1	1	1	—	—	11	11
Zone III[c]	—	—	—	—	—	—	3	3	1	—	—	—	4	3
Total	11	17	5	7	7	—	24	12	4	4	1	—	52	40

B. Number of Unions, 1989

Regions/zones	Coffee S	P	Cotton S	P	Tobacco S	P	Cattle S	P	Basic Grains[d] S	P	Bananas S	P	Total S	P
Region I	1	—	—	—	4	—	1	1	—	—	—	—	6	1
Region II	—	—	4	7	—	—	3	8	1	7	1	—	9	22
Region III	1	1	—	—	—	—	2	—	3	—	—	—	6	1
Region IV	1	4	—	—	—	—	3	—	1	1	—	—	5	5
Region V	—	—	—	—	—	—	9	9	4	6	—	—	13	15
Region VI	8	11	—	—	—	—	3	—	1	1	—	—	12	12
Zone III	—	—	—	—	—	—	1	1	2	—	—	—	3	1
Total	11	16	4	7	4	—	22	19	12	15	1	—	54	57

Source: Association of Rural Workers (ATC).

[a]S: Union chapter on a state farm.

[b]P: Union chapter consisting of workers from adjoining private farms.

[c]ATC had no representation in Zones I and II.

[d]In 1989 the rice sector was enlarged to incorporate all basic grains.

reflected the incorporation of workers engaged in the production of all types of basic grains (not only rice as in 1988). The drop in membership, on the other hand, resulted from the 1988 Sandinista austerity program, which led to a reduction in the size of the workforce employed in the state sector. ATC had its strongest representation in the coffee sector. In 1989, 17,447 workers were integrated into eleven unions on state farms and sixteen on private farms. Whereas the cattle sector had more legally recognized unions, they represented fewer (13,014) workers. The most significant decline in membership, although not in the number of union chapters, occurred in the cotton sector. Although ATC had 11,120 members in 1988, only 5,795 workers engaged in cotton production remained affiliated with the union in 1989. The drop in the world market price for cotton hurt state and private producers alike. As a result, ATC lost almost 50 percent of its constituency engaged in cotton production. On a regional basis, the rural workers' movement was strongest in regions VI and II. Region VI was characterized by coffee production, and banana and cotton cultivation predominated in region II. ATC also represented the seasonal agricultural labor force. Although these workers were not officially members, they benefited from the union's work to gain better working conditions and higher salaries. In 1988, there were 69,265 temporary agricultural workers.

Organizational Structure and Internal Democracy

The structure of the organization and its decision-making process, designed to guarantee internal democracy and the effective participation of rural workers in the life of ATC, were modeled after the structures of the Sandinista party.[69] According to ATC's 1979 "Declaration of Principles," its internal organization was supposed to be governed by the principle of "democratic centralism which implies the consultation and the taking into account of the base structures in all important decisions that affect the life of the Association."[70] Although this kind of democratic centralism envisioned in the organization's charter was basically adhered to, the union's internal decision-making process was deficient from the perspective of formal democracy. Internal democracy was basically restricted to the base level, where the members of the local union-chapters had some measure of control over their leaders. Only at the base level did members elect the leadership of the union chapters in biannual elections.

Organizational structures at the regional level were rather weak. Their members were appointed by the national leadership. Starting in 1982, ATC developed a regional structure that coincided with state and party subdivisions. The basic organizational units were the Comités Zonales de Trabajadores Permanentes (Zonal Committees of Permanent Workers, CZPT). It was the main task of these committees to coordinate the work of the union chapters in a particular zone. By 1983, twenty-three CZPTs existed, which in turn sent representatives to regional assemblies.[71] The process of setting up regional structures, however, was not completed until 1984. For example, the regional committees for regions II and IV were set up in October 1983 and August 1984, respectively.

At the national level, the union was directed by an executive committee whose members were elected by ATC's national congress (the organizational structure is shown in table 3.5). The national executive committee had initially six members (it was later expanded to thirteen), which represented organization, labor matters, records, women, political education, and international relations. The committee was headed by Edgardo García, ATC's secretary general. National and regional ATC leaders were professionals, paid by the organization. The national executive committee made all important decisions regarding the daily functioning of the organization. It reported to a national council. This council approved the budget and was in charge of major policy decisions when the congress was in recess. The national council consisted of the national executive committee and the members directing the federations incorporated in ATC.

The national leadership was not uniformly elected, and the length of the leadership's mandate was not determined. Edgardo García, the current secretary general of ATC, was originally elected at the organization's first national congress in 1978. When ATC held a national congress in 1984, García's leadership was ratified by the attending delegates without formal elections. Neither was the length of his mandate established. In general, the Sandinista Front presented a slate of candidates for executive committee positions, from which the delegates to the national congress could choose.[72]

The national congress was supposed to be convened every two years, yet these assemblies were not held at regular intervals. This was significant, since the national assembly constituted the primary authority for long-term decisions. According to the revised 1992 statutes, the congress now meets every three years.[73] At the March 1992 congress, the delegates approved several changes in ATC's organizational structure. Most

Table 3.5. ATC's organizational structure, 1983–1992

A. 1983–91
National:
National Congress
National Council
National Executive Committee
Regional/Departmental:
Regional/Department Assembly
Regional/Department Council
Regional/Department Executive Committee
Level of Zone: Zonal Committee of Workers
B. 1992
National:
National Congress
National Council
National Executive Committee
Regional/Departmental:
Regional/Departmental Assembly
Regional/Departmental Council
Regional/Departmental Executive Committee

Source: Association of Rural Workers (ATC).

significant was the institutionalization of formal democratic procedures. For the first time, all national ATC leaders were elected in secret direct elections.

Initially, the nature of ATC's base structures was complex. In order to accommodate the needs of its diverse constituency, the rural workers were organized into union chapters and the small farmers and semiproletarians into cooperatives. Following the exodus of the small farmers in 1981, ATC's primary structures were the local union chapters established on private and state farms. In 1985, there were approximately 450 base structures.[74] An important case study describes the union structure on the Oscar Turcios Chavarría state farm, which produced tobacco, basic grains, and vegetables in northwestern Nicaragua.[75] According to Edgardo García, 60 percent of the union chapters were located on private farms. However, union chapters in the state sector were numerically much stronger than those in the private sector.

In the mid-1980s, ATC implemented two important reforms. After the initial structures of the organization were institutionalized, the leadership realized that the problems of the rural workforce differed according

to work sector. As a result, the union chapters at the base level were organized by crop. The 1985 reorganization according to work sector corresponded at the national level to the commissions for cattle, tobacco,
basic grains, cotton, and coffee, where ATC delegates represented the
interest of the rural proletariat. In a second major development, union
structures on individual state farms were integrated into the Sindicatos
Únicos de Empresa (Union Executive Boards, or SUE), which represented
the base structures on all state farms that formed part of a particular state
enterprise. In the private sector, one encountered frequently small union
chapters on neighboring farms. These chapters were consolidated into
strong Sindicatos de Empresas Varias (SEV).[76] This process was the result
of ATC leadership's decision to incorporate base structures established
on private and state farms into a small number of strong unions. Thus,
workers who were represented by distinct base structures joined together
in a single union chapter, while officially maintaining the autonomy of
their original organizations. In 1985 the rural workers grouped into
forty-three unions representing state enterprises and seventy-one unions
composed of numerous base structures located on private farms.[77] Four
years later, in 1989, the distribution of unions between the state and private sectors was almost even, fifty-four and fifty-seven, respectively.

On the state farms, ATC pushed for worker participation. Partially
with international aid, ATC set up two educational centers to provide its
members with the technical training necessary to participate actively in
the management of the state farms. A central institution that facilitated
input from the rural workers was the Consejos Consultivos (Consulting
Councils, or CC). Through these institutions, union representatives shared
in the administration of a particular state farm. Although participation in
these structures was a valuable experience, the union members were limited by their low educational level, resistance by management, and organizational deficiencies within ATC.[78] Further, ATC representatives did
not have the same weight as management in determining the outcome of
decisions, and their participation was frequently restricted to lower-level
decision making.[79] In addition to the consulting councils, union representatives had seats on the Consejos de Producción (Production Councils), which operated at the level of the state enterprises. In this forum the
workers had the opportunity to discuss the economic plan for a particular enterprise. Finally, ATC also held national assemblies that united all
workers engaged in a particular productive activity.

Union leaders benefited from participating in the management of the state sector. Foremost, they gained access to valuable facts. In cases in which private producers wanted to hide or distort information essential for salary and benefits negotiation, union officials could use the knowledge acquired in the state sector to strengthen their bargaining position.[80] The state farms also served as laboratories to overcome class conflict between the white-collar management and administration workers and the manual laborers. García affirmed that the opening of ATC to employees in the administrative sector of the state farms was helpful in deemphasizing class contradictions, but it was not possible to completely resolve them.

Relations with the Labor Movement and Agricultural Producers

One of the first challenges facing ATC was that of establishing its recruiting territory in competition with other labor unions. For example, ATC had to compete in the organizing of tobacco workers with CST and the Confederación de Unificación Social (Confederation for Labor Unification, or CUS).[81] The task was complex, since ATC had to vie with unions that favored the revolutionary project, such as CST, and organizations that opposed Sandinista policies, particularly CUS and FO.

CST came in conflict with ATC over the right to organize workers in agroindustry. In particular, sugarcane workers were initially organized by both organizations. CST argued that ATC should focus its recruiting efforts on the rural workers employed on state and private farms and that workers in agroindustry were the domain of CST, since they were part of the industrial workforce. In order to avoid endangering the worker-peasant alliance, ATC gave in to the pressure applied by CST and ceased its organizational efforts in the industrial plants. This resulted in the loss of almost twenty thousand sugarcane workers to CST.

Once these initial turf fights were resolved, the leadership could focus its energy on obtaining the important goal "to develop the worker-peasant alliance so it could be the driving force . . . in the process of deepening the revolution."[82] ATC's decision not to compete with CST in agroindustry hurt the organization, since it left ATC to organize the most marginalized sectors—workers on state and private farms and semiproletarians. Though both organizations supported the revolutionary project of the Sandinista Front, they differed in their ideological outlook, with CST being more radical. For example, CST, with an explicit socialist orientation, was affiliated with the Federación de Sindicatos Mundiales

(World Federation of Unions, or FSM), which incorporated predominantly unions from east-bloc countries.[83] ATC, on the other hand, was affiliated with the Organización Regional Interamericano de Trabajadores (Interamerican Regional Organization of Workers, or ORIT), which included the United States and Canada.

CST and ATC, both Sandinista organizations, were at a disadvantage when they competed with unions that opposed the revolutionary project. ATC frequently faced the dilemma of whether to support the demands of its members for shorter work days and higher salaries or to urge the workers "to carry out the admittedly capitalist tasks of the revolution."[84] In the state sector, ATC leaders could convincingly argue that the workers were benefiting the country as a whole when they did not give priority to their personal demands, since the surplus they produced was used to finance revolutionary programs. Their task was more difficult in the case of private farms, where harder work by the laborers had one main result—the enrichment of the employer. A content analysis of *El Machete,* the monthly magazine of ATC, demonstrates that the organization chose to support the overall goals of the revolution rather than sectional interests. The single issue raised consistently in every edition of the magazine was how to raise production, regardless of who owned the land. ATC's efforts to motivate its members to raise productivity allowed the ultra-left Workers' Front to make inroads into the rural proletariat. The position of the Workers' Front, denouncing the allegedly bourgeois Sandinista project and demanding immediate pay raises, initially appealed to the workers.

The agricultural producers had a two-pronged strategy against ATC. Large and medium farmers tried to convince their workers that there was no need to join ATC since they were willing to provide all benefits commonly demanded in contract negotiations. This policy was easy to implement, with the organization's moderate demands in the first years following the Sandinista victory. Rosendo Díaz, secretary general of the Unión de Productores Agropecuarios de Nicaragua (Union of Nicaraguan Agricultural Producers, or UPANIC), the organization of the agrarian bourgeoisie, affirmed that ATC was not considered a threat by the employers. He maintained that the union had little autonomy and was basically a branch of the Ministerio de Desarrollo Agropecuario y Reforma Agraria (Ministry of Agricultural Development and Agrarian Reform, or MIDINRA).

Anti-ATC feelings were not limited to the sectors in the agricultural community that were critical of the Sandinista revolution. Even among pro-Sandinista producers, no love was lost for ATC. The antiproducer rhetoric of the class-conscious ATC leadership of the early 1980s was still fresh on the minds of the producers.[85] ATC officials argued, however, that they could detect differences in their relations with UPANIC, the movement of the rural bourgeoisie, vis-à-vis farmers who supported the UNAG. UNAG members were more likely to agree to social benefits for their workers in contract negotiations, and, equally significant, they honored these contracts once they were signed. Although relations with UNAG members were generally constructive, Edgardo García, ATC's secretary general, characterized them in these terms: "Not everything is gold that shines" (García, 1989). Daniel Núñez, the president of UNAG, described the relations between ATC and UNAG in a 1989 interview: "Today, both the UNAG and the ATC have sat down to discuss dialectically the policy of national unity. We've had differences with the ATC, it hasn't been a honeymoon, but we are aware that when fighting for the same goals differences can contribute to development."[86]

García argued that the decidedly antagonistic relations between workers and the rural bourgeoisie in the early 1980s improved over time. Nevertheless, an important group of producers remained hostile. In light of its difficulties with members of the rural bourgeoisie, it is not surprising that the organization frequently opposed the Sandinista policy of national unity. ATC leaders argued that large producers who benefited from government policies such as cheap credit and other economic incentives deposited their capital in foreign bank accounts, while claiming they had not enough funds to pay their workers the minimum wage. The farmers, on the other hand, held ATC responsible for the considerable decline in productivity since 1979. Though the organization attempted to educate its members regarding the importance of increased productivity, the workers, who had finally rid themselves of the repressive measures of the former regime, were taking their "historic vacation," by greatly reducing their working hours.

Party, State, and the Rural Proletariat

ATC was explicit in recognizing FSLN as its revolutionary vanguard. Article 23 of the organization's charter stated: *"The ATC recognizes in the FSLN its revolutionary vanguard and consequently declares itself a Sandinista organization."*[87] Further, the organization coordinated its work at all levels according to the directions given by FSLN and carried out all orientations of the Sandinista National Directorate.[88] Apart from a relationship based on ideological grounds, there was also a financial one. ATC could not maintain itself on the funds generated from membership dues and international donations. Although no exact figures were available, ATC sources acknowledged that the Sandinista party contributed a large share of the union's budget. In 1989 Sandinista support for the farmers' movement was 25 percent of UNAG's budget. Since ATC was financially less independent than UNAG, one can safely assume that the party contributed at least that much to the rural workers' union.

The close relationship between ATC and FSLN raised concerns that there was a lack of independence from the Sandinista party. Rural workers, even when supportive of the Sandinista Front, frequently objected to this close relationship and many chose not to join the union. They wanted to see their interests represented by a more independent organization. Further, ATC did not appeal to workers who were interested in joining a union but opposed the Sandinista project. In 1985 the majority of the ATC membership belonged to the FSLN, although members affiliated with opposition parties could be found in the ranks of the organization.[89] The fact that a diverse ideological spectrum was represented in the rank and file, though significant from a pluralist perspective, did not change the close association between ATC and the Sandinista Front. All ATC representatives in Nicaragua's National Assembly (1984–1990) were FSLN members, and ATC's secretary general, Edgardo García, was a member of the Sandinista Assembly, the party's highest decision-making body apart from its National Directorate.

This symbiotic relationship made it difficult for the union to challenge the revolutionary authorities when this was necessary to defend the rural proletariat. Frequently, ATC assumed a low profile in its relations with FSLN and the state, with its leadership negotiating behind the scenes instead of voicing dissent in public. Before 1981, however, one could find instances of ATC militancy. In its first years, the rural workers' movement publicly confronted the revolutionary authorities to protect the interests of its members. In 1980, for example, after the Sandinista Front had brought land invasions to a halt out of concern for the private sector and the policy of national unity, ATC organized a demonstration in Managua and demanded that no occupied land be returned to the bourgeoisie.[90] According to García, large producers, encouraged by the government's initial weak response, had started to reclaim even properties that had already been integrated into the state sector. Following ATC's mass mobilization, the FSLN decreed in March 1980 that land already taken over would remain in the state sector, while future land invasions were put under sanction.[91] Further evidence that suggested a certain degree of ATC autonomy was the organization's policy regarding large landowners. Before the creation of UNAG, the Sandinista leadership favored the integration of agricultural producers into the rural workers' movement, even when the size of their landholding made them members of the rural bourgeoisie.[92] But, for reasons analyzed above, medium and large producers were excluded from the organization. The class-consciousness of the ATC leaders proved to be stronger than the orientations given by the Sandinista party.

Even in those early years of the revolution, however, ATC's independence was in doubt because of the organization's ties with the state, particularly with MIDINRA. Jaime Wheelock, head of MIDINRA, told an ATC audience in 1979 that the movement had a permanent place in the ministry and that its word "was almost as good as law."[93] This symbiotic relationship continued throughout the 1980s and, though it provided the ATC with a considerable amount of influence, was not without problems.

The majority of the ATC membership was composed of rural workers on state farms. This resulted in a situation in which the revolutionary authorities fulfilled two functions in regard to the agricultural workers. First, they represented the interest of the society as a whole, which included the rural proletariat. Second, and most significant, the state assumed the role of employer vis-à-vis the ATC membership. At times, both functions entailed the need to oppose legitimate demands, and it appears that this particular combination placed ATC in double jeopardy. For example, with the increasingly difficult economic conditions of the late 1980s, the Sandinista government was forced to implement austerity measures that hurt the working class. Further, in its efforts to improve the efficiency of the public sector, the exigencies of the state economy often took precedence over the needs of the rural proletariat employed on state farms. It appears that the revolutionary authorities demanded greater sacrifices from the rural proletariat than were expected from other sectors of society. ATC leaders frequently argued that the Sandinista government neglected the rural sector and directed scarce resources toward the cities. Austerity policies were particularly harsh on rural workers with fixed incomes. For example, the base salary of an agricultural worker that bought 100 percent of a basket with eight basic products in

February 1988 acquired only 60 percent of the same basket in June and a mere 16 percent in July.[94] Urban workers faced similar problems, yet their salaries were somewhat higher than those in the rural sector. In 1985, for example, a rural worker had a minimum salary of 3,500 cordobas per month, whereas an urban worker was paid 4,500.

ATC had great difficulties in pressuring the state to implement policies benefiting its constituency, since it was deprived of its main bargaining tool—the strike. In the early 1980s strikes were outlawed under emergency provisions implemented better to fight the counterrevolution. Yet even when strikes were legal, the ATC leadership argued that work stoppages were not in the workers' interest. According to ATC officials, union members did not initiate a single strike in the state sector. Deprived of its best weapon, the ATC had to resort to "salary strikes" instead. According to the union's secretary general, in instances when state farm managers refused to supply the workforce with the eight essential products agreed to in the basic union contract (corn, rice, cooking oil, soap, sugar, beans, milk, and eggs) the workers refused to accept their wages. This was certainly a dramatic way to publicize and denounce problems in the state sector, but the cost to the rural proletariat was prohibitive.

An important example that demonstrated the lack of ATC leverage vis-à-vis the state was the inactivity of labor inspectors when notified of irregularities in workplaces. Not only were they not sympathetic, they often sided with the employer against the worker.[95] Laws regulating work norms in the coffee harvest were often not observed, and ATC leaders who denounced abuses at times lost their jobs. The labor inspectors, having been informed of irregularities, frequently did not bother to show up to inspect the farms.[96] ATC was simply not strong and militant enough to convince either the employers or the government inspectors that they would incur high costs by not responding to the demands and complaints of the organization. ATC had to fight an uphill battle, since it demanded rights for a sector that was not well represented among state and party officials. ATC leaders often pointed out that the backgrounds of the revolutionary leadership and of most state functionaries were not working-class. If they were not children of professionals, they tended to share backgrounds as agricultural producers. Thus, it was not surprising that rural workers experienced great difficulties in making their voices heard.

The record of a decade of revolutionary rule indicated that ATC was more likely to defend the overall goals of the revolutionary project than to press the specific demands of its membership. The conditions of the rural workers did improve in the areas of education, social security, and health benefits. Salaries and general living conditions, however, remained below comparable urban standards. This situation led to complaints by some workers that they had exchanged their old landlord for a new one—the state. Some sectors within the agricultural proletariat had difficulty accepting the view advanced by the Sandinista government that the workers constituted the state in revolutionary Nicaragua and that this situation in itself represented a fundamental change in the relations of production. Many workers preferred immediate material benefits over deferring their legitimate demands in the interest of the revolution. Despite this difficult situation, ATC members frequently demonstrated a highly developed social consciousness. For instance, they defended the interest of the people against actions by government bureaucrats. At times, Sandinista officials attempted to reallocate resources from a state farm in order to satisfy the needs of a particular constituency. These actions were often the results of political pressures, be it that a refugee camp needed food or a Sandinista cooperative requested access to a state farm's machinery park. Many officials believed that they had the right to dispose of a state farm's resources. The workers held a different view, arguing that the officials had no right to take from the "people's property" but had to pay like everybody else.

The perception that ATC served primarily the interests of the Sandinista government was also related to the organization's involvement in tasks sponsored by the revolutionary authorities. Particularly ATC's contribution to the fight against the counterrevolution carried an enormous price tag. The rural workers' movement played a crucial role in the war effort. Before the military service law extended the defense of the country to all sectors of society, union members participated voluntarily in the Batallones de Infantería de Reserva (Reserve Infantry Battallions, or BIR), Sandinista army units that constituted a central line of defense.[97] In 1984, 30 percent of the ATC membership was mobilized.[98] At times, only women and children were left behind on the state farms. The defense of the revolution had a negative impact on the union's development. First, many ATC members were killed in action or wounded. According to ATC, more than three hundred ATC leaders were assassinated by January 1985 alone. The contras seemed to target the best cadres of ATC. Many times they killed union officials with a distinguished record. Second, union leaders who joined the war effort were sorely missed in the movement's organizational effort. The employers frequently took advantage of their absence "to divide or neutralize the unions."[99] Finally, ATC acquired the reputation of being a recruitment agency for the Sandinista army. This was reason enough for many members of the rural proletariat to keep aloof from the union.

Conclusion

ATC's performance over a decade of representing the interests of the rural workers can best be evaluated if we divide the history of the organization into two distinct periods, from 1978 to 1981 and from 1982 to 1990. The two phases are set apart by one important event—the emergence of UNAG.

From its foundation in 1978 until 1981 when UNAG was formed, ATC was a model grassroots organization, representing effectively its constituents' interests. The association adjusted well to the transition from an illegal union under Somoza to an important mass movement under the Sandinistas. The impressive increase in membership in the first two years after the insurrection constitutes strong evidence for the appeal the organization enjoyed in the countryside. ATC played an important role in the first years of the revolutionary process by gaining political representation for the peasantry on the Council of State and defending with militancy the interests of its constituents. The organization's greatest achievement during this period was the crucial role it played in the design and implementation of the agrarian reform.

The problems for ATC started when it took on too great a task for the capacity of the organization—the incorporation of small farmers into the organization. The often conflicting interests of the rural workers and the agricultural producers resulted in 1981 in the exodus of the small farmers and the constitution of UNAG. With UNAG's emergence, the rural workers' movement entered into a crisis. After 1981 the close relationship with the revolutionary authorities at times impeded ATC's organizational growth. The same ties that benefited the organization initially and helped it to become the most powerful grassroots organization in the countryside started to work to the union's detriment. ATC's policy of giving priority to the general needs of the revolution over the specific interests of its members resulted in a loss of credibility among the rural proletariat. Further, the close relationship with the state made it difficult for the organization to represent the interests of the rural workers, because of the government's leverage as the employer of the majority of ATC's members.

The limitations of ATC were evident; however, the record of the association also showed several significant achievements. The organization's greatest success was to have organized a great number of rural workers. Further, the association succeeded in organizing landless workers into work collectives to acquire collectively land from the state sector for the production of basic grains during the off-season for export agriculture. Also, the movement made great progress in achieving equality for rural women. For the first time in Nicaragua's history, women received the same salary as men. Women also obtained the right to register personally on the payrolls. Under the Somoza dictatorship, their husbands or fathers used to register for them and were paid the woman's salary. Despite the economic limitations of the Sandinista government, day care centers were being constructed and poor children were fed in rural eating places. ATC was successful in obtaining financial support from international sources to fund its projects, intended to improve the living standard of the rural proletariat. According to Francisco Camas, head of International Relations, in the late 1980s, twenty-seven nongovernmental institutions together provided an average of $1 million per year for various union activities. The most significant contributors were unions and other nongovernmental organizations from Holland, Denmark, Canada, and Switzerland.

ATC faced a new challenge when the Chamorro government took power. Not only was its main protector, the Sandinista party, out of power, but the move toward privatization that the new regime had initiated deeply affected its members who were employed in the state sector. Following the 1990 change in government, the state sector was dissolved. ATC was partially successful in protecting the workers. When a conglomerate of sixteen state cattle enterprises was dissolved in mid-1991, the workers received 32 percent of the 525,000 acres.[100] In the case of the state cotton and coffee sectors, ATC obtained a similar percentage of the land,[101] benefiting 6,300 permanent rural workers.[102] By 1992 ATC had established 140 union chapters on these worker-owned enterprises.[103] In the private sector, 238 chapters had survived.

ATC membership declined to 35,607 in 1992 (see table 3.6 for detailed information). Of those members, 16,434 were employed in the private sector, 16,000 formed part of the new worker-controlled enterprises, Área de Propriedad de Trabajadores (Area of Workers' Property, or

Table 3.6. Permanent workers affiliated
with ATC, 1992

Department/region/productive sector	Total
Region I	3,110
Leon (Cotton)	3,172
Chinandega (Cotton)	2,768
Chinandega (Bananas)	5,250
Managua	1,590
Region IV	3,101
Boaco	1,184
Chontales	1,098
Matagalpa	7,194
Jinotega	3,820
Cattle	1,520
Rice	1,800
Total	35,607

Source: Association of Rural Workers (ATC).

APT), and 3,173 ATC members had formed cooperatives.[104] Further-more, 35,214 unemployed workers continued to be attended by the union.[105] The union leadership considered this group to be part of ATC, although legally they could not be members since they were unemployed.

The ATC leadership realized that it had to shed its partisan image in order to represent the workers effectively in the new political climate. In this regard, it is significant that the revised 1992 statutes make no reference to the relationship between the Sandinista Front and the union. Under the Chamorro government, the rural workers suffered from a range of new policies that raised the cost of basic consumer goods, drastically reduced social services, and eliminated subsidized transport.[106] In addition, many laws protecting the rural proletariat were no longer enforced. In an effort to protect its constituents, ATC reached out to demobilized fighters of the Nicaraguan resistance and the Sandinista army. The formation of these alliances contributed to the process of national reconciliation and strengthened ATC's leverage vis-à-vis the government. Although the task of protecting the rights of the rural proletariat under Chamorro is daunting, ATC has so far demonstrated a newly acquired militancy.

_____

Chapter 4

Agricultural Producers: The Dialectics of Popular Hegemony and National Unity

> The fundamental force in this country is the peasantry and being part of the peasantry, the small and medium producers represent sixty percent of the production of this country. . . . We [UNAG] are not defining ourselves as a mass organization, rather we are an organization for production. We represent the various productive sectors and employers of the country; the small, medium and large producers.
>
> *Daniel Núñez, 1985*

In its efforts to restructure the political economy of the Nicaraguan countryside, the Sandinista government relied on the support of an important ally—the Unión Nacional de Agricultores y Ganaderos. The organization stood apart from other grassroots movements in successfully embodying the two central policies driving the Sandinista project, namely popular hegemony and national unity. It was a main objective of UNAG to unify Nicaragua's agricultural producers in an effort to revitalize and reform the rural sector. Equally important, this Sandinista grassroots movement represented a major force ensuring that the transformation of the political economy benefited the previously marginalized peasant class.

Emergence of a Sandinista Agricultural Movement

Until 1979 agricultural producers suffered from the same lack of political representation and organization experienced by the rural workers.

Although some sectors of the rural bourgeoisie were organized into producer associations, the majority of Nicaragua's agricultural producers were left without any representation. According to Daniel Núñez, UNAG's charismatic president, who has led the farmers' movement since 1984, these associations were set up and controlled by the Somoza family and the U.S. embassy.[1] A good example of such a movement was the Asociación de Ganaderos de Nicaragua (Association of Nicaraguan Ranchers, or ASGANIC). ASGANIC, a movement of elite cattle producers, was founded in 1955 by Anastasio Somoza's eldest son, Luís. Continuing to act as ASGANIC's head, even after he assumed the presidency of Nicaragua, Luís Somoza was a symbol of the symbiotic relationship between the Somoza regime and elite bourgeois producers.[2] In addition to the organizations of agricultural producers, the Somoza family and their close associates also controlled the processing industries where profits were concentrated.[3] These structural conditions facilitated the exploitation of small and medium producers. For example, the small farmers were forced to sell their products to the associations controlled by large producers who dominated processing and marketing and thus could dictate the price. Further, poor farmers received none of the technical assistance that the state reserved for the capitalist sector.[4]

In the early 1960s medium and large producers who opposed the Somoza regime and had been frozen out of the elite producer organizations started to organize movements of agricultural producers in several regions of the country. One of the first movements to emerge was the Asociación de Criadores de Ganado Brahman (Association of Brahman Cattle Breeders).[5] Another regional organization, the Asociación de Ganaderos de Estelí (Association of Ranchers of Estelí, or ASOGAES), was created in 1971 in Estelí, a region in northern Nicaragua. These regional cattle movements were eventually integrated into the national Federación de Asociaciones Ganaderas de Nicaragua (Federation of Cattlemen Associations of Nicaragua, or FAGANIC), specifically conceived as an alternative to the Somocista organizations. Luís Somoza's brother, Anastasio, Jr., who by then had assumed power, attempted to preempt the emergence of these independent movements. He pressured ASGANIC in the mid-1970s to open its organization beyond the elite club of cattle producers in order to "coopt a vocal bourgeoise opposition."[6] But his efforts were in vain.

In April 1979 an umbrella organization, UPANIC, was constituted at the national level to represent the diverse productive sectors in opposition to the Somoza dynasty. UPANIC included members of the rural bourgeoisie engaged in cattle, coffee, cotton, bananas, milk, sugarcane, rice, and sorghum production. Eventually, these large capitalist producers formed eight UPANIC affiliates, representing their distinct productive activities. The new movement represented a challenge to the associations controlled by the Somoza dynasty, yet it was only significant for the capitalist class, since it failed to incorporate peasant producers.[7] Although UPANIC did oppose the Somoza regime, its opposition had no clear direction and came at a time when the Sandinistas had already established their hegemony over the coalition of insurrectional forces seeking to oust the dictator.[8]

Following the 1979 insurrection, UPANIC sought to broaden its base of support and started to recruit small coffee producers in the Matagalpa region. The leadership abandoned these efforts in 1980, however, when conflicts with the new government sharpened.[9] Up to this point many prominent UPANIC leaders supported the Sandinistas and accepted important positions in the new government. For example, UPANIC's first president, Marco Antonio Castillo, became vice-president of the Banco Nacional de Desarrollo (National Development Bank, or BND).[10] Other members of the rural bourgeoisie, however, opposed the revolutionary government from the very beginning. They objected particularly to the hegemonic control exercised by the Sandinistas in the new power structures.[11] Their criticism was based on the fact that the power of the traditional elite was increasingly circumscribed by the revolutionary authorities. The animosity that some UPANIC sectors displayed toward the new government turned into open hostility when UPANIC's president, Jorge Salazar, was killed in a confrontation with Sandinista police. This incident confirmed the view held by many large producers that the new regime was bent on destroying the rural bourgeoisie. Although the majority of the UPANIC leadership came to oppose the Sandinistas, several senior officials who did not share this critical assessment of the FSLN stayed in the organization in the hopes of keeping UPANIC within the revolutionary process. According to Juan Tijerino, these officials, many of whom had been instrumental in the creation of UPANIC, were encouraged by the Sandinista policy of national unity. They had been convinced that land expropriations in 1979 and 1980 were directed against the Somoza family and its associates but not against the rural bourgeoisie as a class. These differences in opinion among the rural bourgeoisie became a permanent feature in the life of UPANIC and manifested themselves in a national

leadership vehemently opposed to the Sandinistas, whereas several regional UPANIC affiliates enjoyed cordial relations with the revolutionary
authorities.

By 1980 agricultural producers in support of the Sandinista Front
started to demand better political representation. They were reluctant to
join UPANIC, since it represented, particularly in the eyes of small producers, the capitalist class. The poor peasants rejected this bourgeois
organization, despite efforts to attract them through the offer of credit
and access to cheap farm inputs.[12] Although they showed no interest in
joining forces with rich producers who had previously exploited them,
they were equally opposed to becoming part of ATC, the organization of
the rural proletariat. Nevertheless, in lieu of a better alternative, some
farmers did decide to work with ATC, although they had little sympathy
for the union line of the organization. Once inside the rural workers'
movement, these producers started to advocate the formation of a revolutionary organization for agricultural producers.

The organizational drive for a Sandinista farmers' movement was centered in the departments of Matagalpa and Estelí. On December 14,
1980, a group of small and medium producers in the department of
Matagalpa broke away from the local association (the Cooperativa de
Cafateleros) controlled by bourgeois producers and established the
nucleus of a Sandinista agricultural movement.[13] This development
encouraged producers in other regions to explore possibilities for the creation of new organizational structures. About ten thousand farmers
attended the various meetings.[14] The regional efforts led to the constituent assembly of UNAG, held April 25–26, 1981, in Managua. The
Sandinistas played a central role in the emergence of UNAG. Comandante Victor Tirado affirmed that "the FSLN designated a group of *mili-
tantes* [party members] of peasant origin to initiate the drive for this
organization."[15] The revolutionary government was rightly concerned
with the prevailing conditions in Nicaragua's countryside following the
1980 rupture in relations with the private sector. It was imperative for the
Sandinistas to reach out to small and medium producers who had been
influenced by the UPANIC-affiliated rural bourgeoisie.[16] Large producers, who were afraid that they would be expropriated, sought to
strengthen their position by forging an alliance with peasant producers.
The traditional relations of clientelism constituted the basis for their
influence. Holding positions of authority, they had little difficulty in convincing their clients that the revolution would adversely affect rich and

poor farmers alike. UNAG was to serve as the instrument to counter this development.

Narcísco Gonzalez, a producer from Estelí, became UNAG's first president. Gonzalez was elected by the three thousand producers who attended the 1981 constituent assembly because of his strong standing in the regional agricultural community and his distinguished record as a participant in the revolutionary struggle. UNAG's immediate agenda included the elaboration of the movement's bylaws and its *Plan de Lucha,* a platform outlining the main demands of the farmers. The leadership of the new organization successfully secured representation on the Council of State and demanded to be included on all institutions concerned with agrarian reform and agricultural policy.[17]

Changing Objectives: The Peasantry's Needs versus the Bourgeoisie's Interests

UNAG's main task as an organization was to attend to the needs of the agricultural community. These needs were complex and frequently conflicting, a reality that reflected the diverse social fabric of Nicaragua's rural sector. UNAG pursued two main objectives: to organize the agricultural producers politically and to assist them in improving their economic situation. In addition, the new organization sought to modify the state's policies toward its constituents, which had been characterized by neglect. The state had traditionally catered to the needs of sectors that were organized and thus able to exert pressure on the bureaucrats who designed and implemented agrarian policies.[18] Although the small and medium producers were considered backwards, they contributed 50 percent of total agricultural production at the time of UNAG's emergence.[19] This reality needed to be advertised if UNAG was to be successful in the struggle to gain recognition for the significant contribution of its constituents to the country's economy.

The realization of UNAG's stated objectives required a vigorous recruitment drive, efforts to gain political representation on all institutions affecting the farmers' lives, pressure for the implementation of a comprehensive agrarian reform—in short, a fundamental change in the relations of production inherited from the Somoza family. The organization was instrumental in facilitating and guaranteeing easy access to credit, and it supplied farm equipment at favorable prices. The farmers were also encouraged to be active in basic human needs campaigns, involving education, health, and housing. UNAG's members did not wait passively for the government to come in and provide them with basic services. Rather, they participated actively in improving their basic needs situation. In line with the Sandinista concept of democracy, farmers participated in adult literacy campaigns, joined health brigades to eradicate infectious diseases, and built low-income housing. UNAG worked closely with the other grassroots movements in accomplishing these tasks.[20] Seeking to improve the social conditions in the rural sector, UNAG, together with MICOIN, established rural supply centers to serve affiliated production cooperatives.[21] These stores provided essential products, including oil, sugar, salt, soap, and rice, at government-controlled prices.[22] UNAG members were also active in improving the rural infrastructure, particularly in repairing roads that opened up remote rural areas and gave the peasants improved access to urban markets.[23]

Working on behalf of the producers, the UNAG leadership faced a constant dilemma. It had to balance the conflicting interests of its diverse constituency: peasants engaged in subsistence farming, members of the rural bourgeoisie, individual farmers, cooperatives, and Sandinista production collectives. It has been argued that UNAG showed sophistication in representing "a heterogeneous collection of demands concerning prices, roads, credit, land and co-operatives."[24] The organization accomplished this by incorporating specific demands from its constituency into a broad programmatic platform that provided the leadership with room for maneuver.[25] The immediate appeal the organization enjoyed among the producers translated into a rapid growth of membership. By 1982 UNAG already had a membership base of forty-two thousand farmers.

Despite immediate Sandinista recognition for UNAG, the participation of small and medium producers in Nicaragua's political life remained limited.[26] It is interesting to note that the Sandinistas initially failed to realize their main objective in supporting UNAG, namely, to build it into a bulwark intended to withstand the efforts of a sector of the rural bourgeoisie that was bent on destroying the revolutionary project. UNAG was conceived as a strategic link within the policy of national unity, offering even large producers a role in the new society and thereby breaking up the united front of the capitalist class. Equally important, the government needed "to reactivate production of traditional export crops (cotton, coffee and sugar), which accounted for the special attention given to the large agrarian bourgeoisie."[27] Although the need to incorporate large producers was obvious, UNAG remained an organization of cooperatives and small farmers. Until 1984, capitalist producers were excluded from the organization. It became increasingly evident that the initial failure of the farmers' movement to play a constructive role in forging national unity resided with UNAG's leadership.

Under the inherited leadership of former ATC professionals, the organization focused on strengthening the cooperative sector and emphasized the recruitment of small producers. Until 1983 UNAG organized the peasantry around an agrarian reform, centered on building agricultural cooperatives, and "had not yet found the mechanisms for all sectors of the countryside to participate in the organization."[28] The de facto exclusion of large landowners from the organization during its first years violated the principles established in the movement's charter. The initial program of UNAG stated: "The UNAG is a national organization, pluralist in character, *open to all agricultural producers, regardless of religion, political affiliation or size of landholding.*"[29] The bias against big producers was mainly a function of the view of former ATC cadres, who had joined UNAG in 1981 when the rural workers' movement broke apart. These officials belonged to the rural proletariat and shared a history of struggle against the agrarian bourgeoisie. Having suffered years of exploitation at the hands of rich landowners, they perceived any farmer with a sizable landholding as the class enemy. These officials "called anyone bourgeoisie who had ten cows, or had managed to buy a truck, or a house in a town like Santo Domingo, Río Blanco, Jalapa."[30] Wilberto Lara, UNAG's second president (1982–1984), represented a good example of someone holding this position. A committed revolutionary, he could not transcend his proletarian background. During his tenure, UNAG was scorned even by those members of the rural bourgeoisie who, though open to the changes brought about by the revolution, rejected UNAG leadership's antibourgeois rhetoric. This class bias, in many cases unwarranted, limited the development of the organization and had serious consequences for the revolutionary process. Large landowners, crucial to a viable alliance between FSLN and the bourgeoisie under the policy of national unity, felt alienated, and many turned against the Sandinista revolution.

Mistakes, committed by union officials and government representatives alike, broadened the social base of the counterrevolution beyond members of the rural bourgeoisie and those sectors of the peasantry that had benefited from Somocista policies. Particularly producers from the departments of Boaco and Chontales favored the contras' cause. Taking advantage of this situation, the contra leadership moved their center of activity from the northern regions into the country's interior. UNAG leaders acknowledged that during the 1980s "the small and medium producers in those areas, cattle ranchers and coffee farmers, were influenced by the counterrevolution, and in some case, we must admit, became a social base."[31]

In an effort to reinvigorate the policy of national unity in Nicaragua's rural sector, the UNAG leadership began a discussion in October 1983 concerning the active recruitment of "influential producers."[32] This important redirection of policy that ended the exclusion of the agrarian bourgeoisie was consolidated with the election of a new leader. In July 1984 Daniel Núñez left his position as regional director for MIDINRA and assumed UNAG's presidency. This event entailed two major developments. From the perspective of internal democracy it was significant that UNAG's members participated in the election of the new leader. Daniel Núñez was selected by the Sandinista leadership, yet he was supported and proposed as a candidate for the presidency by the producers of region VI. Following extensive discussions of his candidacy at the base, Núñez was elected by acclamation in a national assembly of the farmers' movement. Although the producers had some input in the selection of their leader, the farmers' choice was limited since Núñez was the only candidate.

The second major development, related to the rise of Núñez to UNAG's presidency, was the participation of large producers in the July 1984 assembly. Their presence was a symbol for the attention the rural bourgeoisie was getting from the new leader. Núñez ushered in a new era, beginning UNAG's rise to become the most important Sandinista grassroots movement. The new president had a crucial advantage over his predecessor. Enjoying a reputation as an outstanding rancher (Núñez had one thousand heads of cattle in the 1970s), he was trusted by the capitalist sector. At the same time, he counted with the respect of small and medium producers. He gained the admiration of the poor peasantry when, in the wake of the successful insurrection, he donated his farm to the revolution. Núñez had a distinguished history as a member of the Sandinista Front and enjoyed the revolutionary leadership's confidence. Having joined the struggle against Somoza as part of the revolutionary Christian movement, he was captured by the Guardia Nacional on December 21, 1974. His captivity was to be short. Núñez was among a small group of political prisoners (including Daniel Ortega) that Somoza was forced to release on December 30, following the successful FSLN raid of a Christmas party at the house of Somoza's minister of agriculture, José María "Chema" Castillo. In the course of this attack, several high-ranking Somocista officials and foreign dignitaries were captured, forcing Somoza to give in to the guerrillas' demands. The fact that Núñez was among the eighteen prisoners who were released and flown to Cuba suggests that the Sandinista leadership early on recognized his value to the revolution. Few people understood the problematic of the rural sector equally well, had his charisma, or could count on the support of poor peasants as well as capitalist producers.

Núñez was able to refocus UNAG's policy toward the incorporation of large producers. This policy shift was particularly important from the perspective of forging national unity in the countryside. The Sandinistas were convinced that the cooperation of the agricultural bourgeoisie was essential to their ambitious project's success. Fortunately for the new government, historical precedents demonstrated that some members of this class were prepared to accept change in the interest of furthering the development of the country. For example, Jeffrey Gould affirmed that during the 1960s in Chinandega province, "the vanguard of the agro-export bourgeoisie supported land reform [under Somoza, while] other powerful sectors of the elite adamantly opposed it."[33]

The total number of large producers (defined as owning more than 350 hectares) was small. It consisted of about 700 people, most of them affiliated to private sector organizations in opposition to the Sandinistas.[34] From 1984 until the Sandinistas transferred power in 1990, UNAG was able to attract about 8 percent of this group.[35] The capitalist producers were insignificant numerically, in terms of both total UNAG membership and the number of agricultural producers in Nicaragua. In 1984 UNAG represented 85,000 of an estimated total of 240,000 agricultural producers.[36] Nevertheless, the large producers represented the most advanced productive sector and were a power to contend with.

The UNAG leadership realized that the recruitment of large landholders needed to proceed with caution in order to ensure that the integration of capitalist producers would not be to the detriment of the small and medium farmers. A distinction was made between large "bourgeois" producers and large "patriotic" producers. Only the latter group, mostly part of the *chapiollo* sector, was actively recruited. The chapiollo, called *kulak nicaraguense* by Ortega and Marchetti, was generally a first generation member of the rural bourgeoisie who had gained his status by confronting the rural oligarchy, particularly over control of the agricultural frontier.[37] The chapiollo "resembles the landlord, by exploiting the labor force with precapitalist methods, and the peasant, by living like he does and working with and besides him while he exploits him."[38] UNAG leaders and Sandinista officials argued that these patriotic farmers differed in several significant ways from the traditional rural bourgeoisie. In the opinion of UNAG's president, the chapiollos were deeply rooted in the domestic culture, whereas the bourgeois sector was mainly oriented toward the United States. Frequently illiterate, the chapiollos showed no desire to travel to the United States on shopping sprees, following the example of the "sophisticated" rural bourgeoisie; instead they shared a deep emotional attachment to their land and were satisfied to stay inside Nicaragua. Further, they were not absentee landlords but personally took charge of production on their farms.[39] This reality distinguished the chapiollo from the traditional bourgeois producer who worked as a lawyer, doctor, or businessman in the city during the week and returned to the *finca* only for the weekend. During his absence, the farm was in effect managed by a *mandador*, or overseer.

Admiring the nationalist fervor unleashed by the Sandinista revolution, the chapiollos had less difficulty accepting that the new government sought a fundamental change in the status quo, which required a complete restructuring of the prevailing relations of production. Also, many chapiollos were rooted in an anti-imperialist tradition and had supported the FSLN during its guerrilla days in Nicaragua's mountains.[40] Whereas the recruitment of the chapiollos was essential from the perspective of forging national unity, UNAG's focus on the recruitment of rich peasants was not without consequences. Most significantly, the chapiollos came to dominate the decision-making structures of UNAG. For example, in 1989, members of agricultural cooperatives constituted only 33 percent of UNAG's national council, which consisted of 156 producers. The rest of the council was composed of individual producers (mostly large cattle ranchers) and union professionals who were also mostly chapiollos.[41] According to 1989 membership data, UNAG numbered 30,919 individual producers and 98,458 members of cooperatives.[42] Based on their numerical weight, the cooperatives, which represented mostly poor and small farmers, should have been allocated a greater percentage of national council seats.

Further, it has been argued that the incorporation of the chapiollos strengthened their political power in the *comarca*, the rural hamlets of their origin, vis-à-vis the poor peasantry.[43] This reality was in conflict with the pronounced Sandinista goal of strengthening grassroots democracy and resurrected power structures from the days of the Somoza regime.[44] Further, problems were not restricted to the political sphere but could be observed in the economic arena as well. The relationship between large and small producers was characterized by tensions that were often exacerbated by the situation of scarcity prevailing in Nicaragua. The difficult economic reality forced UNAG and the revolutionary authorities to make tough choices. For example, the UNAG leadership needed to choose whether to satisfy the demands of key patriotic producers or solve problems of the small and medium farmers. Many small farmers complained about priority treatment given to large producers. Since the cooperation of the capitalist farmers was vital to the revolutionary project, they were often allocated scarce resources, such as jeeps or tires. The peasants watched the capitalist producers driving their jeeps for leisure, while they many times were not able to secure transport facilities to get their own crops to market.

The poor peasants were not the only sector criticizing the consequences of the government's policy of national unity. Dissent was also voiced by the patriotic producers. The chapiollos, having joined the revolutionary project under the policy of national unity and benefited from it, were against Sandinista efforts to broaden the scope of the national unity policy. They were particularly against the inclusion of those sectors of the rural bourgeoisie, organized in UPANIC, that were in opposition to the revolution. They argued that efforts to incorporate the UPANIC affiliates were fruitless and that scarce resources allocated to them were wasted. Thus, national unity was under attack as the result of internal disputes within UNAG and fundamental disagreements between UNAG and the revolutionary authorities over the extent and the direction of this key policy. Marvin Ortega, an astute observer of the process of agricultural transformation, maintained that frequently during the 1980s "the policy of agricultural development and national unity took precedence over the identification that the revolution had with the peasants and vice versa."[45]

In its efforts to develop into a unifying force in the Nicaraguan countryside, UNAG lost sight of the central task of guaranteeing that the transformation of Nicaragua's political economy would benefit the marginalized peasant sector. Criticized over the emphasis given to the needs of the rural bourgeoisie, UNAG modified its policies in 1986 and redirected its attention to the plight of the poor, in particular the landless peasantry. The

UNAG leadership addressed the problem of the landless peasants at the movement's first National Congress, held in Managua April 25–27, 1986. The *Main Report,* a document presented to the delegates evaluating UNAG's performance during the first five years, contained several self-critical statements. The landless peasantry received particular attention. Indicating a redirection of policy, the document stated explicitly that under a revised policy, the organization was to focus on "small, medium and some large farmers, *as well as the landless farmers.*"[46] Landless farmers were a large group. In 1985 this sector was estimated at 100,000 people.[47] Although UNAG's leadership started to give priority to the plight of the landless peasantry, the organization continued to be caught in the unfolding dialectic of national unity and popular hegemony.

In the mid-1980s, land pressure from the landless peasantry and from farmers with insufficient land resulted in invasions of private farms in several regions of Nicaragua. The situation was further complicated by the land hunger of displaced agricultural producers from the war zones who had been forced to resettle in safer areas. The war resulted in 350,000 internal refugees. The invasions were often supported by local UNAG representatives and Sandinista party officials. From the perspective of the national leadership, these local officials had succumbed to pressure or sought short-term gains in prestige. Local UNAG leaders, however, maintained that they acted out of a sincere commitment to help the poor peasantry and criticized those UNAG leaders who defended the interests of the rich farmers. At times, poor peasants affiliated with UNAG even invaded properties belonging to large capitalist producers who were also part of the movement.

The peasants' rage was the result of increasing inequalities in Nicaragua's rural sector. While the poor peasants were off fighting the contras, the rural bourgeoisie gained political power in the comarca and enriched itself.[48] Until 1985 the peasants were alone in their struggle. Instead of coming to their aid, UNAG's national leadership, dominated by chapiollos, exerted pressure on its local staff and the revolutionary authorities to remove the invaders, arguing that the problem of land pressure could not be solved by illegal invasions. This position gained UNAG leaders the appreciation of the rural bourgeoisie, but it created antagonism on the part of impoverished and displaced farmers.

While the UNAG leadership sought to implement a general policy of protecting large producers from illegal invasions to ensure a climate of stability, the ideological climate started to change. The revolutionary authorities realized that in spite of all incentives offered under the policy of national unity, the rural bourgeoisie was not prepared to play a constructive role in the Sandinista development project. In light of this reality, government policies favored once again the core supporters of the revolution—poor farmers and the rural proletariat. The work of those in the UNAG leadership who had been seeking to convince the authorities of the need to address the plight of the rural poor finally became easier.

As so many times before, the people at the grass roots initiated these changes. In 1985, local UNAG officials, having experienced the difficult situation of the peasantry firsthand, headed a movement of landless peasants who demanded a solution to the problem of land scarcity in the region of Masaya.[49] The events surrounding Masaya heralded a radicalization of Sandinista agrarian reform policies. The new policies became law in January 1986, when a reform to the agrarian reform law was decreed. The revised law was designed to allow for a deepening of the agrarian reform in order to benefit the poor peasantry. It was primarily directed against a sector of the rural bourgeoisie that had previously been protected from land expropriations under the policy of national unity. These producers, who owned up to 350 hectares in the Pacific region or up to 700 in the interior, could now be expropriated not only when they had abandoned their farm but also when they had idle, underused, or rented land.[50] As table 4.1 indicates, in the wake of these reforms, the pace of expropriation accelerated dramatically.

Whereas 345 properties encompassing 119,218 hectares had been affected during the last two years that the old law was in effect (1983–1985), 1986 saw 449 properties with a total of 134,628 hectares expropriated. It is interesting to note that the increase in expropriations was not sufficient to satisfy the land hunger of the peasantry. In 1985, 9,537 families received 165,099 hectares, yet only 65,419 hectares were expropriated.[51] Thus, increased land pressure in 1985 forced the Sandinista government to reduce the state sector by 100,000 hectares in order to satisfy the strong demand for land. Despite expropriations in 1986 that amounted to almost twice the area of 1985, the revolutionary authorities continued to be forced to buy land or reduce state holdings. In 1986, 50,000 additional hectares were needed to satisfy the needs of all intended beneficiaries. That year, 11,626 families received 197,112 hectares of land. Thus, the pace of land expropriations could not keep up with the demand for land.

From 1985 to 1987, thousands of rural families received land. UNAG

Table 4.1. Number of properties and area affected by agrarian reform, 1981–1988 (in manzanas; 1 manzana = 1.75 acres)

A. Impact of Agrarian Reform Law, 1981–85

	1981		1982		1983		1984		1985	
Regions/zones	No.	Area	No.	Area	No.	Area	No.	Area	No.	Area
Region I	—	—	84	24,231	70	43,202	17	4,937	29	7,047
Region II	—	—	73	72,582	44	35,271	36	39,941	70	58,451
Region III	—	—	—	—	—	—	2	440	—	—
Region IV	13	16,412	16	8,539	85	51,111	7	4,305	93	12,052
Region V	—	—	61	82,097	13	28,601	19	13,547	13	7,722
Region VI	20	11,369	29	26,744	32	18,780	25	13,687	30	5,570
Zone I	—	—	2	825	—	—	—	—	—	—
Zone II	—	—	—	—	—	—	—	—	—	—
Zone III	—	—	1	1,948	4	11,116	—	—	2	2,555
Other[a]	—	—	2	163	3	817	—	—	2	58
Total	33	27,781	268	217,129	251	188,898	106	76,857	239	93,455

B. Impact of Revised Law, 1986–88

	1986		1987		1988		Total	
Regions/zones	No.	Area	No.	Area	No.	Area	No.	Area
Region I	41	51,275	28	7,483	3	1,870	272	140,045
Region II	114	47,084	30	4,872	18	1,262	385	259,463
Region III	2	205	—	—	1	379	5	1,024
Region IV	168	33,581	4	2,320	2	100	388	128,420
Region V	71	38,807	57	27,851	2	28,515	236	227,140
Region VI	52	19,324	23	12,142	3	1,447	214	109,063
Zone I	—	—	—	—	—	—	2	825
Zone II	1	2,050	—	—	—	—	1	2,050
Zone III	—	—	—	—	1	6,000	8	21,619
Other[a]	—	—	—	—	—	—	7	1,038
Total	449	192,326	142	54,668	30	39,573	1,518	890,687

Source: CIERA, La reforma agraria en Nicaragua: Cifras y referencias documentales (Managua: CIERA, 1989), vol. 9, table 2, p. 40.

[a] Includes properties that cross regional boundaries.

gained in prestige since its members represented the majority of the bene-ficiaries. Nevertheless, the organization continued to face the difficult dialectic of national unity and popular hegemony. The case of La Verona, a farm located in the department of Matagalpa, illustrated UNAG's per-sistent dilemma. Displaced peasants from the war zone, led by former agricultural workers of La Verona, invaded this farm of a medium producer in 1987. Since the owners of the farm were efficient producers, UNAG defended their property rights against the demands of the peasants. The Supreme Court of Nicaragua, acting on an appeal by the owners, ordered the eviction of the invaders. Yet in a severe blow to the independence of Nicaragua's judicial system, Comandante Jaime Wheelock, the minister of Agrarian Reform, ignored this judgment and gave the occupying peasants title to the land. According to "Chico" Javier Saenz, UNAG's regional president, the leadership reluctantly accepted this fait accompli, and the cooperative formed by the peasants on the invaded property became a UNAG affiliate. In the opinion of Ariel Bucardo, UNAG's vice-president, the movement's leadership faced a dilemma—to support the property rights of one person or the necessities of one hundred families. Confronted with this choice, UNAG favored the interests of the peasant producers over the property rights of a capitalist farmer.

Yet things were about to change once again. The number of expropriated farms in 1987 was only 32 percent of what it had been a year before, and the area affected by the agrarian reform declined from 134,628 to 38,268 hectares. This indicated a shift in government policy in favor of the bourgeoisie. The landless peasantry's suspicions were confirmed in 1988, when Jaime Wheelock declared the end of the Sandinista land reform program. The decision was obviously related to the government's attempt to seek once again the cooperation of the bourgeoisie. Indeed, in 1988 only thirty properties were expropriated, and 1989 witnessed a mere three cases.[52] In this final stage of the revolution, the Sandinistas again shifted their policies and "sought *reapproachment* with the private sector in a last ditch effort to resuscitate the economy."[53]

Organizational Structure

All grassroots movements, as well as the Sandinista Front, had organizational structures at every administrative level of government—local, regional, and national. This resulted in distinct advantages and disadvantages. The main advantage consisted in improved communication among the mass organizations, as well as between these movements and the revolutionary authorities. This system made it easy to identify the channels for communicating grievances and exchanging views. On the other hand, it suffered because of its rigidity.

During the 1980s the makeup of UNAG's organizational structure changed several times. The movement was initially built around municipal and departmental structures, following an established tradition. When the government decided in 1983 to consolidate the departments of Nicaragua into six regions and three special zones, UNAG followed suit. The elimination of existing traditional structures resulted in rivalries between departments. In Boaco and Chontales, consolidated into region V, one of the fights was over the location for the headquarters of the regional office. Similarly, UNAG members and officials from the department of Jinotega objected to the fact that the UNAG office for region VI, which comprised Jinotega and Matagalpa, was established in the latter department. Resistance to this organizational structure persisted throughout the 1980s. As shown in table 4.2, following the electoral defeat of the Sandinista government, the union reverted to its initial municipal and departmental structure.

At the local level, agricultural producers, seeking to affiliate with UNAG, initially had the choice of only three structures: Sandinista Production Cooperatives, Credit and Service Cooperatives, and Base Units of Private Producers. This policy—a uniform system in the name of efficiency—did not take account of the complexity and idiosyncracies of Nicaragua's farming community. The rich diversity of association in the countryside was the product of a long history of struggle. Farmers who had grown accustomed to their established structures were reluctant to join new, foreign ones in order to affiliate with UNAG. Many producers were not interested in joining any structure at all; instead they wanted to affiliate with the movement as individuals. At times, UNAG organizers even had to resort to blackmail in order to "convince" producers to become part of the new base organizations. The establishment of Credit and Service Cooperatives constituted a victory of the UNAG leadership over the even more restrictive policies of the revolutionary government, which favored the Production Cooperatives.[54] Further flexibility was introduced with the recognition of "Dead Fence" Cooperatives, which incorporated loosely associated private farms.

The development of these cooperative structures became a central task of the farmers' movement and is a good indicator for the attention UNAG gave to the plight of the marginalized peasant class under the policy of popular hegemony. The expansion and consolidation of the cooperative sector was to a great extent the result of UNAG's efforts. The cooperatives, until 1981 in the care of ATC, constituted the majority of UNAG's base structures and members. In 1989, the organization claimed

Table 4.2. Evolution of UNAG's organizational structure, 1983–1992

A. 1983–91		
National	**Regional**	**Level of Zone**
National Assembly	Regional Assembly	Zonal Assembly
National Council	Regional Council	Zonal Council
National Executive	Regional Executive	Zonal Executive
Committee	Committee	Committee
B. 1992		
National	**Departmental**	**Municipal**
National Congress	Department	Municipal Assembly
National Council	Assembly	Municipal Executive
National Executive	Department Executive	Committee
Committee	Committee	

Source: National Union of Farmers and Ranchers (UNAG).

to represent 30,919 individual producers and 88,085 farmers who were incorporated into more than 3,554 production and service cooperatives (see table 4.3 for detailed information).[55] Compared to ATC's organizational efforts in the cooperative sector, the 1989 numbers are not impressive. By mid-1980, ATC had already organized 73,854 peasants into 2,512 cooperatives.[56] The picture is deceiving, however, since more than half of the reported 2,512 cooperatives in existence in 1980 were production cooperatives that were still in the process of creation and had not yet been firmly established.[57] Subsequently it became evident that many were not viable. In the ensuing consolidation process, scores of these early structures disappeared.

Five different types of cooperative association existed at the time the Sandinistas lost power. The five forms of association were the Cooperativas Agrícolas Sandinistas (Sandinista Production Cooperatives, or CAS); the Colectivos de Trabajo (Work Collectives, or CT); the Cooperativas de "Surcos Muertos" ("Dead Fence" Cooperatives, or CSM); the Cooperativas de Credito y Servicio (Credit and Service Cooperatives, or CCS); and the Tiendas Campesinas (Peasant Store, or TC). The two most significant cooperative forms of association were the Credit and Service and the Production Cooperatives. Whereas the members of a Production Cooperative hold all means of production in common, individual farmers, who preferred a much looser form of association, frequently joined forces in a Credit and Service Cooperative in order to have better access to government services. The latest, and economically most important, form of cooperatives

Table 4.3. Cooperatives affiliated with UNAG, 1989

A. Number of Organizations

Regions/zones	CAS	CT	CSM	CCS	TC	Other	Total
Region I	206	49	10	383	30	7	685
Region II	216	81	10	265	16	—	588
Region III	138	97	29	54	7	—	325
Region IV	302	64	—	178	32	20	596
Region V	120	14	11	73	27	3	248
Region VI	164	18	46	464	54	9	755
Zone I	11	10	5	79	7	72	184
Zone II	14	—	1	5	8	—	28
Zone III	50	58	—	27	10	—	145
Total	1,221	391	112	1,528	191	111	3,554

B. Number of Members

Regions/zones	CAS	CT	CSM	CCS	Other	TC[a]	Total
Region I	4,762	376	269	13,587	62	12,723	19,056
Region II	3,483	1,110	190	7,803	—	5,181	12,586
Region III	2,049	680	808	1,192	—	2,877	4,729
Region IV	6,053	400	—	6,407	795	10,625	13,655
Region V	2,240	179	230	1,694	78	9,203	4,421
Region VI	4,586	162	1,276	20,003	169	15,203	26,196
Zone I	558	135	166	2,666	1,374	3,127	4,899
Zone II	364	—	28	164	—	726	556
Zone III	949	429	—	609	—	2,039	1,987
Total	25,044	3,471	2,967	54,125	2,478	61,704	88,085

Sources: A: Cooperative Enterprise of Agricultural Producers (ECODEPA); B: National Union of Farmers and Ranchers (UNAG).

Note: CAS: Sandinista Production Cooperative.

CT: Work Collective.

CSM: "Dead Fence" Cooperative.

CCS: Credit and Service Cooperative.

TC: Tienda Campesina (Peasant Store).

[a]TC members are not included in the total figure. The great majority of the peasant store members are simultaneously members in one of the four other types of cooperative association. Thus, to include them in the membership total would mean to count them twice.

to emerge was the Peasant Store. Together, the cooperatives played a central part in Nicaragua's economy. In the mid-1980s they contributed 40 percent of the GNP and two-thirds of productive employment.[58]

A central problem in the evolution of the cooperative movement was the multitude of state and private organizations attending to the needs of this sector. In 1985, according to UNAG, thirty-four distinct institutions (state, private, foreign, and religious) catered to the needs of the cooperatives. In the case of the state agencies involved, it appears that the Sandinistas were driven by the paternalistic desire to maintain control, although this contradicted their own attempts to foster grassroots democracy.[59] The UNAG leadership consistently demanded to be given sole responsibility for this sector. In region VI, for example, UNAG professionals had very limited contact with the Sandinista Production Cooperatives, which were mainly attended by agrarian reform officials and representatives of the Sandinista party. This lack of coordination in attending to the needs of the cooperatives led to much confusion and a lack of identification of the farmers with their union. Members of cooperatives, officially affiliated with UNAG, often did not consider themselves part of the farmers' movement.[60]

In 1989, agrarian reform officials argued that UNAG should concentrate on representing individual producers and that the cooperatives should form an independent federation.[61] The idea for such a federation was supported by the directorate of the Sandinista party. The UNAG leadership, on the other hand, viewed this proposal as "an attempt to weaken the peasant movement and to increase the state's influence."[62] Faced with strong opposition from UNAG's National Council, the Sandinista leadership backed down. Nevertheless, following the election of Violeta Chamorro to the presidency of Nicaragua, UNAG created the Federación Nacional de Cooperativas Agropecuarias (National Federation of Agricultural Cooperatives, or FENACOOP). Ariel Bucardo, UNAG's vice-president, who heads the new federation, argued that FENACOOP will enhance the survival chances of the cooperative movement in the new ideological and economic climate. Initial progress was slow. In 1992, UNAG leaders acknowledged FENACOOP's continued structural weakness in several regions of Nicaragua. Although it is important for the cooperatives to have an institutional framework that works on their behalf, it will be a challenge to overcome the suspicion many farmers hold vis-à-vis the federation.

It took several years for UNAG to recognize that the idiosyncrasies of the peasant communities required more flexibility in terms of organizational structures. By the mid-1980s, however, the organization shed its image of rigidity and started to take the demands of the grass roots into account. As a result, UNAG's organizational structures were no longer imposed from above; rather, they reflected the distinct realities of the regions (see table 4.4 for detailed information). For example, in region V, large private farmers predominate. The agrarian reform hardly affected the traditional land-tenure structure in this area, and the private farmers were proud of their independence. Agricultural producers of this region were not likely to join the cooperative movement. Membership figures for 1985 provide evidence for this fact. In that year, more than fifty percent of all agricultural producers who affiliated with UNAG as individuals and not as members of cooperatives or producer organizations came from the departments of Boaco and Chontales. Out of a total of 24,576 individual producers affiliated with the organization, 13,820 came from region V. The cattle farmers of Boaco and Chontales would have been lost to UNAG had the organization's new flexibility not made it possible for this sector to affiliate as individuals. Another group of farmers, independently minded as well, sought to associate with UNAG through the village committees the producers had formed. After initial resistance by UNAG organizers, the village committees were recognized as legitimate UNAG structures. In the region of Boaco and Chontales, the committees functioned along with the established base structures. They constituted important organisms in the region, unifying the community and playing a significant role in increasing production levels. In 1985, 5,491 individual producers were integrated in 560 committees.

In sharp contrast to initial policy, the organization eventually permitted the producers to join in almost any form they elected. In 1985, UNAG was represented by 3,185 base structures at the grassroots level, with an additional 73 associations and commissions of ranchers and coffee growers affiliated with the organization. As shown in table 4.3, by 1989 the cooperative structures alone had increased to 3,554.

Quite similar to ATC's experience, the various commissions and associations were eventually consolidated and organized according to the main productive activities of the Nicaraguan farmer. These coffee, cattle, or cotton associations met once a month with representatives of the government institutions involved in the rural sector to discuss issues of concern to the farming community. Also, every association appointed a delegate to regional and national commissions representing the various productive sectors. These national commissions, whose membership included all relevant government ministers, had decision-making power and played a central role in the political economy of the rural sector.

Table 4.4. UNAG's base structures and membership, 1984–1985

A. Base Structures and Members, 1984

Regions/zones	Base organizations			Total members	UNAG officials
	CAS	CCS	UPB		
Region I	157	501	20	15,492	44
Region II	194	253	52	12,890	46
Region III	130	51	11	3,090	19
Region IV	274	109	—	8,907	59
Region V	65	112	232	16,400	41
Region VI	93	490	—	22,612	85
Special Zone I	39	71	—	2,997	17
Special Zone II	18	5	3	608	20
Special Zone III	52	5	13	1,697	19
Total	1,022	1,597	331	84,693	350

B. Base Structures, 1985

Regions/zones	Base organizations						Total	Associations/ Commissions
	CAS	CCS	CT	SM	CC	UPB		
Region I	146	459	25	—	—	2	632	16
Region II	247	259	—	—	—	—	506	2
Region III	107	38	61	—	6	—	212	10
Region IV	198	133	45	—	—	—	376	27
Region V	69	144	—	—	560	—	773	18
Region VI	93	371	24	12	—	21	521	—
Special zone I	12	36	—	—	—	—	48	—
Special zone II	15	13	9	—	—	—	37	—
Special zone III	51	9	14	—	—	6	80	—
Total	938	1,462	178	12	566	29	3,185	73

Source: National Union of Farmers and Ranchers (UNAG).

Note: CAS: Sandinista Production Cooperative.

CCS: Credit and Service Cooperative.

UPB: Base Unit of Private Producers.

CT: Work Collective.

SM: "Dead Fence" Cooperative (loosely associated private farms).

CC: Village Committees.

The cooperatives are collectively affiliated with the UNAG. In addition, most of the cooperatives' members are also individually affiliated.

The Question of Internal Democracy

A central question regarding the viability of Sandinista democracy, with its emphasis on the participation by grassroots movements, concerned the internal democracy of the various organizations. Here one encountered serious limitations. In the case of UNAG, formal democratic procedures were not institutionalized. Although the local leaders of UNAG's base structures were frequently chosen by the membership, the candidates were generally preapproved by UNAG officials. The grass roots had even less input in the selection of their leadership at higher levels. The members of UNAG's regional and zonal executive committees were appointed by the movement's leadership. In the case of the selection of national leaders, the Sandinista party played an important role. Although UNAG's national executive committee was formally chosen by a national congress, consisting of delegates from all regions of Nicaragua, all candidates were Sandinista party members and had been preapproved by the party's leadership. Further, until 1986, the term of UNAG's executive committee was not established. New organizational rules, drawn up for the first National Congress of UNAG, established five-year terms.

When confronted with the organization's deficiencies regarding internal democracy, UNAG officials argued that the absence of elections at the intermediate level was mainly the result of a shortage of qualified and interested producers who would consider running for office. Therefore, the national leadership felt justified in appointing the regional executive committees. Although there certainly was a shortage of capable leaders in the 1980s, the absence of elections was most likely a reflection of the national leadership's desire to exert strict control at the intermediate level. In the eyes of UNAG officials, the institutionalization of formal democratic principles was not a priority while the country was facing military aggression and an economic crisis. This reality limited the possibility for UNAG members to control and remove their representatives. It contributed to the bureaucratization of the organization and perpetuated the predominance of the chapiollos in the decision-making structures of the union.

UNAG members had equally little influence over the organization's full-time activists who worked at the grassroots level. These paid professionals were hired by the union's leadership. Farmers commonly complained that these professionals were not sufficiently autonomous from local FSLN or government officials and were likely to succumb to pressure. Further, UNAG organizers were often not producers themselves, which made it harder for them to gain the confidence of the farmers. Co-mandante Tirado, who was in charge of relations between the mass orga-nizations and the Sandinista Front, was aware of this problem and em-phasized the need for UNAG, like other mass organizations, to educate its own cadres in order to move toward more democratic structures. In the late 1980s, UNAG leadership corrected several of these organizational shortcomings by incorporating an increasing number of producers into its national council, thereby reducing the number of professionals in this body. In 1984 professionals constituted 60 percent of the council's mem-bers. Five years later, their participation had been reduced to 28 percent.[63] Albeit slowly, the farmers assumed greater control of their movement.

Despite the shortcomings of UNAG's internal organization from a formal democratic perspective, the movement had in fact a "bottom-up" approach to policy formation. This was amply demonstrated by the func-tioning of base assemblies. These meetings, held on a regional basis, pro-vided impressive examples of grassroots democracy at work. Every year hundreds of local assemblies were held in order to collect opinions and register the producers' problems. Whenever possible, problems were dealt with on the spot. Important issues affecting the farming community as a whole received special attention. First, a consultation process was conducted at the local level. For a period of several weeks the producers shared their concerns with the union representatives. The next stage in-volved the convocation of a regional assembly. The questions that need-ed to be dealt with at a regional or national level were taken up in this regional assembly with representatives of UNAG, the government, and the Sandinista party.

The base meetings were true exercises in popular democracy. They served not only to deal with problems at the local level but also to com-municate to the rural community issues affecting the country as a whole. Frequently, UNAG's professionals needed to explain unpopular govern-ment decisions. The war and the economic crisis during the 1980s forced the revolutionary authorities to implement policies that encountered resistance by the agricultural community. UNAG was in effect a mediator between the needs of Nicaraguan society and the necessities of its con-stituents. Prior to a meeting, UNAG officials consulted with the pro-ducers to obtain an understanding of a particular community's problems. The organization then brought in representatives of all pertinent govern-ment agencies to face the producers. In a frank exchange of views, the farmers articulated their difficulties, and the government officials tried to respond to their concerns. A typical meeting assembled representatives of FSLN, the local government, the credit system, the Ministry of Agrarian Reform, and the Ministry of Transport.

The issues discussed at these base meetings varied from one community to the other. Whereas the price of milk and meat was frequently debated in the cattle region of Boaco and Chontales, the price of coffee was an issue of contention in the mountainous region of Matagalpa and Jinotega. Certain issues, however, that concerned the majority of the agricultural producers came up in every meeting. These included credit policy, the scarcity of farm supplies, and the shortcomings of the local bureaucracy. The meetings were open to all producers, and many nonmembers attended, indicating the farming community's faith in the effectiveness of UNAG. Nonmembers, attending these meetings, did so in the belief that UNAG could solve their problems. When asked why they chose not to join the organization if they thought that it effectively represented their interests, these farmers expressed concern that this would compromise their independence. Members of the rival organization UPANIC, in particular, disliked UNAG because of its close association with the Sandinista Party.

Caught in the Crossfire: The Impact of the War

The most important factor that restrained the development of the Sandinista farmers' movement was the counterrevolutionary aggression sponsored by the United States. In accordance with the instructions that the "CIA Manual" provided to the contra forces, members of Sandinista grassroots movements became prime targets.[64] By 1989, 6,500 UNAG leaders and members had been assassinated, and 1,326 buildings (10 percent of all buildings) in cooperatives were destroyed.[65] Some 3,000 farmers were abducted, and about 350,000 peasants were uprooted and forced to resettle in safer areas because of the war.[66] Even after a peace agreement between the Sandinistas and the contras was signed in March 1988, the killing in the Nicaraguan countryside continued. The contras frequently targeted important leadership figures within UNAG. For example, Alfonso Núñez, a brother of UNAG's president and a central figure in the development of the Peasant Stores, was assassinated in November 1986. The loss of high-ranking UNAG officials further compounded the problem of a general lack of educated leadership figures, vital for the growth of the organization. In this context one can easily understand the UNAG president when he maintained in 1985 that the organization's "principal problem is the war."[67]

At the height of the counterrevolutionary war, many agricultural producers left the organization fearing for their lives. UNAG's membership used to fluctuate considerably at the regional level, in accordance with rising or decreasing contra activity. The development of UNAG from 45,000 members in 1982 to more than 125,000 by 1990 was characterized by substantial regional differences. The membership statistics have to be taken with a grain of salt, however, since UNAG stopped issuing membership cards in 1984. It abandoned this practice once the cards became virtual death certificates because of contras targeting farmers affiliated with the Sandinista movement. Thus, the organization had no reliable way to establish the number of affiliated farmers. Usually, a producer was considered a member if he or she used the movement's services and was identified as being supportive of the organization by local UNAG officials. Initially, more than 50 percent of UNAG's members were located in the departments of Matagalpa and Jinotega, where the movement originated.[68] In 1985 regions I, V, and VI were almost equal in strength, with a membership base of over 20,000 each. From 1985 to 1987, however, the UNAG grew by almost 50 percent in region VI, remained stable in region I, and lost more than one-fourth of its members in region V (see table 4.5 for detailed information). These considerable differences in the regional development of the farmers' movement were related to several factors, the most important being the counterrevolutionary aggression. The loss of more than 6,000 members of a total of 21,352 in Boaco and Chontales coincided with the rise of contra activity in the region. UNAG members were prime targets of the counterrevolution. Caught in the crossfire between the Sandinista army and the contras, many farmers chose to assume a lower political profile. The organization's positive development in Matagalpa and Jinotega, on the other hand, was facilitated by a decrease in contra attacks, as well as a particularly capable regional leadership.

The war split the peasant community. A considerable number of farmers, initially mostly from the border regions to Honduras and later on also from the interior, joined the counterrevolution. Peasants who had received plots of land under various Somocista colonization projects were a main base of support.[69] This sector had not participated in the insurrection and opposed the new Sandinista policies. The farmers particularly resented changes in the traditional relations of production

Table 4.5. Membership in UNAG, 1985, 1987

A. 1985

Regions/zones	Members of base organizations[a]						Associated members[b]	Individual members	Total
	CAS	CCS	CT	SM	CC	UPB			
Region I	3,526	14,083	2,711	—	—	180	1,730	—	22,230
Region II	4,518	7,905	—	—	—	—	115	1,205	13,743
Region III	1,695	1,154	477	—	—	—	2,124	1,190	6,640
Region IV	3,588	3,179	340	—	—	—	2,153	2,323	11,583
Region V	1,130	731	—	—	5,491	—	180	13,820	21,352
Region VI	2,429	15,570	317	238	—	1,200	—	3,246	23,000
Zone I	765	1,790	—	—	—	—	—	1,997	4,552
Zone II	223	321	53	—	—	—	—	306	903
Zone III	1,253	236	—	—	—	198	—	489	2,176
Total	19,127	44,969	3,898	238	5,491	1,578	6,302	24,576	106,179

B. 1987

Regions/zones	Members of base organizations[a]				Associated members[b]	Individual members[c]	Total
	CAS	CCS	CSM	CT			
Region I	8,070	11,856	330	333	n.a.	2,834	23,423
Region II	4,293	9,789	396	1,013	96	3,310	18,897
Region III	2,250[b]	2,272[d]	—	800[d]	—	943	6,265
Region IV	5,364	5,939	—	499	2,207	1,947	15,956
Region V	2,559	927	—	—	—	11,491[d]	14,977
Region VI	4,114	22,251	1,489	—	504	4,768	33,126
Zone I	298[d]	1,586[d]	—	202[d]	—	565[d]	2,651
Zone II	1,082	1,109	—	515	—	—	2,706
Zone III	1,092[d]	398[d]	—	255[d]	—	760[d]	2,505
Total	29,122	56,127	2,215	3,617	2,807	26,618	120,506

Source: National Union of Farmers and Ranchers (UNAG).

Note: CAS: Sandinista Production Cooperative.

CCS: Credit and Service Cooperative.

CSM: Dead Fence Cooperative.

CT: Work Collective.

CC: Village Committees.

UPB: Base Unit of Private Producers.

[a]Members of the various base organizations are affiliated with UNAG through their base structures and as individuals.

[b]Associated members are affiliated with UNAG as members of their coffee and cattle associations.

[c]Individual members affiliate with UNAG but do not belong to any base structure.

[d]Total as of July 6, 1987.

that they viewed as beneficial. New organizational structures, such as the emerging Sandinista production cooperatives, were viewed with hostility.[70]

The contra army grew substantially during the 1980s. At the time of the 1990 peace accords, 22,500 fighters demobilized. Joaquín Lovo, the vice-minister of government, maintained that this number is somewhat inflated, since about 5,000 peasants appeared to have "joined" the contras at the last minute to take advantage of the benefits (building materials, food, and so forth) that the international agencies, overseeing the disarmament process, handed out to the demobilized fighters. Although the counterrevolution attracted considerable support among the peasantry, a much greater number of farmers actively defended the Sandinista revolution. The majority of the agricultural community elected to stay on the sidelines.[71] Many times, these farmers were caught between a rock and a hard place. Bands of counterrevolutionaries would visit their farms and demand food at gunpoint. This was often construed by the Sandinista army as support for the contras, and shortsighted military commanders at times imprisoned these peasants. Similarly, the contras punished farmers who took their milk to market, fed Sandinista troops, or were engaged in any activity that could be considered support for the revolution. This situation led to increased polarization in the countryside, with many farmers blaming the government for their predicament. Those that took up arms and joined the contras were swayed by anticommunist propaganda, religious fervor, family ties to Somoza's Guardia Nacional, economic benefits (in 1985, a contra foot soldier was paid the equivalent of ten times the president's salary at the black market rate), and incidents of Sandinista repression.

Daniel Núñez, UNAG's president, was a central figure in denouncing Sandinista abuses. In several instances he demanded to be arrested himself unless the authorities were prepared to release a particular producer who had been taken into custody on the charge of being a contra collaborator. Because of his intimate relations with the Sandinista leadership, Núñez had considerable success in limiting abuses by local officials. Nevertheless, many abuses did occur. Núñez argued that these abuses, committed by narrow-minded local officials, severely damaged the reputation of the Sandinista revolution. In an interview, he recounted an incident in the early 1980s in the town of El Cuá in which a Sandinista functionary with an industrial worker background caused havoc because he did not know how to relate to the peasantry. Having entered into a confrontation with one of the leading producers in the area, he proceeded to confiscate his land. As a result of this misguided action, 200 farmers rallied to the producer's aid, and all of them joined the contras. The Sandinista leadership, mostly of urban background, never fully understood the Nicaraguan peasantry. Greater sensitivity on behalf of the leadership could have prevented many incidents that turned the farming community against the revolution. Fortunately for the Sandinistas, several high-ranking party officials did enjoy the trust of the peasantry. Comandante Victor Tirado, a member of the party directorate, was one of them. El Viejo (the old one) had earned the peasants' support during his years in the mountains. When one observed him, addressing a gathering of farmers in his low, soft voice, it became immediately clear why the party put him in charge of relations with the grassroots movements. He knew how to communicate with the peasantry, and it was obvious that their respect for each other was mutual.

Starting in 1985, the contras lost some of their initial support. Having failed to defeat the Sandinista army on the battlefield, the contra leadership changed its tactics. Following the instructions of the CIA, counterrevolutionary task forces attacked agricultural cooperatives, assassinated Sandinista officials, and victimized the civilian population. This changed their image in the rural population. The majority ceased to consider them a credible military force and started to view them as terrorists.[72] The peasants in support of the Sandinistas made a major contribution to the contras' strategic defeat, fighting in the army and the rural militia. Agricultural cooperatives, located in the warzone, were converted into "self-defense cooperatives" and halted the contras' advance with their weapons in hand. The cooperatives paid a high price for defending the revolution. By 1987, 61 percent of Sandinista war dead were members of cooperatives, as were 71 percent of those wounded and 77 percent of those abducted.[73]

Hedging Your Bet: Political Pluralism in a Climate of Conflict

In order to represent the interests of the agricultural producers before the state and to facilitate political participation by its members, UNAG had to be a representative and pluralist organization with a high degree of autonomy from the revolutionary authorities. In the mid-1980s, UNAG's representativeness was in question.[74] Yet most observers agree that in contrast with other Sandinista grassroots movements, UNAG succeeded in overcoming initial deficiencies and evolved into an effective champion of its membership's interests. A comparative analysis of the Sandinista organization and UPANIC, the movement of the rural bourgeoisie, demonstrates the strength of the UNAG.

It has been estimated that in 1980 Nicaragua's farming community was comprised of 553,966 persons who were engaged in productive activities. By 1987 the farmers had increased to 641,047.[75] If we use the figures for the farming community as our base, UNAG represented 8 percent of the farmers in 1980 and 19 percent in 1987.[76] These figures do not do justice to the importance of the organization, since UNAG represented the interests of both its members and the agricultural producers in general. Also, some observers have argued that the work of UNAG affected not only the producers but also their families. If one includes the family members of the affiliated producers in the calculations, UNAG "influenced" 65 percent of the peasant population in 1987.[77]

In several regions of the country, producers were affiliated with both UNAG and UPANIC, the organization of the political opposition. According to the leaders of the two organizations, neither one favored this development, since both regarded these producers as opportunists. In the early 1980s, UNAG's president flatly denied the existence of double affiliations. Asked in 1984, whether there were producers affiliated with both UNAG and UPANIC, he replied: "No. Either one is in the UNAG or one is not. We cannot accept double affiliations, because we would be dishonest. However, there are producers who have been there [with UPANIC] and are now with us."[78] Notwithstanding these denials, double affiliations were standard practice.

Economic realities were thus frequently more important than political affinities in determining whether a large producer would support the Sandinista government.[79] The insecurity generated by the war was the main reason that many large producers reconsidered the cost of ideological purity. Astute producers sought protection by seeking joint membership in UNAG and UPANIC. Evidence suggests that, as a UNAG member, one was less likely to be in danger of having one's land expropriated.[80] The position of these bourgeois producers was informed by pragmatism and contrasted with the strictly ideological stand taken by the UPANIC leadership. The views of UPANIC's national leaders, who were critical of the revolutionary process, often differed from the ones held by regional UPANIC affiliates.[81] Of the eight UPANIC affiliates, three stood out as having member organizations with independent positions: FAGANIC;

the Confederación de Asociaciones de Algodoneros de Nicaragua (Confederation of Nicaraguan Cottongrowers, or CAAN); and the Fondo de Desarrollo de la Industria Lactea (Development Fund for the Milk Industry, or FONDILAC).

Conflicts between the national UPANIC leadership and some of its affiliates sharpened during the heated pre-electoral climate of 1989. Even within the national leadership, ruptures started to occur. For example, Rafael "Payo" Martínez, the influential president of FAGANIC, publicly distanced himself from Violeta Chamorro in November 1989 and took a nonpartisan position regarding the upcoming elections.[82] One of the most interesting and significant cases of public dissent was the challenge to UPANIC's leadership posed by Juan Diego López, the president of the dairy producers organized in FONDILAC. Like Martínez, a member of UPANIC's governing board, he nevertheless ran on the FSLN ticket for a seat in the National Assembly.[83] López's candidacy on the FSLN slate was not a complete surprise. His good relations with the Sandinistas were publicized when he participated in a private-sector delegation that the government sent to Stockholm in mid-1989 with the mission to raise funds for Nicaragua's faltering economy. The UPANIC leadership had vehemently argued against his participation, out of fear it would lend legitimacy to the Sandinista aid request. Outraged over López's show of independence, UPANIC unsuccessfully tried to expel him.[84] The López case, though the most prominent, was not a rare occurrence. A number of farmers affiliated with UPANIC were FSLN candidates in the municipal and national elections.[85]

The disagreements between leaders of the rural bourgeoisie hurt the organizational development of UPANIC. Some farmers abandoned the organization and joined UNAG.[86] The reputation UNAG enjoyed among the capitalist class fluctuated according to the state of relations between the rural bourgeoisie and the Sandinistas. UPANIC's relationship with the revolutionary authorities alternated between periods of mutual respect and tacit cooperation and times of fierce antagonism. For example, during 1984–1985 relations improved considerably. UPANIC's leadership held the view that the government had finally given the producers decent prices for their products, and they acknowledged that land invasions had become a rare occurrence. Thus, the rural bourgeoisie could produce under conditions of relative tranquility. This situation changed drastically in mid-1985, when a wave of land invasions occurred around the town of Masaya. The UPANIC leaders were outraged over these invasions, which they considered to be politically motivated and arbitrary. As a result, relations started to deteriorate.[87]

The pattern of cooperation and conflict was repeated in the late 1980s. Government efforts to elicit the bourgeoisie's cooperation, evidenced by a halt in land expropriations and official declarations that the agrarian reform had ended, were followed by the spectacular July 1988 expropriation of the most important capitalist enterprise in Nicaragua, a sugar mill belonging to the Pellas family. In the opinion of Ramiro Gúrdian, UPANIC's president, the government intended the following message to the private sector: "I take the largest one, so anyone can be next."[88] The last incident of what could be considered a politically motivated expropriation under the Sandinistas occurred in June 1989. Three eminent UPANIC members were expropriated when they used a meeting of the national coffee commission to challenge the government politically.[89] UNAG leaders criticized the government's decision to expropriate but also condemned UPANIC's attempt to politicize the meeting. In the eyes of UPANIC, these incidents demonstrated that the government could not be trusted, whereas the Sandinistas argued that the bourgeoisie abused times of relative calm to advance its political agenda.

UPANIC's importance was not based on its numerical strength but must be understood in light of the policy of national unity. The organization's leverage was owing to the important role of the rural bourgeoisie in the agro-export sector, an area of vital importance to Nicaragua's economy. Reported estimates for the UPANIC membership ranged from 6,000 to 11,000.[90] Almost all members were medium or large producers. The core of UPANIC consisted of about 700 large producers who together controlled 13 percent of the country's arable land in 1989.[91] Thus, their weight—in terms of total land under control—corresponded roughly to the combined acreage of farms controlled by the Sandinista state in 1989.

In contrast with the organization of the rural bourgeoisie, UNAG represented a broad spectrum of agricultural producers and played a significant role in facilitating their participation in Nicaragua's political system. Beginning in 1981, the farmers' movement became an actor in the national political arena when it was assigned two seats on the Council of State. Following the 1984 changes in leadership, UNAG played an increasingly important role in the country's political economy. As noted above, several observers of the 1984 electoral process feared that the grassroots organizations would lose significance in a representative political framework, having been deprived of direct representation.

In the case of the UNAG this fear was unwarranted. Following the 1984 elections, nine representatives of the National Assembly (out of a total of ninety-six) and seventeen substitutes were UNAG members. Of these twenty-six representatives, seventeen were FSLN delegates, with the remainder belonging to other parties.

The political affiliations of the UNAG representatives in the National Assembly were themselves illustrative of the healthy pluralism within this social movement. It is important to note that of the seventeen delegates representing the FSLN, several were actually not members of the party. Juan Tijerino, third secretary of the National Assembly (1984–90), belonged to this group. A cofounder of UPANIC, he worked in both UNAG and UPANIC in 1983 and was chosen for the FSLN slate because of his excellent reputation among producers. Tijerino argued that he spoke to the legislature foremost as a producer, not a party member, which gave him a position of independence compared to other representatives in the National Assembly. The nine other UNAG representatives who were not FSLN delegates were members of the Liberal and Conservative parties. Among them was Constantino Pereira, the 1984 vice-presidential candidate of the Liberal party who was elected to UNAG's national executive committee in 1992. The fact that UNAG represented a broad party spectrum is evidence that the organization was indeed pluralist and representative.

The Struggle for Autonomy: Party, State, and Agricultural Producers

One important consideration regarding UNAG's role within the new political system was the union's relationship to the Sandinista party and the state. The revolutionary leadership did not share a common view on the role of the grassroots movements in the emerging political economy. Comandante Carlos Núñez, president of the National Assembly (1984–1990), was an advocate for participatory democracy. He criticized the grassroots movements for not representing the interests of their constituents with enough militancy before the revolutionary authorities. Other sectors within the government, however, sought complete control over the grassroots movements and voiced opposition whenever they assumed autonomous positions. The tension between these two views presented a daily challenge for UNAG as the organization pushed for more autonomy. The leadership of the farmers' movement frequently emphasized that UNAG was not "a Sandinista mass organization" but corresponded to the need of the agricultural community for an organization representing its interests. Daniel Núñez, seeking to establish that UNAG was qualitatively different from other Sandinista organizations such as the Sandinista Neighborhood Committees, pointed out that UNAG was the only one of the six main grassroots movements to have emerged *after* the successful insurrection in 1979. Though it is true that the farmers' movement was not created by the Sandinistas during the struggle against the dictatorship, neither did UNAG emerge on the sole initiative of agricultural producers seeking better representation in the unfolding revolutionary project. As discussed above, Sandinista militants, acting upon party orders, initiated the organizational drive that led to the emergence of UNAG. Thus, from the very beginning the Sandinista party influenced the development of UNAG. The Sandinistas' clout led to strong objections by senior UNAG officials who resented attempts by the revolutionary authorities "to use the UNAG as if we were a mass organization."[92] Although strong evidence indicated that UNAG indeed differed from other Sandinista organizations, the farmers' movement did not enjoy complete autonomy.

UNAG recognized the Sandinista Front as its revolutionary vanguard. The movement's initial bylaws stated: "The UNAG is an independent organization, which supports the tasks of national reconstruction and *recognizes the FSLN as the vanguard of the revolutionary process.*"[93] It is no secret that UNAG leadership and FSLN shared a common ideology. For example, UNAG actively supported FSLN during the election campaigns of 1984 and 1989–1990. In 1984 it mobilized thousands of producers from all over the country, who ratified their support for the FSLN in a mass rally held in Managua. The concrete link between the party and UNAG was Comandante Víctor Tirado. Tirado played an important role in the determination of UNAG's policies as well as in the selection of UNAG presidents. A member of UNAG's executive committee served as the liaison between the union and the Sandinista Front, and a representative of Comandante Tirado participated in meetings of UNAG's board of directors. Further, UNAG's president, Daniel Núñez, was a member of the Sandinista Assembly, which consisted in 1991 of ninety-eight high-ranking Sandinista officials. At the 1991 FSLN congress, two other members of UNAG's national board of directors (Ariel Bucardo and Benigna Mendiola), as well as three regional presidents (Roberto Laguna, Hermógenes Rodriquez, and Byron Corrales) were also elected to the

Sandinista assembly.[94] Thus, it was evident that UNAG and the Sandinista Front shared many objectives and enjoyed mutual support.

The Sandinista party had considerable impact in the development of the farmers' movement. FSLN exerted its influence by putting loyal Sandinistas into leadership positions and by providing financial support. Sandinista militants, paid by the FSLN, could be found in UNAG at all levels. According to Comandante Tirado, financial help from the party was of particular importance during the union's first years. The level of support decreased in the late 1980s, when the economic crisis forced the Sandinistas to cut funding to the grassroots movements. In 1988 the party reduced funding for UNAG by 50 percent.[95] As a consequence, UNAG had to lay off 250 professionals. Daniel Núñez pointed out that this measure alone (there were others to follow) reduced UNAG's professional staff by more than half. Even at reduced levels, support from the party continued to be substantial. According to internal documents of the organization, Sandinista funds constituted 24 percent of UNAG's annual budget in 1989 (see table 4.6). This support was essential, since the producers affiliated with UNAG contributed only 15 percent of the movement's operating expenses. The rest came from international donors, foremost Holland and Sweden.

In an attempt to reduce the party's influence, the farmers' movement introduced a project for self-financing at its National Congress in April 1986. Even though UNAG had collected membership dues in the past, the dues were considered voluntary contributions and did not begin to cover the organization's expenditures. UNAG had to rely primarily on international aid and funds provided by the revolutionary authorities. By 1986 the leaders of UNAG were confident that the membership was prepared to assume the financial responsibility of the organization. Although the members were slowly assuming a greater share of the financial burden, UNAG was not able to finance itself from membership contributions. This situation did not reflect the farmers' unwillingness to support their union. Instead it reflected the difficult reality of a country at war. For most of the 1980s, UNAG had no accurate count of its members and thus experienced problems in assessing dues. The contra aggression made it dangerous for farmers to support the union openly. Further, the economic conditions prevailing in Nicaragua, particularly galloping inflation, made any form of dues collection a futile exercise. Daniel Núñez was convinced that "the day the war ends, we [UNAG] will self-finance ourselves."[96] Núñez' optimism was not quite justified. In 1993 UNAG had yet to estab-

Table 4.6. UNAG's budget, 1989–1990 (US$)

	1989	1990
Income		
Member dues	45,000	50,000
Member contributions[a]	85,000	100,000
Support from government	210,000	190,000
External support		
SCC	115,610	75,000[b]
HIVOS	375,000	525,000
NDR	21,150	—
Other	16,450	—
Total	868,210	940,000
Expenses[c]		
Events and assemblies	107,450	100,000
Personnel services	355,760	456,840
Nonpersonnel services	220,000	1,031,880
Supplies	140,000	331,510
Investments	45,000	498,500
Total	868,210	2,418,730

Source: National Union of Farmers and Ranchers (UNAG).

Note: SCC: Swedish Cooperative Center.

HIVOS: Dutch Aid Agency.

NDR: Norwegian Aid Agency.

[a]These contributions are solicited to cover expenses of special events.

[b]Support from January to June under current agreement between UNAG/SCC.

[c]Projections based on expected minimum needs of UNAG.

lish its actual numerical strength by completing a 1990 initiative to affiliate its membership formally.

Comandante Tirado affirmed that much of the Sandinista party's financial aid went to support UNAG's professionals. The organization started in 1981 with a total of 157 paid organizers, a number that grew to 387 by 1987.[97] Most of these union promoters were Sandinista militants who had received formal training. While the UNAG was in charge of teaching organizational techniques, the FSLN was responsible for political-ideological training.[98] In addition, a substantial number of professionals received training in the exterior. More than 500 completed courses in Cuba, sponsored by the Asociación Nacional de Agricultores Pequeños (Small

Farmers' Association, or ANAP), UNAG's sister organization.[99] The Nordic countries that sought to counter the Cuban influence initiated a program in the mid-1980s that exposed dozens of UNAG officials to the Scandinavian experience. In general, one could speak of a symbiotic relationship between FSLN and UNAG professionals. Comandante Victor Tirado affirmed in 1989 that of the 11 members of UNAG's Executive Committee, six were militants of the party. Among the 125,000 producers who supported UNAG in 1990, approximately 10,000 (most of them affiliated with the cooperative movement) were members of the Sandinista Front. As Tirado pointed out, the Sandinista militant "gives directions to other members regarding the lines of the Revolution, clarifies the policies of the Revolution, [and] guaranties the defense of the peasantry's interest."[100]

It is essential to note that the Sandinista militants in UNAG were generally highly committed individuals who sacrificed themselves to contribute to the realization of the revolutionary project. UNAG's rapid growth would not have been possible without their dedication to work under the most adverse conditions. Many militants were also "natural" leaders who commanded the support of their communities, even in areas in which the FSLN had lost support. Their political leverage with the Sandinista authorities greatly benefited the farming community. Daniel Núñez, in particular, is a highly respected, charismatic Sandinista leader, whose personal commitment has been a central factor in the success of UNAG. Yet the close relations between UNAG and the party also had their price.

At times the farmers perceived UNAG professionals as agents of the state. This was particularly the case in matters regarding military service.[101] UNAG officials sought to convince the producers to fulfil their duty and comply with the military service law. The farmers were naturally reluctant to risk their lives fighting the contras and frequently chose not to attend meetings sponsored by UNAG out of the fear that the organization was in collusion with the military authorities. This situation made producers wonder whether the state's or the producer's interests came first in the eyes of UNAG professionals and led to distrust between UNAG and its members. An illustrative example was Horacio Bonilla, a Sandinista militant who served as UNAG's president in region V. Although he enjoyed considerable power because of his direct access to the Sandinista leadership, he had little support among local producers, since they had been given no input in his selection as UNAG's regional president. In fact, Bonilla was placed in his position by the Sandinista party. Most farmers considered him a party hack, whose loyalty tied him to the FSLN, not the peasantry.

The question of loyalty was perceived as a problem by many producers. In simple cases, militants had to neglect their work in UNAG because the party instructed them to focus on other activities, such as the 1990 election campaign. The priority given to partisan activities during election campaigns was a phenomenon that could be observed in all Sandinista grassroots movements.[102] More serious conflicts of interests arose when the position of the party forced the militant to violate the principles of grassroots democracy. Such cases occurred in the selection of peasant store leaders and in the elections of UNAG officials. In several instances, high-ranking UNAG officials pushed candidates who enjoyed the confidence of the party but were rejected by the grass roots. These conflicts, which could be observed throughout Nicaragua, were the result of "the subordination of the specific demands by the base to the general lines set forth by the party and the government: national unity, defense, production, or elections."[103]

Whereas the UNAG leadership was solidly Sandinista, the movement was politically by far the most open of all Sandinista grassroots movements, and its constituents represented a diverse political spectrum. Comandante Tirado noted that "even though it [UNAG] receives support from the government and the Sandinista Front, it maintains as a movement an independent position, which allows it to be an organizational alternative for all producers, and not only for those who sympathize with Sandinismo."[104] Arquímedes Rivera, the director of the peasant store project (1986–1990), and a Sandinista militant, emphasized that one should not confuse the positions of the UNAG leadership with the organization as such. Whereas the leadership was clearly pro-Sandinista, UNAG sought to represent producers regardless of their political views. He further pointed out that in case the membership did not like the political position of the leaders, it had the power not to reelect them. At the time, however, the leadership was not fully accountable to the base, since competitive elections within the union had yet to be institutionalized. The UNAG leadership is certainly entitled to its political views, as are union leaders in all countries. Problems arise, however, when the leadership uses the organization as its political platform. The election campaign of 1989–1990 illustrated this problem.

In 1989 the FSLN faced a dilemma—to continue the process of

strengthening the autonomy of the Sandinista grassroots movements begun in 1987 or to rely on the mass organizations for the difficult task to gain reelection. Not surprisingly, the survival of the revolutionary project was given priority over concerns regarding the possible conse-quences of this action for the development of grassroots democracy. Particularly in the rural sector, the Sandinistas had little choice. The war, the difficult economic situation, and misguided policies of regional Sandinista officials had eroded support for the government. In region V, Agustín Lara, the head of the regional government, had antagonized the rural community to the point that senior UNAG officials considered him "the most important asset of the counterrevolution." Many Sandinista leaders were convinced that only UNAG could deliver the peasant vote necessary for an electoral victory. This situation explains the high incidence of UNAG leaders on the Sandinista slate. In region V, for example, the Sandinista ticket was headed by Daniel Núñez, with UNAG members representing 50 percent of the candidates to the National Assembly.[105] In the municipal elections, farmers affiliated with UNAG constituted 60.8 percent of all FSLN candidates.[106]

The producers who campaigned on behalf of the Sandinista Front enjoyed the support of the local peasantry, and their candidacies reas-sured the large producers that the views of the farming community were considered important. Members of the rural bourgeoisie looked favor-ably upon the Sandinista strategy to run candidates with a farming back-ground. FAGANIC's president, expressing his satisfaction with the inclu-sion of producers on the FSLN ticket, commented on the candidacy of Juan Ramon Aragon, a large cattle producer and member of UNAG's national board of directors who was nominated for the National Assembly: "I have no objection, and regarding whether or not he is a Sandinista, when the hour comes he will have to look after the interests of the ranchers."[107]

In the eyes of many producers, UNAG became exceedingly politicized during the election campaign. This process took many forms. For example, grassroots meetings were often converted into political rallies, and UNO supporters were at times harassed. Although many UNAG officials supported Daniel Núñez and FSLN in the election campaign, the majority of the membership did not. The UNAG leadership and the members of the Sandinista production cooperatives were solidly Sandin-ista, whereas individual producers and members of credit and service cooperatives overwhelmingly supported the Chamorro candidacy. Grassroots participation declined as a result of this "politicization," and peasant leaders were alienated. They perceived the electoral campaign as an attempt by UNAG's leadership to impose its views on the base. In light of the outcome of the February 1990 elections, the strong support for UNO among the UNAG membership constituted a fortunate fact. It was a major factor in ensuring the relatively smooth adaptation of UNAG to the new political climate.

The farmers' movement demonstrated a greater degree of independence from the FSLN than one observed in the case of the other main mass organizations. Its leaders were not afraid to oppose Sandinista policies when they ran counter to the interests of the farming community. UNAG leaders used the representation on government bodies to press their case. For example, in the National Assembly, UNAG's president headed the agricultural commission, which had great influence in determining agricultural policy. A key factor in UNAG's success at challenging the party line, compared with that of its counterparts, was the economic clout of its constituents. In 1989 UNAG members produced 55 percent of all coffee, 50 percent of all cotton, and 60 percent of the beef that was exported.[108] The producers' weight was not limited to the economy but was equally evident in the political arena. Comandante Victor Tirado affirmed that "without the UNAG, without the political and ideological unity of the workers and peasants, it would have been impossible to confront the war and to maintain the economy at levels of survival."[109]

A closer examination of the record of the organization shows that UNAG evolved over time into an increasingly autonomous movement. This becomes quite clear if one analyzes the organization's behavior in cases where the interests of its constituents were in conflict with those of the FSLN or the state. The available evidence supports the view that UNAG used its considerable leverage to stand up for its members, even in defiance of the Sandinista Front. For example, in the spring of 1985, the government wanted to implement a major resettlement program for peasants living in northern Nicaragua, then a war zone. The objective of the revolutionary authorities was to create a free-fire zone for the Sandinista army and to dry up any support the counterrevolutionaries enjoyed. UNAG strongly objected, since its constituents did not want to resettle, despite the daily aggression. In heated debates, UNAG persuaded the revolutionary authorities to change the scale and implementation of the evacuation program substantially, avoiding a potential repetition of the Miskito problem and attending to the wishes of the producers. UNAG's leverage in this case was related to the fact that the government depended on the organization to carry out the actual resettlement. The government had to rely on UNAG as the only organization capable of convincing the producers of the need to leave their farms.

UNAG was also instrumental in ensuring that all forms of cooperative association would be voluntary, an issue of great controversy in revolutionary Nicaragua. The organization recognized the strong individualism of the Nicaraguan peasantry and favored the distribution of land in a variety of forms. UNAG's leadership argued that the imposition of a rigid model of cooperative association would be a mistake.[110] If the peasantry could not be convinced to work the land collectively, they should be given the choice to receive properties as private individual producers. Many agrarian reform officials argued, however, that the creation of a system of family farms would be in conflict with the goals of the Sandinista project.[111] UNAG's position was reinforced in 1985, when extensive land invasions occurred in Masaya. Subsequently, the government increased the distribution of land to individual producers. The 1986 modification of the agrarian reform law finally resolved the conflict between agrarian reform officials and UNAG in favor of the farmers' organization. The revised law took account of pressures by the peasantry and UNAG to provide land to peasants as individual producers.

When the government was unwilling or incapable of providing solutions to problems that affected the producers, UNAG frequently took matters into its own hands. The high prices for farm inputs constituted such a case. Comandante Jaime Wheelock, minister of agriculture and agrarian reform, acknowledged that the prices for essential agricultural inputs, such as seeds, fertilizer, and farm equipment, rose in an exorbitant manner after the Sandinistas took power.[112] The government was unable to prevent speculation in agricultural inputs and failed to establish an effective state distribution system. Responding to the crisis, UNAG devised a solution. With the financial help of Western European governments, the organization established a country-wide network of supply centers that provided the most essential products to UNAG members at cost.

The farmers' movement also successfully applied pressure on the government to solve the debt crisis of Nicaragua's rural sector. In 1983, UNAG headed a campaign that achieved the cancellation of the debt owed by basic grain producers.[113] Several years later, the farmers' movement once again had to address the question of farm debt. In 1988 the Sandinista government instituted a major economic reform in an effort to control inflation, which was running at 30,000 percent. A new currency was issued, in effect devaluing the Nicaraguan cordoba by 1,000 percent. A one million cordoba short-term debt was thus reduced to 1,000 cordobas. In order to guarantee the solvency of the banking system, President Ortega issued a decree outlining long-term debt revaluation procedures. UNAG argued that the new law favored speculators who had acquired short-term debt, while it punished productive farmers with long-term commitments. For example, a one million cordoba short-term debt incurred for the business of buying and reselling calves could be paid back easily, since it amounted only to 1,000 cordobas. On the other hand, producers who had acquired long-term debt for raising cattle saw their loans revalued by a multiplier of fifty. Following considerable base pressure by cattle producers, particularly from region V, President Ortega promised to rescind the decree. When the banks nevertheless proceeded with the revaluation of long-term debt, the producers were outraged, charging the president with breaking his word. UNAG, supported by Comandante Carlos Núñez, continued to fight this government policy, and a solution was finally reached in July 1988. The producers with long-term debt were allowed to repay their loans the same year, thereby avoiding revaluation. This concession of the government alleviated the debt burden of the cattle producers while avoiding a solvency crisis of the banking system. UNAG's prestige in the farming community soared to new heights. The organization had once again demonstrated its capacity to change government policies opposed by its constituents.

UNAG's struggle for autonomy was most evident at the local level. Officials of the organization often complained about pressures applied by the Sandinista Front and the state. The government sought to exert control through its bureaucracies such as MIDINRA. Party and government representatives tended to have urban backgrounds and viewed problems affecting the countryside in global political terms, whereas UNAG members looked at the same issues from the much narrower, parochial perspective of a producer. Further, people with urban backgrounds were convinced of the rural sector's backwardness and justified their authoritarian measures with the need to enlighten the peasantry. In the first years of the revolution, most Sandinista leaders considered the peasantry "backwards" and argued that to "modernize" the small producers they had to be integrated into the cooperatives and the state sector.[114] Many state officials considered the peasantry incapable of understanding the changes required in the transformation of the traditional relations of production.[115] The farmers, on the other hand, tried to get the revolutionary authorities to "understand the problematic of the countryside."[116] As part of this process, UNAG professionals and members learned to understand the larger national problematic, and the revolutionary authorities sought to comprehend the local perspective. When this approach failed and state and party officials imposed their views in an authoritarian manner, UNAG appealed to the regional and national authorities for help. The organization also sought to discredit these government officials by whatever means available, even by accusing them as counterrevolutionaries.

UNAG's strong and independent positions, often challenging the revolutionary government and the FSLN, led to many conflicts. Whereas these disagreements were evident at the local level, clashes at the national level were rarely made public. In this context, it is essential to note that although the party at times limited the autonomous development of the farmers' movement, the Sandinistas deserve credit for having demonstrated a genuine interest in the organizational growth of UNAG. The Sandinista leadership was particularly interested in fighting instances of corruption, favoritism, and paternalism in the grassroots movements. According to reliable sources, the Sandinista party criticized UNAG in a 1988 internal report. One criticism concerned financial irregularities in the administration of the peasant store network. Thus, though relations between UNAG and the revolutionary authorities were not without conflict, they were generally constructive.

The Impact of International Solidarity

In its efforts to gain greater autonomy from the Sandinista party and the government, UNAG needed to rely on the help offered by the international community. The organization was very successful in obtaining financial support and technical assistance from international aid agencies, private funding institutions, and Western European governments. UNAG strengthened its international reputation when it was recognized by the International Labor Organization as a representative of Nicaragua's private sector. The farmers' movement became also a member of the Central American and Caribbean Cooperative Federation and was eventually trusted with leading it. In terms of the viability of Sandinista democracy, UNAG was considered a test case by the Socialist International and European governments supportive of the Sandinistas. Seeking to strengthen the participatory aspect of Nicaragua's revolutionary project, bilateral and multilateral donors provided substantial financial support to UNAG. In 1985 the list of major donor countries was headed by Sweden, followed by Italy, Holland, France, and Belgium. By 1989 organizations of agricultural producers from Norway, Finland, Canada, and the United States also made significant financial contributions to their Nicaraguan counterpart.[117] Swedish and Italian support was particularly significant, since it went beyond a mere financial commitment. Italy supported and advised a training center in León, where UNAG members were taught basic organizational and farming skills. Swedish aid played a leading role in the most significant contribution by international donors, namely support for the peasant stores. Between 1985 to 1987, UNAG received approximately US$22 million from international donors for the peasant stores.[118] Total international aid in 1987 for all of UNAG's projects, including the peasant stores, amounted to US$24 million. The most significant contributors were the Swedish Cooperative Center (SCC), followed by Hivos of Holland, Oxfam-England, and Oxfam-America (see table 4.7). The agricultural producers of Norway were the most important new funding source in 1987. The Norwegian contribution was dwarfed, however, by the Swedish aid program. In 1987 the Swedish Cooperative Center contributed more than nineteen of a total of US$24 million in international aid given to UNAG. Nicaragua was among the eighteen most significant recipients of Swedish development aid. Aid for reconstruction started in 1979 and amounted to almost US$200 million by 1989.[119] Although the mining and forestry sectors received the biggest share of aid, Swedish support for UNAG and the peasant stores was substantial (see table 4.8). Assistance included consulting services provided by SCC, direct aid for UNAG's organizational tasks, and the disposition of foreign exchange, essential for the importation of basic farm inputs and consumer products, which were being sold through the peasant stores.

Conclusion

It was of fundamental significance for UNAG to maintain and increase its independence from the FSLN, since many private producers would not join an organization they perceived to be identical with the Sandinista Front. UNAG membership itself did not imply any affiliation with the FSLN. This was underscored by the fact that UNAG members can and do

Table 4.7. International aid to UNAG, 1987 (US$)

Organization/country	Received	Allocated[a]	Total
SCC/Sweden	3,414,142	16,155,000	19,569,142
Hivos/Holland	758,869	270,000	1,028,869
Oxfam/England	178,700	182,870	361,570
Oxfam/USA	225,000	225,000	450,000
Oxfam/Canada	20,731	—	20,731
Fundacion Paulo Freire/Holland	54,543	—	54,543
Rädd Barna/Norway	19,426	358,000	377,426
Hovib/Holland	51,549	23,187	74,736
Freres des Hommes/Belgium	7,000	—	7,000
Terres des Hommes/France			
Desarrollo y Paz/Canada	26,282	—	26,282
Community Aid/Australia	26,000	—	26,000
Union de Productores/Norway	—	1,940,000	1,940,000
Bridgit Lotte-Oxfam/Canada	6,000	38,200	44,200
Total	4,788,242	19,192,257	23,980,499

Source: National Union of Farmers and Ranchers (UNAG).

[a]Most of the 1987 aid agreements between UNAG and international donors are in the form of multiyear contracts.

represent opposition parties in the National Assembly. Without doubt, UNAG continues to be the most effective and significant social movement representing the interests of Nicaragua's farming community. As UNAG tries to adapt to the new economic and political climate, it needs to reconcile the conflicting interests of its constituents, who range from peasant producers organized in cooperatives to wealthy landowners.

The land invasions of the 1980s, in particular, demonstrated the difficulty of integrating these conflicting interests into a coherent policy while preserving a democratic practice. UNAG confronted the same dilemma that the revolutionary government faced in its own hegemonic project— how to ensure the participation of all sectors of the rural community while guaranteeing that the needs of the most marginalized groups are not neglected. The predominance of the chapiollo sector in UNAG's decision-making structures represents a major obstacle in this regard. The recent creation of the national Federation of Cooperatives has the potential to strengthen the cooperative movement vis-à-vis the chapiollo sector. Yet it remains to be seen whether this new organizational structure will translate into increased weight for the poor peasantry in UNAG's decision-making process. Many farmers continued to be suspicious of the leadership's motives and argued that FENACOOP was yet

Table 4.8. Swedish development aid to Nicaragua, 1985–1989 (millions of Swedish crowns)

Bilateral aid projects through SIDA	1985–86[a]	1986–87	1987–88	1988–89[b]	Total
Energy sector	10.8	4.0	12.0	37.0	63.8
Forestry sector	94.2	28.2	32.1	35.0	189.5
Mining sector	156.7	43.6	38.8	39.0	278.1
UNAG/ECODEPA	—	5.0	17.0	22.0	44.0
Culture	—	—	1.6	2.0	3.6
Fund for imports	34.7	45.0[c]	69.8	73.0	222.5
Consulting	18.9	1.5	2.7	3.0	26.1
Women projects	—	—	—	2.0	2.0
Health sector	64.3	—	—	—	64.3
Emergency aid	64.9[c]	15.0[d]	13.0[d]	20.0	112.9
Aid by NGOs	48.0	49.2	35.0	40.0	172.2
Scientific cooperation through SAREC	28.8[e]	8.9	8.9	46.6	
Total	492.5	220.3	230.9	281.9	1,225.6

Source: Swedish International Development Authority (SIDA).

Note: One US$ = 6.30 Swedish crowns (1989 exchange rate).

[a]Includes aid up to 1985–86.

[b]Aid for 1988/89 is in allocated amounts with the exception of the Scientific Cooperation category, which has been paid out.

[c]Includes aid to UNAG/ECODEPA.

[d]Total aid to UNAG/ECODEPA.

[e]Includes aid up to 1986–87.

another attempt to control their resources. These fears are historically justified and can only be allayed by strengthening UNAG's internal democracy.

UNAG made substantial progress in this direction as a result of the organization's ten-year evaluation process, which culminated in the second National Congress in 1992. The farmers' movement formulated important new objectives and rewrote its bylaws. The most important new goals were the "democratization of the economy" and "peasant unity."[120] Essential for the future development of UNAG was the institutionalization of formal democratic principles. Elections for all of UNAG's organizational structures will from now on proceed on the "basis of a direct, individual, *public or secret vote, according to the decision of the plenum.*"[121] Further, the National Council's 160 members, elected by the National Congress, are now supposed to be representative in terms of "territoriality, form of organization and productive sector."[122] The new procedures, implemented the first time at the April 1992 Congress, led to some surprises. For example, in the election to UNAG's National Executive Committee, the delegates unexpectedly selected Martha Heriberta Valle, the head of UNAG's women's section in region VI, while reelecting most of the historic UNAG leaders. As insignificant as such an event might appear, the last Congress could signal a watershed in the organization's development—the point in time when the grass roots start to gain control over their leaders.

Throughout the 1980s, the organization's policies were frequently criticized by sectors within the Sandinista party. They argued that UNAG "supported changes which meant a retreat from socialist objectives."[123] This criticism was the result of UNAG's objection to policies that favored state accumulation over the producers' interests.[124] In this instance, past difficulties have turned into current advantages. However, though the autonomous development of UNAG was a central challenge during the Sandinista revolution, the movement faces new problems under the Chamorro government.

The revolutionary period had its own logic, which left UNAG struggling to adapt to the new environment. Despite the fact that the organization had been founded in 1981, UNAG obtained legal status only in March 1990, following the electoral defeat of the Sandinista government. This belated juridical recognition was of essence for the future viability of UNAG. In another crucial area, UNAG finally embarked on a long overdue drive to determine its actual membership base by handing out identification cards to its current supporters and new members. This process, financed by SCC, began on March 12, 1991, in region IV. In order to obtain a UNAG-identification, a farmer needed simply to request one without having to show any documents.[125] This simple procedure was important if UNAG was to pursue its goal of "peasant unity" successfully, creating a climate in which the organization would be a viable option for producers who had supported the counterrevolution. UNAG has assumed a crucial role in the process of reconciliation under way in Nicaragua.[126] Daniel Núñez argues convincingly that the peasants on both sides were the victims. He stated the prevailing sentiment in the countryside succinctly: "We will not get involved in a new war; we contributed the dead, the others contributed the ministers."[127]

The 1992 organizational data for UNAG reveal a number of interesting developments (see table 4.9 for detailed information): (1) the composition of membership statistics reflects the degree to which UNAG has reinstituted a departmental structure; (2) the process of *carnetización* is

Table 4.9. Organizational data for UNAG, 1992

Department	Municipalities attended by UNAG	Attended cooperatives	Attended producers	Registered members
Matagalpa	9	254	8,684	954
Granada	4	160	4,300	2,057
Madriz	8	159	2,500	450
Jinotega	6	147	5,000	315
Rivas	10	195	7,500	2,120
Nueva Segovia	10	120	6,000	—[a]
Raas	8	23	3,500	450
Masaya	5	131	1,731	1,731
Managua	6	128	1,769	1,478
Leon	10	169	5,570	694
Estelí	6	180	3,600	200
Chinandega	12	486	7,786	523
Boaco	6	48	450	—[a]
Río San Juan	4	23	800	46
Chontales	11	68	2,300	65
Carazo	7	126	3,946	2,261
Nueva Guinea	1	52	2,500	753
Raan	3	35	1,500	250
Total	126	2,504	69,436	14,347

Source: National Union of Farmers and Ranchers (UNAG).

[a]The registration drive had not started.

proceeding slowly (as of March 1992, only 14,347 farmers had become registered members); and (3) the latest UNAG data show a substantial decline in producers attended by the organization, from 120,506 in 1987 to 69,436 in 1992. The overwhelming majority of the remaining members are affiliated with cooperatives. Only about 7,000 individual producers continue to be attended by UNAG. In region VI (Matagalpa and Jinotega), official membership declined from 33,126 to 13,684. The decline was even more drastic in region V (Boaco and Chontales), from 14,977 to 2,750 estimated members. Although UNAG continues to be present throughout Nicaragua (organizational structures exist in 126 out of 144 municipalities) it faces the challenging task to keep its current members and recruit new ones.

UNAG's president understands these new challenges ahead. Under his leadership, UNAG is shedding its image as a Sandinista movement. It is significant in this context that UNAG's new bylaws, passed by the 1992 National Congress, make no reference to the relations between UNAG and the Sandinista party. Political aspects are currently deemphasized, and the business character of the organization becomes the new focus.[128] The UNAG leadership is positioning the union to compete in the new economic climate. It has accepted the new rules of the game. The enemies of the past have become the funding sources of today. In a victory of pragmatism over ideological correctness, UNAG is working with the World Bank and the United States Agency for International Development (USAID) in an effort to find solutions to the problems facing Nicaragua's farmers.

Chapter 5 _____

New Relations of Production:
Cooperative Peasant Stores

> We have a strategy to fight for the democratization of the economy in the countryside. And what is that? To have in our own hands the tools to create development. The ECODEPA is one tool in our hands; the UNAG is another; the National Federation of Cooperatives is yet another. Little by little we'll build the links to guarantee our strategy.
>
> *Daniel Núñez, "The Farmers' View," Envío 10*
> *(January-February 1991).*

The Conception of the Peasant Stores

In its pursuit of a socialist project, intended to improve the living conditions of the poor majority, the revolutionary government sought to introduce new relations of production. In the Nicaraguan countryside this meant replacing the exploitative, authoritarian structures put in place during the Somoza era with new ones based on equality and cooperation. The emerging state agencies, particularly MIDINRA and MICOIN, were not equipped, however, to fill the void left by the disarticulation of the traditional structures. Seeking complete control over agricultural production, the state set prices for farm products and established authorized distribution channels. In order to enforce these policies, controls were set up at the exit of every village.[1] Not only was the peasantry's access to the market restricted, but MICOIN officials arbitrarily confiscated agricultural products from producers who simply transported their harvest home.[2] At the same time, the state proved unable to supply the rural sector with essential agricultural inputs needed for production. The economic crisis and counterrevolutionary aggression further contributed to a situation that was characterized by a deterioration of the living conditions of the peasantry. In response to a system that favored the urban consumer and discriminated against the rural sector, the peasantry decreased production.

In some regards, the hopes of the peasantry for immediate improvements following the defeat of the Somoza dictatorship were too high. An unrealistic expectation prevailed as to the ability of the new regime to improve the standard of living of the poor majority in the short term. Objective difficulties, such as a scarcity of resources and the need to allay the fears of the rural bourgeoisie, which felt threatened by the agrarian reform, were compounded by mistakes of the government. Nevertheless, the peasants were rightly disillusioned about the slow pace of the agrarian reform and the government's control of agricultural prices and marketing. In the eyes of significant sectors of the peasant community, the Sandinistas had failed to deliver on their historic promise—to radically improve the living conditions of the rural poor upon gaining power. By 1984 the Sandinista government was rapidly losing credibility in the countryside, and the counterrevolutionary forces were solidifying support in several regions of Nicaragua. With the government's "strategic alliance with the peasantry" in danger of being severed, the Sandinistas began to implement a series of new policies designed to regain the trust of the rural community and to ensure the survival of the revolution.

A key element of the new strategy was the establishment of a rural supply network with emergency aid from international donors. UNAG constituted the driving force behind the attempt to find a solution to the crisis dominating Nicaragua's rural sector. From its very beginning, the farmers' organization attempted to resolve the problem of the shortages in farm inputs, tools, and basic staples. The UNAG leadership held the view that the supply of farm inputs and the processing and marketing of agricultural products were services the producers should manage themselves through cooperative enterprises.[3] In order to create these new relations of production, UNAG sought and obtained the support of Sweden's farming community in Halland, SCC, and the Swedish government.

Plans for the establishment of an emergency rural supply network took on concrete form by 1984. The following year, President Ortega went on a state visit to Sweden where he obtained several million U.S. dollars in emergency aid from the Olof Palme government.

The rural supply network was intended to benefit the poorest peasant families in the zones of Nicaragua most affected by the war. It consisted of peasant stores at the local level that were linked to a distribution and import agency, ECODEPA. The first peasant stores were set up in region VI, then a war zone whose agricultural production was of great importance to the national economy. The principal goal was to help the agricultural producers organize themselves politically in UNAG and economically in multiple-purpose service cooperatives. It was to be accomplished by pursuing four objectives: (1) to establish a network of cooperatives with the capacity to supply the producers with essential farm inputs and to buy their products at favorable prices; (2) to strengthen UNAG as a union and representative of the peasantry; (3) to strengthen agricultural production; and (4) to promote unity, democracy, and peace. It is important to point out that over time the objectives changed. In particular, the integration of women became a specific goal.[4] Bengt Kjeller, main SCC representative in Nicaragua and principal advisor to ECODEPA (1986–1989), summarized the purpose of the project[5] succinctly: "To develop a cooperative capacity which would strengthen the producers' capacity to obtain better prices for their products and at the same time serve the [needs of the] peasants better."[6] Between 1984 and 1989, the ECODEPA project received almost US$23 million in support from international aid donors. As table 5.1 indicates, the most significant contributors were SCC with US$19 million, Hivos of Holland with US$1.7 million, Oxfam-England and Oxfam-America with US$756,268, and the agricultural producers of Norway with US$641,640.

Initially, UNAG's leadership did not fully appreciate the importance of the project and left the task to set up the first peasant stores mostly to the Swedish advisors and a few committed local UNAG professionals. Following the election of Daniel Núñez to the presidency of UNAG, however, the national leadership of the farmers' movement assumed direction of the project. It is significant that UNAG's national executive committee made the decision to promote the ECODEPA project over the veto of FSLN's national directorate.[7] Alfonso Núñez, the brother of UNAG's president and head of UNAG in region V, was a driving force in the early

Table 5.1. International aid to ECODEPA,
1984–1989

Development agency	Amount (US$)
Sweden (SCC)	19,124,889
Holland (HIVOS)	1,762,276
United States and England (OXFAM)	756,268
Norway (NDR)	641,640
Denmark (SUM)	359,419
Belgium (COOPIBOS)	129,419
United Kingdom (War on Want)	61,549
Total	22,835,460

Source: Cooperative Enterprise of Agricultural Producers
(ECODEPA).

stages of the creation of the peasant stores. He paid his commitment to improve the life of the peasantry with his life, when he was assassinated by the contras in November 1986.

In 1985, Arquímedes Rivera, a member of UNAG's national executive committee, was chosen as director general of the emerging cooperative supply network. The first peasant store opened in November 1985 in San Dionísio, a town in region VI. The initial success of the project attracted the attention of agricultural producers from other regions, and they demanded to be given similar support.[8] Although the project was extended to incorporate region V, lack of funds impeded the development of the peasant stores at the national level. This situation improved in 1986 when aid to ECODEPA increased. The three-year cooperation agreement between Sweden and Nicaragua, signed by Foreign Minister Sten Anderson and Comandante Henry Ruíz in 1987, provided the financial guarantee for the establishment of a country-wide network of cooperative stores.

Formal Organizational Structure

The general structures of the peasant stores were approved in April 1986 during UNAG's first National Congress. Upon this general approval, a consultation process was carried out during 1987 and 1988 to discuss bylaws and operating rules in assemblies attended by thirty thousand agricultural producers.[9] The project was given a federal, cooperative structure consisting of three levels.[10] The *tienda campesina* (peasant store, or TC) constituted the base unit. The TC was in essence a service cooperative, open to all producers regardless of whether they belonged to an agricultural cooperative or were engaged in private farming. Upon becoming a member, a producer had to contribute a membership quota. These dues were assessed by the store's executive committee, based on the producer's economic capacity. Total membership contributions between 1985 and 1989 were estimated at half a million U.S. dollars.[11] The store members were the owners of the cooperative. In the few cases in which store operations showed a profit, it was usually invested in improving infrastructure.

The peasant stores of a particular region formed a departmental enterprise called ECODEPA Departamental (Departmental ECODEPA, or ED). The fifteen departmental ECODEPAs in turn, constituted ECODEPA Nacional (National ECODEPA, or EN), which operated as an import agency for farm inputs. These products were then sold through the departmental ECODEPAs to the peasant stores. The ECODEPAs and peasant stores also bought agricultural products from the local producers.

The farmers forming a peasant store constituted the general assembly of members, which was supposed to convene at least every six months. The general assembly constituted the highest decision-making authority at all three levels. As one of its main functions, the general assembly elected the governing body of the store. The *comisión de abastecimiento* (provisions committee, or CA) managed the affairs of the peasant store. These "executive committees" were headed by a coordinator. Together with the other committee members, the coordinator oversaw the work of a hired administrator who performed the daily managerial duties, mainly bookkeeping and attending customers. The final link in the system was the *comité de vigilancia* (oversight committee, or CV), which monitored all operations of the cooperatives and was elected by the general assembly.

At the departmental level, we move formally from direct to representative democracy, since the general assembly of each departmental ECODEPA consisted of the executive committees of all stores in the department, the store administrators, the ECODEPA manager, and the representatives of the local UNAG offices.[12] The two most important institutions at the departmental level were the comisión de abastecimiento departamental (departmental provisions committee, or CAD) and the manager of the departmental ECODEPA. The executive committee consisted of the coordinators of every store in the department, UNAG's regional president (or the UNAG representative for the zone, in cases where the ED was not in the regional capital), and the ED manager. According to the bylaws of the organization, it was the prerogative of the CAD to hire the manager. Initially, however, the managers were selected by the national UNAG leadership. The managers, a vital link in the ECODEPA project, were a central factor in the emergence of the stores. Indeed, the whole system was built with the EDs as a starting point, spreading below to the stores and above to the National ECODEPA.

At the national level, the general assembly consisted of the one hundred members of UNAG's national council and the comisión de abastecimiento nacional (national provisions committee, or CAN) of the National ECODEPA. The CAN had fifteen representatives, elected by the executive committees of the departments. It also included the president of UNAG, as well as the director and the general manager of the National ECODEPA. The director and general manager were nominated by the general assembly of the National ECODEPA. The director was simultaneously a member of UNAG's national executive committee.

A serious deficiency regarding the formal structure of the project was the lack of legal status of the stores and ECODEPAs. ECODEPA obtained its *personería jurídica* first in March 1990. According to Manuel Aburto, as of mid-1992, only 75 of the 122 stores had been legalized. It was not until the impending change in government that the precarious legal situation of the project started to be rectified. Because the stores were not legally recognized, they were governed not by statutes but by internal rules that had no legal force. This formal weakness limited the autonomy and authority of the farmers that represented the peasant stores vis-à-vis both UNAG and the state. It also facilitated undemocratic interferences in local affairs by the leaders of the national ECODEPA. Lacking legal status, a particular store had no legal recourse against arbitrary actions by UNAG or state officials.

Economic Benefits and Changing Priorities

When the rural supply network was initiated as an emergency project in 1985, the needs of the poor farmers were given priority. Another marginal sector that benefited, at least initially, was semiproletarians. This group was made up of agricultural workers on state and private farms who engaged in subsistence farming in addition to their salaried work. Semiproletarians could become store members if the general assembly decided to admit them.[13] It is interesting to note that peasant stores such as Tierra Azul in Boaco, Wiwilí in Jinotega, or Wasaca Abajo in Matagalpa, whose constituency was generally poor, were more likely to admit agricultural workers than stores with a well-off membership. Although semiproletarians could be found among the membership of many stores, their numbers were never significant.

It is evident that the peasant stores were conceived within the policy goal of popular hegemony. In the beginning, the stores carried nine essential products indispensable in agricultural production, ranging from machetes and hoes to nails and horseshoes. In addition, the producers could buy basic food staples and other consumer goods that were in short supply during the mid-1980s. The store products were made available at heavily subsidized prices. In 1989 it was estimated that of the US$22 million given to the project in donations, 8 million had been used to subsidize store products.[14] Thus, the poor farmers benefited from the stores in two significant ways: (1) store products were often sold far below their market price, and (2) essential farm inputs that were in scarce supply were made available in remote areas that were not served by other suppliers. In addition, the stores provided credit to the members and bought their harvest. As the policy goal of national unity gained importance, the stores attended also to the needs of medium and large producers. For example, the stores started to carry farm machinery. These items were essential for capital-intensive production but were of no use to a peasant producer.

The ECODEPA project's impact in the countryside was not reflected in its relative weight in Nicaragua's economy. In fact, in 1989 the national ECODEPA imported only about 3 percent of the capital goods, intermediary goods, and consumer products intended for the agricultural sector.[15] If, however, one examines the role of the project in the distribution of key products that were essential to the agricultural producer, the importance of ECODEPA becomes evident. For example, ECODEPA's market share for backpack sprayers and plastic pails was 100 percent, for rennet pills and horseshoe nails 90 percent, for machetes 34 percent, and for rubber boots 16 percent.[16]

In the early stages of the ECODEPA project, peasants affiliated in great numbers. The number of stores increased from 55 in 1985–1986 to 197 in 1988 (see table 5.2). By 1989, 63,800 producers were members in 191 stores. Following a monetary reform in 1988, austerity measures were instituted in order to control inflation and the unrealistic price

Table 5.2. Development of peasant stores, 1985–1991

Departmental store	1985–86	1986–87	1988	1989	1990	1991
Estelí	—	10	19	16	17	6
Madriz	—	4	12	7	7	5
Nueva Segovia	—	6	7	7	7	5
Leon	—	7	7	8	8	8
Chinandega	—	4	4	8	20	18
Managua	—	5	7	7	12	12
Masaya	—	7	17	20	13	11
Carazo	—	—	—	—	—	8
Rivas	—	7	11	12	12	6
Boaco	10	10	10	10	10	9
Chontales	27	21	21	17	8	8
Matagalpa	13	31	48	47	43	13
Jinotega	5	11	10	7	7	2
Raan	—	6	6	7	6	—
Raas	—	22	8	8	5	7
Río San Juan	—	10	10	10	3	4
Total	55	161	197	191	178	122

Source: Cooperative Enterprise of Agricultural Producers (ECODEPA).

structure was readjusted. As a result, implements needed for agricultural production were easily obtained from a variety of sources, both state and private sector suppliers. The previous shortage of goods was replaced by a money shortage. The new economic reality ended the expansion of the rural supply network. The real crisis for the peasant stores, however, was yet to come. It started in 1990, with the change in government. When the Sandinistas left office in 1990, the rural supply network consisted of 178 stores and 61,392 members. A year later, only 122 stores with 39,555 members were left.

In order to survive in the new economic climate, the philosophy under which the ECODEPA project operated during its first years needed to be revised. Although the move toward economic viability started under the Sandinistas, the restructuring of the project took on even greater urgency with the change in government. From an emergency project that lost substantial amounts of money, it was supposed to evolve into a profitable self-sustaining enterprise. The challenge facing the ECODEPA leadership was substantial. In 1992 the project had US$8,063,479 in capital.[17] Since ECODEPA had received US$23 million in donations at this point, the losses were considerable. These losses should not be attributed to poor management. As noted, the peasant stores were originally conceived as an emergency aid project. Thus, a significant part of the donated funds was supposed to benefit the producers. The other losses (about US$5 million) were mainly the results of inflation. The origins of the project fostered a mentality, however, that made the change toward economic efficiency difficult.

As the new "market-philosophy" continued to transform the ECODEPA project, many of the weakest stores closed. Whereas this market orientation was essential to ensure the long-term viability of the ECODEPA system, many of the intended beneficiaries were disenfranchised. The elimination of subsidized prices for store products affected the poorest customers. There is no doubt that poor peasants benefited hardly at all from the stores once the new policies became effective. This underclass was so deprived that it could not enter the market under the difficult economic conditions of the late 1980s. Most peasants in this group lacked the money to buy the most basic items, such as a machete. The stores attended to the needs of these poor peasants only in the initial phase of the project (1984–1987), when it operated under emergency conditions and store products were sold well below cost if not given away.

The Evolution of Grassroots Democracy

Marvin Ortega has argued that "the internal democracy of the cooperatives is an essential condition for the organizations' independence regarding the state."[18] In the case of the peasant stores, independence also meant freedom of interference from the regional and national ECODEPA and UNAG leadership.[19] Throughout the 1980s, the peasant stores struggled to achieve institutional autonomy and to strengthen their internal democracy. The challenges facing the development of grassroots democracy in Nicaragua were reflected in the daily operations of the peasant stores. One important measure of the institutionalization of democratic procedures was the extent to which the bylaws of the stores were being observed. A more significant criterion, however, was the *quality of participation*.

From the outset, the project faced an important obstacle. In their initial phase, the stores were organized in a top-down fashion. For UNAG leaders who wanted to solve the supply crisis as fast as possible, this was an efficient way to proceed. From the perspective of organizational democracy, however, it was problematic. Little attention was given to familiarizing the producers with the cooperative philosophy of the project. This deficit proved to be difficult to overcome as the project matured.

The frequency of general assemblies and the number of attending members varied considerably across departments. Of the four departments under study[20] (Boaco, Chontales, Matagalpa, and Jinotega), only Boaco complied with the bylaws, which required at least 50 percent attendance for decisions taken by the general assembly to be valid.[21] This suggests that the established requirements were too high. Thus, general assembly meetings were not yet fully institutionalized. Indeed, some studies considered the assemblies the least developed bodies of the ECO-DEPA structure.[22] Reasons for the weakness of the general assemblies were numerous. Most important were the geographical dispersion of store members, their lack of interest, the counterrevolutionary aggression, and Nicaragua's difficult political climate.

One of the most important factors restricting the development of base democracy was Nicaragua's highly charged political climate. Particularly, the period of election campaigns was problematic. During the campaign for the 1990 elections, scheduled assemblies were frequently postponed because they were considered "political" meetings in the highly charged pre-electoral climate. In Boaco, for example, which traditionally had the highest degree of quantitative participation, the impact of the 1989 elections on the institutional framework of the peasant stores was remarkable. Of the department's nine general assembly meetings, scheduled in November and December of 1989, only two turned out to be proper store meetings. Santa Lucia's and Tomatoya's stores carried them out as planned, while all other meetings were either canceled, rescheduled because of low attendance, or converted into electoral rallies.

In the case of Tierra Azul's and Boaco Viejo's stores, only a handful of peasants showed up for the planned meetings, which had to be reprogrammed. Those who did attend complained that the stores no longer served the needs of the members because the prices charged for store products were too high. The Santa Elisa store had to postpone its meeting because its financial records were not up to date. Stores in the towns San José de los Remates and Teustepe also held general assemblies, but their meetings were politicized to such a degree that one could no longer consider them proper store meetings. For example, the San José de los Remates store called a general assembly to inaugurate its new building. The members planned to meet after an electoral rally held in benefit of the regional Sandinista candidates to Nicaragua's National Assembly.

Upon conclusion of the rally, however, the store meeting was canceled and the attending peasants proceeded to the scheduled festive activities, with a bullfight as the main event. The general assembly of Teustepe's store also turned into a political meeting. The assembly was originally called to discuss the prospects for a store project involving the production of cattle feed. Instead, several Sandinista candidates gave speeches. The attending producers were urged to come forward with their problems and concerns. Although several producers took advantage of this opportunity, the store's agenda itself was never discussed.

In the case of executive committee meetings, quantitative indicators showed great diversity across departments. Boaco and Jinotega reported functioning committees for all peasant stores, whereas only 60 percent of Matagalpa's and Chontales' committees were active. Attendance also varied greatly. The executive committees of Chontales were least developed, with only 12 percent of the committee members attending any session. Jinotega did somewhat better with a 41 percent attendance record, whereas Boaco and Matagalpa reported an attendance of about 90 percent.[23] The department of Boaco was most successful in fostering strong executive committees. I will use the store of Teustepe to illustrate this point.

At the time, Teustepe had without doubt the best organized and most active committee of the department. Meetings were generally attended by all members and followed institutionalized procedures. With the coordinator, Alfonso Hurtado, in firm control, every member was given equal time for discussion, and a conscious effort was made to find consensus on all matters. The cordial, constructive atmosphere was surprising, considering the diverse social and political background of the members. When Hurtado complained about his workload and sought to obtain a greater commitment from his colleagues in sharing the burden of running the store, an agreement was concluded, the terms of which obliged every committee member to allocate one day a week to supervision of the store's operations. The support that Hurtado received from his committee was unusual. Most coordinators carried the burden of managing the store alone. Many producers were reluctant to serve on the executive committee because of the time commitment and economic costs involved. For example, when four members of San Buenaventura's committee, including the coordinator, resigned their positions, their resignations were not accepted, since other members proved reluctant to serve in their place.

Many times individual coordinators rather than the executive committee directed the rural supply cooperatives. Although generally committed individuals, the coordinators frequently lacked a democratic mandate. Nationwide, two-thirds of the coordinators were elected by store members, while the remaining third were appointed by UNAG, ECODEPA, or Sandinista officials.[24] The imposition of coordinators in one-third of all cases reflected the fact that in many stores formal democratic procedures had not yet been institutionalized. Even coordinators elected according to the statutes, were frequently proposed to the membership by UNAG representatives. This kind of approval virtually guaranteed appointment.

The personal characteristics of the coordinator constituted the strongest predictor for success or failure of a particular store. Some exceptions notwithstanding, the coordinators sought to foster grassroots democracy. Contrary to the traditions prevailing in other sectors of the cooperative movement, these leaders encouraged effective base participation. It was standard procedure for a coordinator to start a meeting by explaining to the members that they had the right to remove him in case they were not satisfied with his performance. This tradition contrasted favorably with other rural organizations in which the leadership was hardly accountable to the base.

The coordinators' effectiveness in attending to store business was often limited because they were seriously overcommitted. Many of them were community leaders and held a variety of time-consuming positions. Oren Siles presented a typical case. He was the coordinator of Matiguas's peasant store (located in the department of Matagalpa) and a member of the departmental executive committee, held a seat on UNAG's municipal council, and served as the coordinator of the supply commission of Matiguas. This situation reflected the scarcity of capable leaders throughout Nicaragua. It was a strength of the ECODEPA project to attract capable people and to contribute to the formation of new ones. This was particularly the case at the departmental level, where a new elite of grassroots leaders started to emerge.

UNAG professionals and ECODEPA officials often violated important principles of grassroots democracy. Efforts to strengthen the economic viability of the supply network were frequently given priority over ensuring grassroots participation. For example, when producers in the town of Matagalpa created a municipal store, there was little discussion of the cooperative principles underlying the modus operandi of the enterprise. This is significant because familiarity with these principles was a precondition for effective democratic participation. The attending producers appeared to realize this fact. With little or no knowledge of their rights and duties, several farmers objected to the pressure applied by national ECODEPA officials to immediately proceed with the selection of a permanent executive committee. Because of their objections, only a "provisional" committee was elected. Its composition, however, was controlled by the ECODEPA official in charge of the meeting, who subsequently was elected as store coordinator. In general, a tendency could be observed for provisional committees to be converted into permanent ones, without effective member participation. This situation, present throughout Nicaragua, represented an important limitation of grassroots democracy and partially accounted for the difficulties in increasing base participation.

Although some of their actions limited democratic development, ECODEPA officials and UNAG professionals played in general a positive role in the formation of the stores. Many stores required and received initial nurturing and direction from these organizers. Particularly the departmental managers, appointed to their positions by the UNAG leadership, played a significant role. The constructive relationship between the store members of the department of Boaco and Mauricio Solórzano, the departmental manager, was a case in point. Solórzano's role was crucial in ensuring the stability of the department's stores. Whereas other areas showed substantial fluctuations in the number of functioning stores, Boaco closed only one in 1989. Several stores in the department experienced serious crises and would not have survived without the manager's initiative. For example, when the Tierra Azul store temporarily ceased to function (no meetings were convened, and the coordinator did not attend departmental assemblies), Solórzano convened a general assembly and proposed a slate of candidates for a new executive committee. Although these elections were technically deficient (less than 40 percent of the members assisted, with 50 percent required for a quorum), the short-term survival of the store was ensured.

Strict adherence to formal rules was often incompatible with the reality of grassroots democracy. Santa Lucia's store experienced a severe crisis in 1988, when some members of the executive committee, charged with misappropriation of store funds, were jailed. Because many farmers were afraid to speak up and to confront the store leadership, Solórzano convened a general assembly to discuss the future of the store. In this meeting the members chose to elect a new coordinator who was not even a member of the store. Thus, the quality of grassroots participation had to be the essential yardstick for assessing the institutionalization of base democracy, not adherence to formal procedures, which were often designed by bureaucrats with little understanding of the reality of rural life.

In their struggle to keep the stores alive, the executive committees often had to cope with incompetent and insubordinate store administrators. In 1989 Santa Elisa's store had to fire an administrator who was buying sunglasses and toys instead of agricultural supplies. She also shared the store's checkbook with her husband, who misappropriated funds. Boaco Viejo's store, on the other hand, had an administrator who considered himself primarily a Sandinista militant. He informed the executive committee that he would only accept instructions from the Sandinista base committee. It took the members several weeks to "persuade" this individual that they, and not the party, were in charge. Several peasant stores in Chontales, including the ones in Santo Domingo and San Pedro de Lóvago, experienced similar problems with their administrators. San Pedro de Lóvago had an administrator whose whole family joined in robbing the store. They felt secure, thinking that their Sandinista party membership would protect them. These abuses were facilitated by an executive committee that stayed detached from the store's daily affairs. Finally, Aaron Guerrero, the manager of the departmental ECO-DEPA, and Daniel Núñez, the UNAG president, intervened. They installed the directorate of the local cattlemen association as an interim executive committee. Subsequently, the leadership of the cattlemen association chose one of its own members as the new coordinator. Thus the immediate crisis was solved. The fact, however, that the solution required outside help, weakened grassroots democracy. Because of the strong influence of UNAG and the tradition of paternalism prevailing in Nicaragua's rural sector, the farmers tended to defer to the judgment of the union leadership when the stores experienced problems.

The most encouraging evidence for the development of effective grassroots democracy was the experience of the Nueva Guinea peasant store. One of the few cooperatives in Nicaragua with legal status (it had been legally constituted in 1976 under the Somoza government), it represented a well-organized, democratic organization with an active membership. Although the cooperative existed before the initiation of the ECODEPA project, it was inoperative. The peasant store breathed new life into the cooperative. The peasants engaged in "popular education" (signs of the effort to educate the members in the principles of cooperative association were visible on the walls of every building) and participated actively in the daily affairs of the cooperative. The members took great pride in the economic success of their enterprise and were convinced that the key to their success was voluntary grassroots participation.

Relations between the Stores and the Production Cooperatives

The region of Jinotega and Matagalpa demonstrated a particular pattern of development because the established structures of the production cooperatives, affiliated with UNAG, played a substantial role in the development of the local stores. In Matagalpa and Jinotega, the local territorial council of the cooperative movement generally assumed the function of the peasant store's general assembly. The statutes permitted this in cases "where the territorial dispersion, the war situation, or difficult means of communication obstruct the realization of assemblies of the peasant store's members."[25]

Apart from representatives of the local cooperatives, meetings of the territorial councils were usually attended by a UNAG representative, the political secretary of the Sandinista party, as well as officials from the Ministry of Agrarian Reform and the National Bank. With all sectors of the cooperative movement present, the store representatives frequently had a hard time getting everyone to focus on the agenda; however, the inclusive nature of these meetings could also be of benefit. For example, it helped the representatives to plan the store's purchasing needs more efficiently. There were also instances when the leadership of the territorial council was identical with the store management. In these cases, store business tended to dominate the agenda.

The voices of those store members who were private producers were generally excluded from meetings of the councils. Since individual farmers are not part of the cooperative movement, they were only represented if one of them held a seat on the store's executive committee. Further, the territorial councils, in effect, took over the management of the peasant stores, a phenomenon observed throughout region VI. Executive committees never held separate meetings but always convened within the setting of the territorial council. The territorial councils also played a crucial role in the creation of the stores in their jurisdiction. Following the discussion establishing demand for a local store, the council selected an executive committee to begin operations. The peasant stores of Wiwilí, Pueblo

Nuevo, and Las Latas, were all formed in this way. Since the territorial council determined the makeup of the executive committee, the store management lacked independent authority. Executive committees were subsequently confirmed by a vote of the general assembly only when it was deemed necessary to convene one. With measures designed for extraordinary situations evolving into standard procedures, there was no incentive to convene a general assembly, even when conditions permitted it. Thus, store members experienced little meaningful participation in selecting their leadership. This contributed to the alienation of the peasantry from the stores and strengthened the belief of many producers that the stores belonged to the executive committee or UNAG.

In light of these difficulties, it was not surprising that in 1989, only thirty-two of the forty-seven stores in Matagalpa actually functioned. There was an obvious need to further consolidate the rural supply network. Fortunately, such efforts were under way. In an encouraging trend, exemplified by developments in Matiguas, inactive, geographically dispersed peasant stores were consolidated into strong municipal entities. In March of 1989 five stores surrounding the town of Matiguas became part of a new municipal store. The five stores had been experiencing problems, ranging from incompetent administration to decapitalization, suffered as a consequence of the 1988 monetary reforms. In September 1989 the executive committee was restructured during a general assembly, attended by the members of the five old stores. Every one of the consolidated stores received representation on the new executive body. In addition to this consolidation process, the executive committee members of the departmental ECODEPAs became more involved in supporting the stores of their geographical area. Democratic participation at the store level was actively encouraged by the work of the departmental committee. Its members attended store meetings in their geographical area. They provided support to the local executive committee without seeking to take control as is usually the dynamic when higher ranking officials participate in local affairs.

This type of support was particularly needed in the case of stores that were located in zones of armed conflict. A case from the department of Matagalpa illustrates this point. In 1987 La Patriota's peasant store was destroyed by counterrevolutionary forces. Following this incident, Oren Siles, then a member of the departmental executive committee, became active in assisting the rebuilding of the store. The conditions for cooperative development were not favorable in this zone of Nicaragua, where the cooperative movement was marked as Communist by the armed opposition. Upon returning to their farms, peasants who participated in store meetings were frequently threatened by armed counterrevolutionary bands. Simply discussing the principles of cooperative association in these rural hamlets frequently meant a death sentence. Thus, it is not surprising that the executive committee of La Patriota was not enthusiastic in ensuring the store's smooth operation. Oren Siles encouraged the committee members to become more active and facilitated store meetings in the safer climate of Matiguas (the next town).

Most stores were in dire need of special attention. Members were frequently ignorant of their role in the stores, and many did not believe that they were the true owners. This situation reflected deficiencies in the project's education and training programs. The training sections of the ECODEPAs were understaffed, and many lacked the most basic resources, such as adequate transportation. In Matagalpa, the training section consisted of five members, each attending seven stores. Although the training staff was furnished with motorcycles in 1989, which facilitated their outreach, training consisted mainly of teaching the store administrators how to keep appropriate records. Most members were unfamiliar with the basic statutes, and there was hardly ever a formal discussion of the project when store meetings were convened. The members' lack of interest in gaining greater knowledge regarding the cooperative framework of the enterprise was evident at a 1989 meeting of Jinotega's departmental executive committee. A member of the training section virtually had to plead with the coordinators to share their concerns in order to allow him to design his work according to their necessities instead of forcing him to continue to work in a "top-down" fashion.

The Evolution of Departmental and National Structures

The departmental assemblies were less developed than other bodies in the ECODEPA structure. Although they were supposed to convene at least once a year, only half of the fifteen departmental ECODEPAs had ever done so.[26] When assemblies did take place, however, attendance was high. The most developed and important institution at the departmental level was the executive committee. It was in this forum that base democracy had taken root. In 1989 only two departmental ECODEPAs had inactive committees.[27] In departments with a relatively small number of peasant stores, the coordinators of all stores were represented on the committee. This was the case in Boaco and Jinotega, with ten and seven stores, respectively. In Matagalpa and Chontales, on the other hand, five to eight store coordinators, representing all geographical areas of the department, were elected to the committee. The manager, who also served on the committee, had no voting rights. This is significant because it was part of an apparent strategy by UNAG officials to restrict the influence of the departmental managers. In contrast to the departmental level, the national management enjoyed voting rights. Its participation was not considered a threat since the national leadership of ECODEPA was appointed by UNAG. Thus, union officials were in complete control at the project's national level. In the departments, however, the managers defended the institutional autonomy of the departmental ECODEPAs against Managua. They were supported in this task by their executive committees.

Effective control over the departmental ECODEPAs was determined by the respective strength of the CAD and the manager. In this struggle, Chontales' CAD had achieved the most significant advances. It was the prerogative of the CAD to hire the manager and oversee his work. Nevertheless, in the early stages of the project, the national leaders of UNAG and ECODEPA frequently imposed their choices. In June of 1988, for example, the director of the national ECODEPA attempted to transfer Freddy Hernández Rívas, the manager of Chontales, to Managua. The CAD opposed this action. During this conflict, the executive committee sent a telegram to Managua, expressing its support for their manager and rejecting "all arbitrary decisions in violation of the statutes."[28] It took the support of the Swedish advisors and several tumultuous meetings for a victory of base democracy to emerge. Interestingly enough, the CAD had not been pleased with the performance of the manager. Although they supported him against undue pressure, they fired him shortly after. This case represented one of the most important instances of the departmental committees successfully defending their autonomy against national officials.

This type of interference by Managua into local affairs was not an isolated incident. In the case of Boaco, Mauricio Solórzano, the local manager, had to fight several attempts to remove him. Solórzano's problems were mainly owing to his determination to defend ECODEPA's institutional autonomy against UNAG, particularly regarding finances. Rumors were spreading again in the fall of 1989 that Solórzano, having already confronted several crises, was working against UNAG and did not adequately perform his managerial duties. The manager survived this critical situation primarily because of the strong support he received from his executive committee. Solórzano's ability to survive was even more remarkable, since he faced the opposition of Daniel Núñez himself. The continued survival of Boaco's manager constituted evidence for increasing autonomy at the intermediate level.

The managers played a crucial role in setting up the peasant stores. Mauricio Solórzano of ECODEPA Boaco and Francisco Dávila of ECODEPA Matagalpa, in particular, were involved in the creation of almost every store in their department. Because of their importance in the initial stages of the project, it is not surprising that the managers enjoyed considerable influence. Their educational backgrounds (the managers were much better educated than the farmers who were part of the executive committee) and familiarity with the goals and policies of the project also strengthened their position. Criticism of the managers was frequent. It was alleged that they manipulated and controlled the executive committees. Indeed, the managers frequently did control the affairs of the EDs, particularly when the executive committee was weak. At the end of the 1980s, the executive committees began, frequently with the encouragement of the manager, to assert control. Judging from the monthly meetings of the CADs, their development differed across departments. In Jinotega and Matagalpa, the managers were in charge. Instead of abusing their power, however, they encouraged greater participation by the CAD members. In Boaco, the manager and the coordinator of the CAD conducted meetings jointly, whereas Chontales's executive committee appeared to be firmly in charge of its departmental ECODEPA.

After the old manager was fired, the executive committee hired Aaron Guerrero, who had previously held a high-level position at the national ECODEPA. Initially, Guerrero showed little concern for democratic procedures. He tended to control the meetings of the executive committee and decided all major policy issues. Soon, the store leadership and the manager were at loggerheads. The manager ran a business that was supposed to make a profit, whereas the members of the executive committee wanted to keep the prices of store products as low as possible, to make the goods affordable even to the poorest customers. The CAD members who particularly objected to the high profit margin of 25 percent set by Guerrero finally revolted. In a *misa negra* (black mass), they coordinated their strategy and wrested control over the enterprise from the manager. The profit margin was lowered to 15 percent, the accountant was fired (his snoring bothered the CAD members when they were sleeping over at the store facilities on nights before meetings), and the coordinator of the CAD was firmly put in charge of future meetings. The change from a submissive committee into a belligerent one was dramatic. One of the CAD members characterized the new relationship between manager and executive committee succinctly: "*El gerente es el mozo.* [The manager is the servant.]" The secret of the committee's success was the dedication and hard work of the members. Many times they traveled to the departmental capital one day before scheduled meetings in order to shape consensus on an agenda and to check the books of the enterprise. Thus prepared, they presented a united front and had the necessary information to control every move of the manager. The committee generally carried out all agreements concluded at a meeting, which attests to the effectiveness of its members. The described metamorphosis from a submissive committee to one that commanded authority reflected the gain in confidence of many store coordinators. The producers were starting to take control, frequently over opposition from UNAG officials. During the early stages of the project, UNAG organizers used to nominate the CAD members, thus being able to exert control. An extreme case occurred in Chontales, when Danilo Salgado, the regional UNAG president, appointed himself coordinator of the CAD. Until he was removed from his position as UNAG president and resigned from the CAD, affairs at the departmental ECODEPA were conducted according to his views (those of a union official), which did not necessarily coincide with the interests of the producers. Indeed, for some time the executive committee was reduced to a rubber stamp.

Manolo Rodriguez, Salgado's successor as departmental coordinator, was also nominated by UNAG. Yet under his leadership, the CAD was quite strong. The increased autonomy of the CAD reflected the collective strength of the committee, rather than individual leadership. In fact, several of Rodriguez's colleagues considered him weak, since he sought to avoid confrontations with the manager or UNAG officials. In the Chontales case, the stronger members pushed the weaker ones toward more belligerent, autonomous positions. The executive committees of Jinotega and Matagalpa also derived their strength from collectivity, whereas Boaco's coordinator Alfonso Hurtado was a one-man show. Hurtado, tireless in his pursuit of the affairs of the departmental enterprise, represented a shining example of the many capable peasant leaders emerging throughout the ECODEPA system. Hurtado was particularly effective in

supporting the department's peasant stores. Nevertheless, active participation by *all* members of the CAD appeared to be a prerequisite to assure
effective member control over the cooperatives. Despite his considerable
skills, Hurtado was frequently outmaneuvered by the manager. This outcome might have been different had he been able to count on the support
of his colleagues. For example, the manager tended to "forget" meetings
agreed upon with Hurtado if he opposed the agenda. Active participation
by the other members would have rendered manipulations of this kind
impossible.

Elections to Matagalpa's departmental executive committee also indicated a strengthening of grassroots democracy. In May of 1989 the local
manager and Torbjörn Ockerman, the Swedish advisor, proposed a list of
candidates to the general assembly for election to the CAD. The outcome
of this process caught everybody by surprise. Geronimo Escoto, the vice-
coordinator of Wasaca Abajo's peasant store who was not even on the
list of candidates, was elected as the new head of the CAD. Escoto, an
illiterate farmer, was the favored candidate because of his reputation as a
leader. A Western observer might wonder how an illiterate peasant could
possibly fulfill his duties as head of an executive committee. As Matagalpa's manager pointed out, formal education had little to do with effective leadership. The previous CAD had a member with a graduate degree
from a university in Mexico, yet the committee proved inefficient and
had a low degree of member participation. In the same election, Carmelo
Vargas, the coordinator of Wasaca Abajo who was the original candidate
for head of the CAD, became an ordinary member of the committee. This
violated the statutes, which required equal geographical representation
of all stores in the CAD. As one might expect, active democratic grassroots participation does not always adhere to formal rules.

At the national level, only the executive committee (CAN) met on a
regular basis. In 1989 the executive committee convened five times. One
should not infer from these meetings that the CAN had assumed its role
as the most important executive authority within the ECODEPA project.
Instead, the CAN was a rubber stamp, ratifying decisions taken by
UNAG leadership. Thus, institutional autonomy and base democracy
were limited to the local and departmental level. The UNAG leadership
determined the agenda for all meetings of the CAN, which were conducted in a rather authoritarian fashion. The December 1989 meeting
represents a good example of the extent to which UNAG dominated the
national committee. When the department coordinators convened in

Managua, they learned that the meeting had been closed to "outside" observers on the orders of UNAG's directorate. This unilateral decision, whose main purpose was to exclude Bengt Kjeller, the principal Swedish advisor, enraged several coordinators. Although they insisted that Kjeller be allowed to attend the meeting (they considered him an advocate of their position), their view did not prevail.

Social Class and Ideology: National Unity versus Popular Hegemony

In the late 1980s there was considerable controversy within the ECODEPA project regarding the intended beneficiaries of the peasant stores and the extent to which they had benefited. This discussion was hardly surprising in light of the fact that both the definition of the beneficiaries and the general objectives of the rural supply network changed over time. Under the terms of the 1987–1990 aid agreement between UNAG and SCC, "the peasant families living in regions affected by the war . . . constitute[d] the principal beneficiary" of the project.[29] Following the end of the war, refugees returning to take up production were also supposed to receive support. Although the term "peasant families" is vague and incorporates agricultural producers from all social strata, it was a well-established priority of the project to benefit primarily the small and medium producers.

According to the statutes, every agricultural producer had the right to become a member "independently of sex, [political] affiliation, religious belief, status as individual or cooperative producer, or size of farm."[30] In 1989 the composition of the store constituency varied considerably across the four departments. In general, small producers constituted the overwhelming majority of the store members.[31] Rich farmers were a small minority. For example, in Boaco's peasant stores, large producers constituted 3–4 percent of the membership.[32] The membership also differed with regard to the relative weight of individual farmers versus members of cooperatives. Matagalpa and Jinotega's peasant stores were characterized by a predominance of peasants belonging to Sandinista production cooperatives, whereas individual producers were in the majority in Chontales.

It has been recognized that the ECODEPA project succeeded in integrating producers with different class backgrounds.[33] The peasant stores provided an important forum for individual producers and members of production cooperatives to exchange ideas. This contributed to reducing

prevailing tensions between the two sectors. The general lack of communication prevailing in Nicaragua's countryside fostered deeply rooted
suspicions between the private and the cooperative sectors. The resent-
ment some private producers felt vis-à-vis the production cooperatives
was not without foundation. Particularly in the distribution of scarce
farm inputs and access to credit, production cooperatives were given priority treatment by the state. Despite some improvements in relations,
peasant stores whose membership consisted predominantly of individual
producers nevertheless were reluctant to award the production cooperatives full membership rights. Whereas the production cooperatives were
granted membership, they were frequently not informed of planned
meetings and faced great difficulties in obtaining representation on the
executive committee. This discrimination violated the statutes, which
envisioned the representation of all sectors on the executive committee.[34]
Members of production cooperatives not only complained that "the producers with more money rule" but maintained that the products sold in
the stores were too expensive for their limited means. This view was supported by Aaron Guerrero, Juigalpa's manager, who argued that the
ECODEPA project was not designed for the poor peasantry but benefited
mainly medium and large producers.

At times, large producers attempted to gain control of the stores. For
example, in San José de los Remates, large producers affiliated with
FAGANIC, gained control of the executive committee. Subsequently,
they excluded small producers from joining. This prompted the department manager to intervene. He closed the store until a new committee
was elected. Large, capitalist producers played a limited role in the
stores. Of more concern were the actions of the chapiollos. Not surprisingly, their predominance in the union's affairs translated into influence
within the ECODEPA project.

During the late 1980s the peasant stores of Boaco and Chontales were
controlled by chapiollos. Even in region VI, where the production cooperatives were numerically strong, chapiollos exerted control in many
stores. In particular in the case of the store coordinators this was not a
surprising development. The coordinators, as all other members of the
executive committee, were not remunerated for their work but held
strictly honorary positions. Therefore, only relatively well-off producers
could afford to neglect their farms and donate time to advance the rural
supply network. Following the change in government, it became clear that
the ECODEPA project was increasingly controlled by rich producers. The

neoliberal economic program implemented by the Chamorro government tended to favor large private producers, while marginal sectors, in particular the production cooperatives, lost the government support that had made them viable. The UNAG leadership, dominated by chapiollos, tended to defend the interests of the rich producers over those of the marginal peasant sectors.

The change in government raised another important issue—the place of the rural supply network in the new ideological climate. The stores were open to agricultural producers, regardless of their ideological convictions.[35] Yet the majority of the members were affiliated with UNAG that supported the Sandinista revolutionary project. In 1988 ECODEPA officials estimated that about 30 percent of the membership was not affiliated with UNAG. This figure was contested by representatives of the rural bourgeoisie who opposed the Sandinista government.[36] In their view, UNAG imposed ideological membership criteria, thus excluding many large producers from the benefits of the supply network. Yet this perception by the national leadership of UPANIC was itself a reflection of ideological considerations rather than an accurate description of reality.

The UPANIC leadership represented a group of large private producers that considered it impossible to work together with the Sandinista government. During the ten years of the revolutionary government, these farmers sought a share of political power before they would agree to economic cooperation.[37] As discussed, their views did not represent the class position of all members of the rural bourgeoisie. Several UPANIC affiliates enjoyed good relations with the ECODEPA project. Particularly the milk producers organized in FONDILAC and the cattle ranchers of FAGANIC participated actively. Juan Diego López, the president of FONDILAC, personally supported San José de los Remates's peasant store. According to the manager of ECODEPA Chontales, members of FAGANIC, including the president of the organization, Rafael Martínez, enjoyed well-established commercial relations with the ECODEPA project. There might have been exceptional cases of producers being excluded from the ECODEPA project based on political motives, but this was hardly established policy.

More important than the controversy concerning the rural bourgeoisie's access to the ECODEPA project were the ideological orientations of the store members. Most of them were affiliated with UNAG. This did not mean, however, that they supported the Sandinista government. On the contrary, support for UNO during the 1989 election campaign was considerable. Particularly in Boaco and Chontales, the majority of the store members favored the opposition. Political support for UNO reflected the sentiments of the electorate in the two regions and translated into a devastating defeat for the Sandinista Front. The opposition won eight of the ten seats to the National Assembly and control of all municipalities.[38] The Sandinistas did somewhat better in Matagalpa and Jinotega, where the ruling party obtained four National Assembly seats while UNO gained seven. At the municipal level, however, the Sandinistas lost badly, winning only three out of twenty-seven towns.[39]

During the electoral campaign, meetings at the store level were often characterized by their heavy political content. Sandinista supporters, at times, objected to allowing participation by members of the opposition. Yet it was more common to find Sandinista and UNO supporters working side by side. Several stores had coordinators who were candidates on the Sandinista ticket while other members of the executive committees ran on the UNO slate. This reality indicated that the peasant stores were characterized by political pluralism. The apparent contradiction of producers actively participating in a project sponsored by a Sandinista grassroots movement while supporting the political opposition was not perceived as such by the majority of the store constituency. Many producers indicated that they supported the goals of the revolutionary project while being critical of the Sandinista government. Moreover, a vote for UNO was not necessarily an endorsement of the opposition but was foremost intended to end the massive killing and economic deprivation resulting from a decade of U.S.-sponsored aggression. The war caught the peasantry in a no-win situation, a reality particularly evident in Chontales. Producers, suspected by the Sandinista authorities of collaborating with the contras, endured many hardships. It was not uncommon to find cases such as the town San Pedro de Lóvago, where, according to local officials, at one point more than 50 percent of the members of the local cattlemen association, including its president, were jailed by the Sandinistas. On the other hand, thousands of peasants were assassinated by the counterrevolution for being "Sandinista sympathizers."

Whenever there were serious disagreements between store members, great efforts were undertaken to resolve them in a constructive fashion. In the November 1989 meeting of Jinotega's departmental executive committee, one coordinator reported that a UNAG professional who was a candidate for the local town council on the UNO ticket was spreading propaganda against the town's peasant store. In the ensuing discussion, a member of the committee argued that opposition supporters should not be able to participate in the ECODEPA project. In his view, the peasant stores were sponsored by the Sandinista Front, and since the opposition was against all revolutionary projects, their supporters should not be benefiting from the stores. This position was strongly rejected by Irene Rivera, the coordinator of Wiwilí, who held that the peasant stores belonged to the people and were intended to benefit all sectors of the peasantry, regardless of their ideological convictions. Rivera then proceeded to startle his colleagues and announced that he too favored the Chamorro candidacy. In fact, he was running for the town council of Wiwilí on the UNO ticket. Support for UNO was so persuasive that some stores actively supported the opposition's election campaign with store resources, including trucks. The opposition was also represented at the regional level. Apart from the departmental executive committees, UNO had support within the management, with one of the managers belonging to a party that formed part of the opposition alliance. Even the contras took the ideological diversity of the membership into account. Although some stores were destroyed in counterrevolutionary attacks, they were not primary targets.

The store leadership was engaged in a conscious effort to prevent a further politicization of the ECODEPA project. In this spirit, Juan Calero, the coordinator of the Muelle de los Bueyes store, started a meeting of the local general assembly, held during the 1989–1990 election campaign, with the following remarks: "Here Liberals, Conservatives, Marxists, Communists—everyone is welcome. . . . We do not talk politics here, we talk about work."[40] In the difficult pre-electoral climate, coordinators also sought to protect the store membership from abuses by local authorities. A UNO supporter affiliated with the Teustepe store who faced imprisonment on trumped-up charges went free once the store coordinator intervened on his behalf. In another instance, the executive committee of San Pedro de Lóvago pleaded with Vice-President Sergio Ramírez to secure the prison release of one of the store members who was a candidate for UNO.

The membership of the peasant stores had a diverse class background and represented a broad political spectrum. Although the project benefited a diverse strata of Nicaragua's agricultural sector, it suffered from the contradictions arising from the policy goals of national unity and popular hegemony. With the chapiollos in control, marginal sectors, particularly landless peasants and women, were not adequately represented.[41]

UNAG and ECODEPA: The Union and its Economic Branch

According to the 1987 aid agreement between UNAG and SCC, it was an important objective of the project "to strengthen the UNAG as a union and democratic organization, representative of the peasantry and the producers of Nicaragua."[42] UNAG's role in the development of the rural supply network was emphasized in the 1989 statutes of the peasant stores: "The peasant stores and the ECODEPA are part and instruments of the Nicaraguan peasant movement led by the UNAG."[43] Daniel Núñez, UNAG's president, was the coordinator of the national executive committee, and the regional UNAG presidents held seats on the departmental committees. The eminent role of UNAG in the ECODEPA project reflected the union's initiative and commitment in the creation of the rural supply network.

The two institutions reinforced each other. The development of the peasant stores would not have been possible without the political clout and organizational support of the farmers' organization. In turn, the ECODEPA project's economic resources facilitated UNAG's evolution into a more autonomous movement. Yet the objectives and goals of UNAG as a political movement and ECODEPA as a business enterprise differed, requiring the establishment of concise institutional boundaries. Throughout the late 1980s, the lack of a clearly defined relationship led to conflicts "between and among the two organizations and the technical advisors."[44] There were mainly two distinct views regarding the proper relationship. The UNAG leadership perceived ECODEPA as an integral part of the union and considered it in organizational terms one of several of the union's sections. The majority of donors involved in the project, together with many ECODEPA and store leaders, shared a different opinion. They emphasized the institutional autonomy of the ECODEPA project within an organic conception. The peasant stores represented the heart, with UNAG constituting a political and ECODEPA representing an economic arm. The latter view prevailed in region V, where ECODEPA and store officials favored strict institutional separation. Aaron Guerrero, ECODEPA Chontales's manager, argued that, particularly in the administrative sphere, a clear separation between UNAG and

ECODEPA was essential. These differences in conception had important implications for the development of the ECODEPA project.

A central source of conflict concerned the financial relationship. Under the terms of the aid agreement, UNAG was supposed to receive financial support for its activities from a Cooperative Development Fund, established with profits from the sale of merchandise throughout the ECODEPA system. The transfer of money from this fund to UNAG generally took place "in an unprogrammed fashion" and left UNAG short of the support required to maintain its activities.[45] When the union did receive funds, the organization almost never accounted for their use, which led to frictions and further restricted the flow of funds. Most peasant stores utilized existing UNAG infrastructure. Indeed, UNAG contributed both manpower and buildings. As noted, union officials were actively involved in initiating the peasant stores. Many UNAG officials considered the stores "children of UNAG" and felt justified in relying on their resources. Particularly in the early stages of the project, UNAG officials disposed of ECODEPA resources with liberty. Many times this was done to advance the political objectives of the union. In the case of Santa Lucia's peasant store, the local UNAG organizer distributed scarce products to farmers who were not even store members in an attempt to obtain their support for the union. In another incident, a UNAG professional attempted to supply a resettlement camp with valuable zinc for roof construction, over the opposition of Teustepe's executive committee. ECODEPA resources were also used to maintain and establish traditional patron-client relationships. There were cases of UNAG's leadership ordering the ECODEPA management to distribute scarce products to particular individuals free of charge. Eduardo Baumeister, who participated in several evaluations of the ECODEPA project, maintained that UNAG's reliance on the assets of ECODEPA not only drained resources from the project but allowed store and ECODEPA leaders to blame the precarious economic condition of many stores on UNAG interference, when in fact most problems were results of deficient management.

The representatives of the peasant stores and the regional ECODEPA management, seeking to assert their control over the emerging structures, objected to interference into their internal affairs. The demands by UNAG officials, often perceived as unreasonable, were generally rejected by the executive committees. As a result of these conflicts, many UNAG officials were alienated and withdrew from active participation in the emerging cooperative enterprise. In Boaco and Chontales, the disengagement of UNAG officials from the project was still evident in 1989, while Matagalpa and Jinotega experienced a greater degree of cooperation between the two institutions.

During the late 1980s, financial relations between UNAG and ECODEPA were multifaceted. In many instances, financial support for UNAG was established on an ad-hoc basis. This irregular use of project funds led to criticism from the peasant store constituents. Although the support given to UNAG at the local and regional levels was slowly being institutionalized, irregularities continued. In one such instance, ECODEPA León was ordered by the UNAG leadership to provide the necessary funds for the acquisition of a private home for the regional UNAG president.[46] In region VI the peasant stores of Matiguas, San José de Bocay, Pueblo Nuevo, and Waslala paid the salary of the local UNAG organizer. This was a reasonable arrangement, since the UNAG professionals in the two departments spent considerable time working on behalf of the stores. The Waslala store also paid the salary of UNAG's local secretary and contributed 1 percent of the store's net profits to the union. At the departmental level, ECODEPA Matagalpa contributed 1 percent of its net profits, whereas Jinotega and Chontales provided no official regular support. Boaco approved aid on a case by case basis. In February 1989, for example, the executive committee agreed to a UNAG request of three million cordobas to support expenses incurred by UNAG's National Council during a meeting in Managua.[47] The departmental enterprise also paid the salary for the secretary in the regional UNAG office.

The UNAG leadership strongly resented the debate over the financial relationship between the union and the ECODEPA project. Daniel Núñez emphasized that the peasant stores would not exist without the initiative of UNAG. As noted, the union was very successful in obtaining financial support and technical assistance from international donors. Up to US$10 million were annually contributed in foreign aid.[48] Yet, the considerable financial support UNAG received from international donors went mainly to the ECODEPA project and left the union short on funds. According to Núñez, UNAG professionals received salaries that barely allowed them to survive, and 250 of them had to be laid off in 1988. In contrast, many ECODEPA employees received higher salaries than their counterparts in comparable state or private enterprises.[49]

More serious than these difficulties in the financial relationship between the two organizations were actions by the union that undermined the institutional autonomy of the ECODEPA project and limited effective grassroots democracy. As I noted above, the UNAG leadership was in firm control of ECODEPA's national executive committee. Further, there were instances of interference in the regional and local decision-making process. Analyzing the relationship between UNAG and ECODEPA, one needs to distinguish between the following sectors within the union: the national leadership, UNAG professionals, and the agricultural producers who served the union in local leadership functions.

Problems arose usually from actions taken by UNAG's leadership. Within the leadership there appeared to be a split between members, such as Daniel Núñez, who had a background as a producer, and pure union professionals (paid UNAG employees). The loyalty of the professionals was exclusively with the organization, whereas the former group had primarily the interest of the producers at heart. The agenda pursued by the professionals was not always in the true interest of the store constituency. Francisco Gutierrez, UNAG's president in Boaco, maintained that the professionals were generally more interested in the short-term political leverage that UNAG derived from the ECODEPA project than in ensuring the long-term viability of the peasant stores. Also, they were reluctant to relinquish control over any aspect of the organization, including the peasant stores. Thus, the professionals, rather than the UNAG leaders in general, were at the root of the frictions between UNAG and ECODEPA.

At the grassroots level, however, there was close coordination between the union and the business enterprise, since the UNAG and the ECODEPA leaders were often identical. Many store coordinators were presidents of the local UNAG office or held other positions in the union. These local leaders showed greater concern for the institutional autonomy of the peasant stores than UNAG's national leadership. For example, when the executive committee of Teustepe's peasant store discussed a request by Daniel Núñez that the committee hire a particular individual as store administrator, several store leaders expressed concern about being told by UNAG's president whom they could employ. The issue was further complicated by the fact that the administrator was also to carry out secretarial duties for the local UNAG office. In order to ensure that it would have complete authority over the new employee, the executive committee decided to stipulate in her contract that she was employed by the peasant store and not UNAG.

Generally, local leaders became more assertive in resisting attempts to interfere in their internal affairs. In their struggle to gain full institutional autonomy, the executive committees usually put pressure on UNAG's national leadership to control overzealous local professionals. The departmental executive committees were instrumental in supporting individual peasant stores in this endeavor. Cases such as Acoyapa, where local UNAG organizers attempted to take over the peasant store, were usually resolved once the departmental committees notified the national UNAG office. The assertiveness of some executive committees intimidated several UNAG professionals to the point that they no longer participated in store or ECODEPA meetings. In the case of weak committees, however, UNAG professionals could interfere with impunity. In December 1989 UNAG's president in Chinandega reportedly ignored all institutional procedures and fired the manager of the departmental ECODEPA. Although the executive committee objected, it did not take any actions to reverse this decision.

The ECODEPA project strengthened the union in several regards. The rural supply network attracted sectors of the peasantry that used to be indifferent or hostile to the Sandinista revolutionary project. UNAG, considered the "parent" of the peasant stores, received credit for the improvements that the ECODEPA project brought about in the peasant economy and was able to strengthen its standing in the rural community. One indication of UNAG's appeal was the fact that the farmers' movement recruited 14,000 new members between 1985 and 1987, a period when other grassroots organizations declined in membership. Most of this growth took place in region VI, where the peasant stores were initiated. Overall, the peasant stores furthered the general consolidation of the farmers' movement rather than contributing to significant growth in membership. It is interesting to note that in region V, UNAG actually lost 6,000 members during 1985–1987. As discussed in the previous chapter, the considerable loss of members in region V was the result of an increase in counterrevolutionary aggression. Many producers left the farmers' movement, fearing that their association with a Sandinista organizations would make them a target. It speaks for the strength of the ECODEPA project that the membership of the stores continued to expand under these difficult conditions. As table 5.3 shows, the number of members increased from 49,800 in 1986–1987 to 63,800 in 1989. Even in zones of conflict, farmers joined the stores in increasing numbers. In Chontales, part of region V, store membership increased from 4,000 to 7,200, whereas Matagalpa reported an increase from 5,000 to 8,300 members.

Table 5.3. Evolution of peasant stores membership, 1986–1991

Departmental store	1986–87	1988	1989	1990	1991
Estelí	3,000	4,000	7,900	10,223	3,515
Madriz	1,000	3,000	2,400	2,407	2,627
Nueva Segovia	1,000	2,000	1,200	961	1,914
Leon	4,000	3,000	3,500	3,514	1,548
Chinandega	400	1,000	1,800	3,919	3,460
Managua	4,000	2,000	2,500	2,478	1,615
Masaya	4,000	7,000	7,900	4,911	3,163
Carazo	—	—	—	—	3,396
Rivas	9,000	4,000	4,200	4,634	4,961
Boaco	2,000	3,000	3,100	3,123	3,350
Chontales	4,000	7,000	7,200	3,680	2,877
Matagalpa	5,000	8,000	8,300	7,985	2,510
Jinotega	9,000	8,000	7,500	7,540	1,504
Raan	2,000	3,000	3,100	3,127	—
Raas	400	1,000	600	1,469	1,880
Río San Juan	1,000	2,000	2,600	1,421	1,235
Total	49,800	58,000	63,800	61,392	39,555

Source: Cooperative Enterprise of Agricultural Producers (ECODEPA).

Only Jinotega's stores contracted somewhat during this time period, suggesting that the peasantry considered the project to be basically apolitical.

Most important, the experience of the ECODEPA project strengthened the process of internal democratization within the union. The producers, having gained confidence in the running of their cooperatives, started to demand greater participation in the decision making of UNAG. As a result, the farmers' movement began to discuss ways to strengthen the participation of its base structures in the life of the organization and to limit centralized decision making. In one instance, agricultural producers affiliated with Teustepe's peasant store objected to the conduct of the local UNAG leadership, which had been imposed by Managua, and did not respond to their demands. Under mounting grassroots pressure, the UNAG leadership agreed to new elections. The farmers chose Alfonso Hurtado, who had gained their trust with his performance as the peasant store's coordinator. Teustepe represented an important development: local producers, elected by their peers, started to replace paid professionals installed by Managua. This process at the local level, in turn, resulted in pressure for effective democracy at the regional and national level. Not surprisingly, these pressures met with resistance.

A central debate during 1989–1990 concerned a UNAG proposal to restructure the cooperative enterprise. Sentiments ran high, with regional and local ECODEPA leaders seeking to preserve the current system and several members of the national management together with UNAG leaders advocating change. On the surface, the argument was over the economic role played by the departmental ECODEPAs and the need to integrate the peasant stores more fully into the cooperative movement. The real fight, however, concerned the institutional autonomy and democratic development of the project. UNAG and ECODEPA officials at the national level argued that the profit margin applied by the departmental ECODEPAs unnecessarily increased the cost of the merchandise to the final consumer and that crucial resources were wasted by an inefficient, overly bureaucratic, departmental management. The departmental profit margins did indeed increase the final cost to the consumers. It is interesting, however, that a 1989 study of the economic health of the ECODEPA project concluded that the departmental ECODEPAs had relatively low operational expenses, whereas the national ECODEPA experienced problems controlling its operating costs.[50] The UNAG leadership proposed to increase the profitability of the enterprise and lower the cost of products sold to the peasantry, by reducing the departmental ECODEPAs to simple warehouses or branches of the national ECODEPA.[51]

Many departmental coordinators and managers perceived UNAG's proposal, presented in terms of economic reorganization, as an attempt by the union to gain effective control of the ECODEPA project at all levels. Their objections to the proposed changes were numerous. The managers, who obviously had a personal stake in this discussion, argued convincingly that, at their current stage of development, most peasant stores would not survive without the organizational and financial support provided by the departmental ECODEPAs. The departmental enterprises granted the stores credit, and, as discussed, the managers were helpful in assisting the store coordinators. Few stores had administrators who were capable of managing affairs independently under the difficult economic conditions prevailing in Nicaragua. Francisco Berrios, Jinotega's manager, predicted that only two of the department's peasant stores, El Cuá and San José de Bocay, would survive without the institutional support provided by the departmental enterprise. Berrios proved prophetic indeed: by 1991 all stores but two had closed (see table 6.5).

The UNAG leadership decided this debate in its favor. On November 18, 1990, ECODEPA's general assembly unanimously approved new statutes. In the new organizational structure, the departmental ECO-DEPAs lost their autonomy and were converted to branches of the national ECODEPA. Although the new structure was likely to make the ECODEPA project economically more viable, it limited the development of grassroots democracy. The new design affected the very heart of the ECODEPA project—its democratic, participatory structure. According to the 1990 statutes, the peasant stores could no longer be considered the owners of the enterprise. Further, the entrepreneurial freedom and initiative of the departmental managers, considered a major factor in the success of the enterprise,[52] was eliminated. In its attempt to find a balance between "pure democracy and economic efficiency," the national leadership gave priority to the economic viability of the project. Miguel Barrios, the new general manager of ECODEPA, recently stated his view on the subject: "The democratic principles of cooperation should be used to strengthen the development of the activities and services of a cooperative, but never to delay decision-making or contribute to the dispersion of authority."[53] Finally, increased centralization under the 1990 statutes was in direct opposition to the goal to strengthen the peasants' control over their economic affairs.

A Changing Relationship: The Peasant Stores and the State

The success of the stores was based on the project's ability to import the farm implements needed by the agricultural producers and to distribute them widely. Until 1990, the project's access to foreign exchange constituted a crucial advantage vis-à-vis the state agencies that suffered from a chronic shortage of hard currency. Further, the limited supplies the state agencies did import were usually not made available to the average agricultural producer. Under the policies of the Sandinista government, the needs of the state farms received highest priority. Next in line were CAS and sectors of the rural bourgeoisie whose continued participation in the revolutionary project needed to be encouraged with the allocation of scarce resources. The services that the ECODEPA project provided to the peasantry made it a competitor with several state agencies. As noted above, these agencies failed in creating a viable rural infrastructure to substitute for the elimination of the inherited structures of domination and exploitation. Initially, the ECODEPA project encountered lack of support if not outright resistance from state agencies such as MIDINRA and MICOIN. According to UNAG officials, these institutions and their officials resented the fact that an independent supply network had started to challenge the state's influence over the life of the peasantry.

Following an evaluation of the impact of the ECODEPA project on the rural distribution system, relations started to improve. In 1988 an agreement was signed between ECODEPA-UNAG and the state agencies involved with the rural sector. This agreement recognized the farmer stores as the principal rural supply network and emphasized the importance of increased state support.[54] The officials of the various state agencies who conducted the evaluation recommended that the state agencies lend their support to the peasant stores.[55] They also noted that the stores deserved to be treated at least as well as any private enterprise. For example, Servicios Agrícolas Gúrdian, a private enterprise belonging to an important opposition figure, was assigned hard currency for imports, whereas the ECODEPA project had to rely exclusively on donor funds.[56]

Under the Sandinista government, problems between the state sector and the ECODEPA project could be encountered at all levels. These difficulties were the result of different conceptions regarding the role of the peasantry in the transformation of the Nicaraguan countryside. The state agencies sought to control the peasantry, whereas the philosophy of the peasant stores was to encourage grassroots participation.[57] As one producer put it: "They [the State] come with the objective to help, but also to take control of everything."[58] For example, MIDINRA officials viewed the Centros de Desarrollo Cooperativo (Centers for Cooperative Development, or CDC)—officially intended to complement the stores—as instruments for either taking over the stores when the opportunity presented itself or controlling them. CDCs usually attacked the weakest stores in the department. In some instances, such as in Wiwilí, the local CDC tried to undersell the peasant store in order to drive it out of business. Although the Wiwilí store managed to survive, the tactic proved successful in the case of the Cafen peasant store in Boaco. The store closed down in 1989 and subsequently reopened as a CDC. This picture of conflict contrasts with the close cooperation between stores and CDCs in some towns. These harmonious relations were generally based on close personal contacts between state and store officials. For example, Neris Mendoza, the head of the CDC in Teustepe, participated at times in meetings of the store's executive committee, and Don Reinaldo, one of the store leaders, held a seat on the local CDC Council.

The state's monopoly over the distribution and sale of fertilizer constituted another form of control. In the eyes of many ECODEPA leaders, this central agricultural implement was used to lure the producers away from the peasant stores. The issue of the fertilizer monopoly aroused great anger among the store constituency. The situation was particularly controversial, since the fertilizer was a Norwegian donation. Norwegian aid officials affirmed that the aid, more than US$12 million in 1989, was intended to contribute to increased production of food grains and to improve income opportunities for small and medium farmers. Jaime Wheelock, the Sandinista minister of agriculture and agrarian reform, agreed at one point to the demand that the stores be allowed to buy fertilizer for distribution to their members. Yet he revoked this concession before the new policy was instituted. Wheelock's ambivalence was most likely influenced by the lucrative nature of the monopoly. State officials acknowledged that the state agency selling the fertilizer operated for profit and not primarily to the benefit of the producers. The profit from the sale of fertilizer was used to support the operating expenses of the regional MIDINRA offices.

Apart from problems with CDCs, peasant store leaders complained about the limited access to credit and the heavy tax burden. The peasant stores did not have access to state credit on the same terms as other sectors of the agricultural community. In addition, taxes were levied at all three levels of the ECODEPA system. In general, the project paid 60 percent of the total value of its merchandise in taxes.[59] At the local level, the same merchandise was often taxed twice—once on the sale by the departmental ECODEPA and the second time at the store level. During the last months of the Sandinista government, the state agencies came under heavy pressure from UNAG to resolve this situation.

It is broadly recognized that the peasant stores would not have survived the 1980s without the political clout of the union. Daniel Núñez was a major factor in negotiating better conditions for the ECODEPA project. He criticized MIDINRA and other state officials for designing policies at their desks that did not take the reality of the rural sector into account. These problems notwithstanding, Núñez emphasized that "without the Revolution, there would be no peasant stores."[60] Indeed, the ECODEPA project enjoyed the support and appreciation of the Sandinista government. Henry Ruíz, then minister of external cooperation and a member of the National Directorate of the Sandinista Front, stated in 1989: "If the ECODEPA did not provide the services it does to the countryside, the government would have to, and that if this were the case, the services would be far less efficient and more costly."[61]

The future of the peasant stores in the new political climate prevailing under the Chamorro government seemed uncertain at best. Interestingly enough, the ECODEPA project had excellent relations with the state under Chamorro. This was reflected in the recent appointment of Daniel Núñez, to the board of directors of the *Banco Nacional de Desarrollo*. It certainly helped that Miguel Barrios, ECODEPA's new general manager, was Chamorro's nephew. In a society in which family ties transcend ideological and class cleavages,[62] blood ties between the ECODEPA manager and the country's president constituted a distinct advantage. In another important sign of good relations between the new government and the project, Nicaragua's National Bank granted ECODEPA a loan for the import of fertilizer in the amount of US$11.9 million.[63]

Conclusion

In the view of UNAG's president, the ECODEPA project had been essential in "stimulating participatory democracy [and] the democratization of the rural economy."[64] In order to grasp fully the contribution of the ECODEPA project to the development of grassroots democracy in the rural sector, one needs to consider the challenges facing cooperative development in Nicaragua. Most important, during the 1980s the cooperative movement was a central target of counterrevolutionary aggression. Further, until recently the Nicaraguan peasantry had no experience of democratic grassroots participation. Francisco Dávila maintained that it only knew the Somocista, U.S.-sponsored model of cooperative development, which was in the control of the *comerciante*, the middleman. Although the repressive features of the model were eliminated under the Sandinista government, the tradition of paternalism continued to characterize cooperative development. This was particularly the case in the development of the Sandinista production cooperatives. The peasant stores constituted an important break with this tradition. The stores provided the agricultural producers with the possibility of gaining control over their lives by confronting the policies of the state and eliminating the middleman. In a "revolution from below," grassroots participation began to transform UNAG, making it more accountable to the base. This change was supported by an emerging elite of peasant leaders. Their formation, started in the producers' assemblies initiated by the Sandinista grassroots movements, was completed in the executive committees of the peasant stores and departmental ECODEPAs.

As several store leaders argued: "The project has helped us to realize our potential."

Two central deficiencies of the ECODEPA project were the absence of an effective education and training program at the grassroots level and the project's precarious legal status. The majority of the store membership was not familiar with the basic cooperative principles that constituted the nature of the peasant stores. This was problematic, since effective participation requires informed decisions. The 1990 change in government emphasized the urgency of resolving the project's legal status. Immediately following the Sandinista defeat, UNAG started to acquire legal status for the peasant stores and the ECODEPAs.[65]

The change in the orientation of the ECODEPA project, from an emergency aid program to one that assured self-sufficiency, facilitated the adaptation of the peasant stores to the new economic climate under the Chamorro government. Although the change in government did have drastic economic consequences, the fact that the Sandinista government had already moved in the direction of a market economy helped. Of greatest concern for the democratic development of the project was the 1990 reorganization of ECODEPA's organizational structure. It effectively destroyed the original project design that emphasized cooperative principles.

Chapter 6_____

The Struggle Goes On: Rural Women in the Nicaraguan Transition

> [I]n any given society the degree of wo-
> man's emancipation is the natural measure
> of the general emancipation.
>
> *attributed by Friedrich
> Engels to Charles Fourier*

A complete account of the Sandinista revolution in the rural sector requires an examination of its legacy regarding women's emancipation.
Historically, rural women constituted one of the most marginalized sectors of Nicaraguan society. Thus, a revolutionary project based on a policy of popular hegemony should have paid particular attention to the
needs of this sector. In this chapter I examine the situation of rural women during the revolutionary period by focusing on the grassroots movements and give an initial account of the first years of the Chamorro administration. I argue that strategic gender issues were neglected under the
Sandinistas, while women benefited in many ways from the social policies introduced during the revolutionary period. Many of these gains,
however, have been eroded since the Chamorro government took power.

Throughout the eleven years of revolutionary rule, the Sandinista government faced a central question—whether to give priority to the overall
goals of the revolutionary project or to further the particular interests of
any one sector of Nicaraguan society. For most of the 1980s the Sandinista leadership maintained that the defense of the revolution required the
subordination of the fight for women's emancipation. This position was
a key factor in restricting progress toward the full realization of women's

161

rights. The Sandinista experience did not differ from the reality of other revolutionary societies. The subordination of women's issues was standard praxis in the Soviet Union, and "the existing socialist regimes in China, Vietnam, and Cuba reveal many of the same shortcomings of the orthodox Marxist-Leninist approach to women's liberation."[1]

Maxine Molyneux has emphasized that the controversy over the proper strategy for achieving women's emancipation in a revolutionary society is owing to the difficulty in defining women's interests or explaining the roots of women's subordination. She argues that "women's oppression is recognized as being multicausal in origin and mediated through a variety of different structures, mechanisms, and levels, which may vary considerable across space and time. There is therefore continuing debate over the appropriate site of feminist struggle and over whether it is more important to focus attempts at change on objective or subjective elements, on structures or men, on laws and institutions or on interpersonal power relations—or on all of them simultaneously."[2] Molineux makes an important distinction between *strategic* and *practical* gender interests:

> Strategic interests are derived in the first instance deductively, i.e., from the analysis of women's subordination and from the formulation of an alternative, more satisfactory set of arrangements to those that exist. These ethical and theoretical criteria assist in the formulation of strategic objectives to overcome women's subordination, such as the abolition of the sexual division of labor, the alleviation of the burden of domestic labor and childcare, the removal of institutionalized forms of discrimination, the establishment of political equality, freedom of choice over childbearing, and the adoption of adequate measures against male violence and control over women. . . . Practical gender interests are given inductively and arise from the concrete conditions of women's positioning by virtue of their gender in the division of labor. In contrast to strategic gender interests, practical gender interests are formulated by the women themselves who are within these positions rather than through external interventions. Practical interests are usually a response to an immediate perceived need and they do not generally entail a strategic goal such as women's emancipation or gender equality.[3]

Molineux's categories have been employed in numerous studies. Her distinction of strategic versus practical gender interests helps us better to understand Sandinista policies toward women.[4]

Historical Background

Before taking power on July 19, 1979, the Sandinistas had clearly stated their commitment to women's emancipation. According to the 1969 *Historic Program of the FSLN*, the Sandinista revolution would "abolish the obvious discrimination that women have been subjected to compared to men [and] establish economic, political and cultural equality between women and men."[5] Specifically, the revolutionary leadership promised to provide special attention to the needs of mother and child, end the legal discrimination of children born out of wedlock, build day care centers, establish a two-month maternity leave before and after birth for working women, eliminate prostitution, and emphasize women's participation in the revolution.[6] Thus, initially the revolutionary leadership addressed strategic and practical gender interests. Yet revolutionary praxis was much more successful in addressing practical needs than strategic ones.

The reign of the Somoza family was characterized by the legal discrimination of women and the all-pervasive culture of machismo. This culture, which characterized male-female relations throughout Latin America, constituted a general climate of inequality and oppression that manifested itself in physical violence against women, abandoned families, discrimination at the workplace, and women's subordination at the level of private gender relations.[7] When one contrasts the oppressive conditions women were subjected to with the Sandinista promise of liberation, it is not surprising that women joined the revolutionary struggle in great numbers. The motivations of women who became FSLN members differed. Although some actually were familiar with the Sandinista program as it concerned women's emancipation, most joined out of hatred of the Somoza dictatorship or the desire to express their solidarity with family members who were already part of the struggle.[8]

Women represented an estimated 30 percent of Sandinista combatants and held several important command positions.[9] In addition they transported supplies, served as cooks, and cared for the wounded.[10] Women's sacrifices in the overthrow of the Somoza regime proved meaningful. Once in power, the revolutionary government immediately implemented legal reforms benefiting women.[11] A new media law ended the exploitation of women as sexual objects in commercial advertising, and changes in family law gave women equal custody rights over their children, established the right to alimony, recognized "de facto" marriages, and secured the right to inherit for children born out of wedlock. Progressive labor legislation established the right to equal salaries, outlawed discrimination against pregnant women in the workplace, and established pre- and post-natal benefits.[12] In the rural sector, female peasants obtained the right to own land and to participate in agricultural cooperatives on the same conditions as men. Several of these rights—for example, the protection of working women during pregnancies—were written into the 1987 constitution.

In addition to these important legal changes, efforts to end the traditional marginalization of women in the political arena were undertaken. The revolutionary leadership assigned the AMNLAE a crucial role in this task. Through AMNLAE, women obtained representation on the Council of State. AMNLAE's initial direction was to encourage the active participation of women in the revolutionary process. In the mid-1980s, the women's movement claimed to have eighty-five thousand members.[13] A major focus of the organization was the mobilization of women in the various campaigns centered on basic human needs. Female participation in literacy and popular health campaigns was massive. Women constituted 80 percent of all health brigade activists and 60 percent of all teachers (12 percent of the teachers were AMNLAE members).[14] Women were main beneficiaries of these social campaigns, which represented avenues for participation in the emerging socioeconomic structure that formed the foundation of the revolutionary process.

Sandinista policies resulted in substantial changes in the public sphere, yet many problems remained to be addressed. Similar to the experience of Western capitalist societies, attitudes at the level of private gender relations proved most resilient. The continuing difficulties women faced several years after the successful insurrection led to a radicalization of the women's movement. Female leaders argued that it was time to focus on the larger problematic—the lack of progress in achieving specific women's rights, including control over their sexuality and reproductive capacity, and the abolition of a gender-based division of labor. Women were marginalized and suffered male domination. Lourdes Benería and Martha Roldan have emphasized that since the inherited class structure and the prevailing system of patriarchy are often "interconnected and mutually reinforcing . . . patriarchy might be maintained throughout different modes of production."[15] Thus, Sandinista emphasis on socialist transformation was not enough. Patriarchy itself had to be attacked.

This, however, was difficult since it would have set the Sandinistas on a collision course with the church hierarchy and significant sectors of the bourgeoisie who defended the status quo. The Sandinistas argued that they could not afford to antagonize these crucial sectors at a time when the revolution, increasingly suffering under the U.S.-sponsored military attack and economic boycott, was fighting for its survival. Once again, the policy of national unity disadvantaged a sector of society that should have been a primary beneficiary of popular hegemony. The national unity policy, however, was not the sole obstacle. The revolutionary leadership also feared that a drive to alter traditional gender relations radically would encounter resistance from many male supporters. Further, Sandinista leaders themselves, with few exceptions, shared the traditional view of women's role in society. They were more concerned with ensuring the reproduction of Nicaragua's population in light of the war than with advancing women's rights. Although a few high-ranking Sandinistas were female, the nine-member National Directorate of FSLN was exclusively male until 1994.

If we consider these factors, it is not surprising that key demands such as legalization of abortion or greater access to contraceptives were conspicuously absent from Sandinista discourse. The women's movement, following the directions of the revolutionary leadership, also did not advocate a radical feminist agenda. With AMNLAE being reduced to mobilizing women in defense of the revolution, women's participation declined. Some women withdrew completely; others continued the fight by focusing their energy on the struggle for women's rights within peasant, farmer, and worker organizations.

In the mid-1980s, the strategic defeat of the counterrevolutionary forces provided the context for a reassessment of the role of the grassroots movements. In general, the Sandinista mass organizations gained greater autonomy in their relations with the party.[16] During this period AMNLAE went through an evaluation process that resulted in the formulation of AMNLAE's 1987 program. It emphasized the importance of combining the struggle for the revolution's survival with the fight for women's rights.[17] The Sandinista Front joined AMNLAE's efforts in March 1987 with the *Proclama Sobre la Mujer,* a pronouncement outlining its position regarding the emancipation of women in Nicaragua.[18] The *Proclama* included two significant changes in Sandinista thought: (1) it recognized the necessity for changes in private gender relations, advocating shared responsibilities of women and men in taking care of the family and attending to housework; and (2), it emphasized that the struggle for women's emancipation should no longer be subordinated to the revolution's priorities.[19] The Sandinistas acknowledged that despite important accomplishments toward women's emancipation, "discrimi-natory laws and social practices; the subordination of women in society and the family; paternal irresponsibility; physical and moral mistreat-ment; [and] *machismo*" continued to prevail.[20] The change in Sandinista thought reflected the realization that it was counterproductive to per-ceive the struggle for women's emancipation and the defense of the revo-lution as conflicting agendas.

Female Participation in the Rural Workers' Movement

Under the Sandinista government, the most significant changes affecting rural women came as a result of the 1981 agrarian reform and a new law that regulated agricultural cooperatives. These legal measures gave women the right to own land and to participate in cooperatives under the same conditions as men. Equally important, women gained political rep-resentation through their membership in the two main rural grassroots movements, the Rural Workers' Movement and the National Union of Farmers and Ranchers. Throughout the 1980s, more women partici-pated in ATC than in UNAG. The different participation rates reflected the extent to which women had been incorporated into particular sectors of the economically active population. Whereas female participation in agricultural cooperatives (which constituted the main base structures of UNAG) was limited, the number of female agricultural workers in the rural labor force was substantial.

The 1980s were characterized by a "feminization" of the Nicaraguan workforce. This phenomenon had its roots in the 1970s, yet accelerated dramatically over the course of the next decade. Initially, it reflected the difficult living conditions that forced women to join the workforce in order to support their families. Between 1950 and 1980, the number of economically active women grew from 50,000 to 178,000.[21] Female par-ticipation in the Nicaraguan labor force increased from 29 percent in 1977 to 42 percent in 1983.[22] This trend became even more pronounced as a result of the war. With the male labor supply depleted by the military draft and the recruitment of peasants into the counterrevolution, female laborers were sought after.

In the rural sector, female participation in the economically active population (EAP) was about 18 percent in 1977.[23] Based on the fact that in 1992 women constituted 40 percent of salaried agricultural workers, one can safely assume that the relative weight of women in the agrarian

EAP increased over time.[24] The substantial increase in the number of female agricultural laborers over the past decade was reflected in ATC's membership statistics. ATC was open to female agricultural workers on state and private farms who belonged to the permanent or seasonal workforce. By the mid-1980s, the female proportion of agricultural workers affiliated with ATC was already 40 percent. According to official statistics, women represented 28 percent of permanent agricultural workers who were members of the Sandinista union, and they made up 57 percent of the seasonal workforce. The number of women among agricultural laborers affiliated with ATC indicated that the Sandinista union's membership accurately reflected the gender composition of the rural workforce. Most female ATC members were employed on state farms. The proportion of women working in the state sector was more than twice as high as in the private sector (see table 6.1).[25] This indicates that the revolutionary government was more likely to employ women than private farmers.

The proportion of female workers affiliated with ATC remained fairly stable throughout the 1980s. In 1989 women constituted 40 percent of the 135,000 permanent and seasonal agricultural workers affiliated with the Association of Rural Workers.[26] Female laborers represented 35 percent of the union workers with permanent work and 50 percent of the seasonal workforce.[27] Thus, over the course of the 1980s, we find a slight increase in the female proportion of permanent workers and a slight decrease in women's participation in the seasonal workforce, a development that indicates an improvement in the relative security of rural women.

The ATC's female members were deeply affected by the change in government that followed the Sandinista electoral defeat. The privatization of the state sector meant that many ATC members lost their jobs. The number of permanent workers affiliated with the Sandinista union dropped from 48,430 in 1989 to 35,607 in 1992.[28] The decline of the ATC started under the Sandinistas. In 1988 a harsh austerity program was introduced to bring hyperinflation under control (33,000 percent in that year). It included a drastic reduction of the state sector and was the main reason for the union's loss of 3,755 members between 1988 and 1989. This loss in membership accelerated under Chamorro. By 1992, an additional 12,733 workers had ceased to be ATC members. Although some members abandoned the movement in the wake of the 1990 elections because they no longer wanted to be associated with a Sandinista union,

Table 6.1. Female participation in ATC, mid-1980s

	% of female members	% of female workers	% of female temporary workers
Cotton	42	15	58
Coffee	30	25	59
Tobacco	50	47	54
Region I	80	79	100
Region II	44	17	58
Region III	17	21	0
Region IV	33	13	54
Region VI	30	28	76
Private sector	32	14	56
State sector	45	35	57
Total	40	28	57

Source: CIERA/ATC/CETRA, Mujer y agroexportación en Nicaragua, 104.

most left because they lost their jobs. Not surprisingly, women suffered disproportionately. In 1989 the union's female members numbered 15,355.[29] Three years later, only 5,623 female workers remained affiliated with ATC, and the number of male members had shrunk to 29,984 (see table 6.2). Thus, between 1989 and 1992, ATC lost 9,732 female workers and "only" 3,001 male laborers. Female ATC leaders maintained that women were the first to be fired because of economic considerations. For example, employers avoided the potential cost of having to pay maternity benefits. As a result of this process, female membership in the union dropped to 15.8 percent in 1992.

During the first two years of the Chamorro government, ATC was successful in gaining ownership of 136 state farms that were privatized. In 1991, the new Area de Propriedad de Trabajadores (Area of Workers' Property, or APT) consisted of 230,530 acres of land, about 32 percent of the privatized state sector.[30] This was a significant achievement that benefited ATC's female membership, which came to be strongly represented on the privatized farms. Whereas women represented 23 percent of the workers on former state properties, they constituted less than 9 percent of ATC members employed in the private sector (see table 6.3). In 1992, 3,651 female workers were employed on the new worker-owned enterprises, whereas 1,467 worked in the private sector. The distribution of male workers showed a completely dif-

Table 6.2. Distribution of ATC membership by sex, 1992

Department/region/ productive sector	Women	%	Men	%	Total
Region I	825	26.5	2,285	73.5	3,110
Leon (cotton)	238	7.5	2,934	92.5	3,172
Chinandega (cotton)	110	4.0	2,658	96.0	2,768
Chinandega (bananas)	1,700	32.4	3,550	67.6	5,250
Managua	73	4.6	1,517	95.4	1,590
Region IV	225	7.3	2,876	92.7	3,101
Boaco	22	1.9	1,162	98.1	1,184
Chontales	41	3.8	1,057	96.2	1,098
Matagalpa	1,580	22.0	5,614	78.0	7,194
Jinotega	587	15.4	3,233	84.6	3,820
Cattle	22	1.5	1,498	98.5	1,520
Rice	200	11.1	1,600	88.9	1,800
Total	5,623	15.8	29,984	84.2	35,607

Source: Association of Rural Workers (ATC).

ferent picture, with 14,967 in the private sector and only 12,349 on former state farms.[31]

The needs of female workers initially received little attention from the ATC leadership, despite their numerical strength. It has been argued that "the ATC failed to adequately address women farmworkers' concerns during the revolution's first four years."[32] Because of the lack of active female participation in the union's affairs, the male leaders had little incentive to change their priorities. For example, only one-third of female workers who participated in union meetings spoke up.[33] This reflected the continuation of a cultural tradition in which women were subordinate to men. The same tradition also impeded women's access to leadership positions. Although women represented 35 percent of the permanent workers affiliated with ATC in 1989, only 15 percent of the leadership of local union chapters was female.[34] In addition, women rarely held important positions. For example, the union representatives who participated in the management structures of the state farms were almost exclusively male.

In their fight to gain better representation, female workers were supported by the establishment of a Women's Secretariat in 1984. This office provided women with an institutional platform to formulate policies addressing the problems faced by female workers.[35] The work of the Women's Secretariat led to a series of meetings by female workers. For

Table 6.3. Distribution of female ATC members employed in the state and private sectors, 1992

Department/region/ productive sector	Private sector	State sector	Cooperatives	Total
Region I	—	825	—	825
Leon (cotton)	21	217	—	238
Chinandega (cotton)	28	—	82	110
Chinandega (bananas)	—	1,700	—	1,700
Managua	33	40	—	73
Region IV	143	37	45	225
Boaco	15	5	2	22
Chontales	32	—	9	41
Matagalpa	818	395	367	1,580
Jinotega	377	210	—	587
Cattle	—	22	—	22
Rice	—	200	—	200
Total	1,467	3,651	505	5,623

Source: Association of Rural Workers (ATC).

example, in 1986, eight thousand female workers assembled in meetings throughout the country to evaluate their situation and to demand that "their union make women's rights a priority."[36] This process culminated in the Second National Assembly of Female Workers, which passed a list of demands, including increased female quotas for leadership positions, improved childcare facilities, the start of sexual education, and an end to domestic violence.[37] Similar demands were raised in resolutions passed in subsequent meetings of female workers. Between 1985 and 1992, a total of seven national meetings were held.[38]

Female agricultural laborers did benefit from the Sandinista government's commitment to improve the basic needs of the rural population. Particularly education and health care were greatly expanded. Further, the establishment of rural childcare facilities made the integration of women into the workforce easier. Male prejudice, however, relegated them to the low-paying jobs. For example, between 1984 and 1986, ATC trained fifteen women in the use of tractors. According to Dora Herrera, the head of ATC's Women's Section, of these fifteen, only one actually became a tractor driver; the others succumbed to pressure by male coworkers who considered their privileged status threatened. Further, female workers were supposed to receive equal salaries. In practice, however, women were often discriminated against. Eventually, ATC became an effective advocate for women's interests in the public sphere, yet little progress was made in changing the traditional sexual division of labor.[39] In addition to a full workday on the state farms or in the private sector, female ATC members continued to carry the full burden of domestic work.

Interestingly enough, whereas the number of female workers in ATC declined during the course of the transition from the Sandinista to the Chamorro government, female participation in the union's leadership structure was strengthened. This phenomenon should not be attributed to more favorable conditions for women under the new government. Instead, it represented the result of the militant struggle by female ATC members over many years. In 1992, 198 local union leaders were women, representing 19 percent of the grassroots leadership. Although the same proportion of female leaders could be found at the intermediate level, the union's national executive committee had stronger female representation. Five of the 13 members were female.[40] Events during the ATC's 1992 National Congress further illustrate the increasing strength of women within the union. In the elections for a seat on the ATC's National Secretariat, Alba Palacios, the head of ATC's International Relations and the Women's Secretariat, received 254 votes from the 300 delegates. This was the same number of votes cast for Edgardo García, ATC's secretary general, who has held this position since the union's founding in 1978. In the subsequent vote for the position of secretary general, García was successful in his bid for reelection, since he ran unopposed. In light of the strong support received by Palacios, García realized that he would face a tough challenge the next time around.

Since the change in government, women's gains in the social sphere have been eroded. The introduction of school fees and the end to free health care restricted access of female agricultural workers to essential social services. According to ATC data, of the sixty childcare facilities that existed on state farms in 1990, only eleven remained open in 1992. Female ATC members were not just quietly accepting this new reality. Instead they fought to defend their past gains while devising strategies for survival. With the help of international donors, female health clinics were set up to replace lost government services. Further, women's cooperatives were created to help unemployed ATC members to subsist. In the continuing fight to change private gender relations, sex education workshops, which were being conducted since 1988, started to include men for the first time.[41] These workshops constituted evidence for the ATC's effort to address strategical gender interests.[42]

Female Producers in the National Union of Farmers and Ranchers

Female agricultural producers who were affiliated with UNAG experienced many of the problems encountered by their sisters in the rural proletariat. Compared with that of ATC, female participation in the farmers' movement was substantially less significant. Women constituted less than 13 percent of UNAG's membership in 1990 and held few leadership positions. Whereas several women served as presidents of their agricultural cooperatives, all of UNAG's executive committees, from the municipal to the national level, were headed by men. This reality reflected the state of gender relations in the farming community that made women reluctant to assume leadership positions.

International donor agencies played an important role in working with progressive Sandinista sectors to strengthen the role of women within the farmers' movement. For example, financial support from Swedish and Dutch development agencies provided funding for the establishment of Women's Sections at the regional level. The role of international agencies in furthering the cause of women's rights is by no means unique to Nicaragua. A similar development can be observed throughout Latin America.[43] Male UNAG leaders, even those who disagreed with the underlying philosophy of the financial contributions, welcomed them, since they constituted additional resources, and thus leverage, for the organization. In 1987 a Women's Section was established at the national level of UNAG. This body sought to promote the integration of women into the base structures of the farmers' movement and fought to improve the economic and social situation of rural women. The section was headed by Benigna Mendiola, a charismatic peasant leader known for her contribution to the struggle against the Somoza dictatorship. Mendiola represented the Sandinista party in the Nicaraguan legislature and was a member of UNAG's national board of directors. She was also elected to the Sandinista Assembly in 1991. These positions gave her prestige and independence. Despite her potential clout, the Women's Section remained a weak part of the farmers' movement. This situation indicated problems that were institutional in nature. The difficulties facing female producers reflected the low priority the UNAG leadership gave to the needs of female producers, rather than personal deficiencies of the head of the Women's Section.[44] The sexist attitudes of male UNAG leaders, in turn, were suggestive of male-female relations in society at large.

Changes in the legal sphere often did not translate into revised practices at the grassroots level. For example, the 1981 Cooperative Law that established legal equality stated explicitly that women were supposed to be incorporated into cooperatives on the same basis as men. By 1989, however, only 33 percent of all agricultural cooperatives had female members, and women represented only 11 percent of the total membership (see table 6.4 for detailed information). Only the peasant stores showed a higher degree of female participation. Rural women not only suffered from restricted access to the cooperative movement but also were discriminated against as individual beneficiaries of the agrarian reform. When the Sandinistas left power, only 7 percent of individual land titles were held by women.[45] Most of these beneficiaries were mothers or wives of Sandinista soldiers who had been killed in the counterrevolutionary war. In light of the fact that 20 percent of all rural households were headed by women, it is evident that women were not sufficiently incorporated into land distribution programs.

Although about one-third of all agricultural cooperatives had some degree of female participation, in more than half of them not a single leadership position, including secondary ones (e.g., secretary), was held by a woman.[46] By contrast, community organizations involving health and education efforts had female participation levels over 50 percent. Further, in areas traditionally considered to be the domain of women, such as sewing cooperatives, an exclusively female membership existed.[47] This difference in women's participation across organizations was a manifestation of the continued sexual division of labor, which sought to restrict women to their traditional role.[48] Although female participation in the labor force was considerable, it was a reflection of society's needs rather than an indication of equal access to the labor market. For example, women could become part of the agricultural labor force because the demand for male labor could not be satisfied because of wartime mobilization. When they competed with men, however, as in the case of gaining membership in agricultural cooperatives, they tended to be excluded. All kinds of justifications were used to exclude women. Men argued that women could not become members because of the cooperative's insufficient landholdings or their alleged inexperience in farming. The stated economic reasons frequently rationalized ingrained cultural

Table 6.4. Female participation in cooperatives, 1989

Type	No.	% with female members	Women	%	Men	%
CAS	1,221	27.32	3,023	12.3	21,463	87.7
CCS	1,528	52.84	5,437	10.6	46,022	89.4
CSM	112	32.91	191	6.8	2,610	93.2
CT	391	26.83	507	15.2	2,829	84.8
Other	111	25.00	88	8.0	1,016	92.0
Total	3,363	32.98	9,246	11.1	73,940	88.9
TC	191	n.a.	13,500	21.2	50,300	78.8

Sources: UNAG, Autodiagnostico cooperativo, 1989; ECODEPA, Dirección de plan-
ificación, Sept. 1989; MIDINRA, D.G.R.A., 1989.

Note: CAS: Sandinista Production Cooperative.

CT: Work Collective.

CSM: "Dead Fence" Cooperative.

CCS: Credit and Service Cooperative.

TC: Tienda Campesina (Peasant Store).

prejudices. As Mendiola has argued, men refused to accept women as their equals.[49]

In 1989 female members of agricultural cooperatives assessed their situation. More than 3,100 women participated in an evaluation process that allowed female producers to share their experiences and discuss possible solutions. This process culminated in February 1989 in the first national meeting of female producers. At the meeting's conclusion, the women presented a *Plan de Lucha,* which addressed the main problems confronting female producers. Most important, they denounced the fact that agrarian reform titles were issued in the name of the head of the household instead of the couple (thus, when a rural woman was abandoned by her partner she lost access to land). Even when women did hold a land title they suffered frequently from arbitrary actions by government officials, who threw women off their land or subdivided it. Other important issues concerned discriminatory treatment within the cooperatives and a general attitude of male UNAG leaders that did not value the participation of female producers in the organization.[50] Similar problems were addressed during the third national meeting of female producers in September 1991.[51]

On the occasion of UNAG's Second National Congress in April 1992, the leadership, having evaluated the organization's record for the past five years, acknowledged that it had failed to promote female participation in an integral manner. Instead this task was considered the work of the Women's Section.[52] Martha Valle, a member of UNAG's executive committee, maintained that this critical self-evaluation reflected a new thinking by the UNAG leadership vis-à-vis the female membership. For example, in 1992, the national executive committee proposed quotas for elections for leaders at the intermediate level (departments) in order to guarantee female representation. Further, the struggle of female producers received a boost when the national Women's Section obtained financial autonomy because of funding from international donor agencies.[53] These agencies played a crucial role in sponsoring the creation of the peasant stores, one of UNAG's base structures. Female participation in these stores was particularly strong. It had many interesting characteristics and deserves special attention.

The Experience of the Peasant Stores

According to its 1989 statutes, it was a general objective of the ECODEPA project to promote the integration of women.[54] This goal, however, was not part of the original project design and was added only in the late 1980s. Nevertheless, compared to other forms of cooperative association, the peasant stores demonstrated some success in incorporating female producers. In 1989, 191 stores operated throughout Nicaragua, with women constituting 13,500 of the total 63,800 members (see table 6.4). Female participation, at 21 percent, was almost twice as high as the average participation rate in all other cooperative base structures of UNAG (see table 6.4). Following the electoral defeat of the Sandinistas, the number of stores and their membership declined drastically. In 1990 there were 178 stores with 61,392 members. One year later, only 122 stores with 39,555 members had survived. Over the course of this consolidation process, female membership declined from 21 percent in 1989 to 17.5 percent in 1991 (see table 6.5). The data indicate that female participation rates differed considerably from one department to the other.

In general, the relatively high incidence of female membership at the base level in 1989 did not translate into a corresponding share of leadership positions. Few women were represented on the executive committees at the store level. Of the eighty-five peasant stores that participated in a self-evaluation study in the late 1980s, only 24 percent reported

Table 6.5. Development of peasant stores and membership by sex, 1990–1991

	No. of stores		No. of members		1990		1991	
Dept'l store	1990	1991	1990	1991	Men	Women	Men	Women
Estelí	17	6	10,223	3,515	8,138	2,085	2,527	988
Madriz	7	5	2,407	2,627	1,959	448	2,133	494
Nueva Segovia	7	5	961	1,914	760	201	1,432	482
Leon	8	8	3,514	1,548	2,485	1,029	1,320	228
Chinandega	20	18	3,919	3,460	3,047	872	2,934	526
Managua	12	12	2,478	1,615	2,278	200	1,332	283
Masaya	13	11	4,911	3,163	4,670	241	2,812	351
Carazo	—	8	—	3,396	—	—	2,924	472
Rivas	12	6	4,634	4,961	3,763	871	4,230	731
Boaco	10	9	3,123	3,350	2,764	359	2,671	679
Chontales	8	8	3,680	2,877	2,649	1,031	2,618	259
Matagalpa	43	13	7,985	2,510	7,020	965	2,115	395
Jinotega	7	2	7,540	1,504	6,592	948	1,092	412
Raan	6	—	3,127	—	2,451	676	—	—
Raas	5	7	1,469	1,880	937	532	1,410	470
Río San Juan	3	4	1,421	1,235	1,192	229	1,072	163
Total	178	122	61,392	39,555	50,705	10,687	32,622	6,933

Source: Cooperative Enterprise of Agricultural Producers (ECODEPA).

female participation on the executive committee.[55] The department of Jinotega had the worst record. In 1989 there was no female representation on the executive committees of the department's seven stores, despite the fact that 818 female producers had joined the cooperatives, constituting 11 percent of the total membership (see table 6.8). Throughout the ECODEPA project, not a single woman could be found in a leadership position at the regional or national level. The limited number of women in leadership positions raises the question of the characteristics of those who had defied the odds.

According to a study by the Nicaraguan Women's Institute, a low education level did not impede the integration of female producers into the cooperative movement at the level of simple membership.[56] Women in leadership positions, however, had consistently higher education levels than female producers who were merely members.[57] Thus, education levels did play a role in determining women's success in obtaining leadership roles. Interestingly enough, education was not an important factor in the case of male leaders. The members of the executive committees of the departmental ECODEPAs in Matagalpa, Jinotega, Boaco, and Chontales did not have different education levels than the average store member.

Almost without exception, women who were members of executive committees of peasant stores were not only relatively well educated but often held leadership positions in other organizations. Female leaders in the ECODEPA project were also members of the executive committee of other cooperatives or held positions within the UNAG hierarchy. For example, Carina López Herrera, a member of the executive committee of Matagalpa's peasant store, was also president of a credit and service cooperative and a member of UNAG's municipal council. Asunción Flores, another leader, who served on the Camoapa peasant store committee, held a leadership position with the local UNAG office. Thus, women with established leadership credentials enjoyed a definitive advantage in the ECODEPA system. This, however, was also the case for male leaders.

An analysis of the gender distribution throughout the peasant stores, reveals an interesting phenomenon. In the department of Chontales, the nationwide ratio of male-female representation was reversed. In the late 1980s, women represented about 20 percent of the total membership at the national level, whereas the corresponding figure for Chontales was almost 60 percent.

Chontales differed from other areas of the country in two important regards. First, it had a much higher incidence of individual private producers than other departments. And second, beginning in 1985, Chontales became the central theater for counterrevolutionary aggression. As a result, many male agricultural producers withdrew from any kind of participation in the mid-1980s, hiding from both the Sandinista army and the contras. Instead, they sent their wives to join the emerging rural supply network. There appeared to be a general tendency for female membership and participation in store meetings to increase under situations of conflict. This phenomenon could be observed during the politically charged pre-electoral climate of 1989, when female producers participated at a much higher rate in store meetings than corresponded to their numerical strength among the members.

In the wake of the 1990 demobilization of the Nicaraguan resistance, male membership in the peasant stores remained stable, while women left in great numbers. By the end of the year, female membership had decreased to 28 percent, and one year later it was a mere 9 percent (see table 6.6). Whereas the number of women dropped precipitously, male

Table 6.6. Development of peasant stores in Chontales, 1988–1991

Year	Men	%	Women	%	No. of stores
1988	3,061	40.6	4,475	59.4	21
1989	2,489	41.6	3,501	58.4	16
1990	2,649	72.0	1,031	28.0	8
1991	2,619	91.0	259	9.0	8

Source: Cooperative Enterprise of Agricultural Producers (ECODEPA).

membership rates remained stable. It is not clear from the data, however, whether the apparent stability of male membership rates was owing to husbands entering the stores to replace their wives while other males left, or whether the male members of 1989 were identical to those from 1991.

The peasant stores in Matagalpa and Jinotega, which were also located in the war zone, did not differ in their official gender distribution from other stores outside the areas of conflict. This could be explained by the fact that the majority of agricultural producers affiliated with the stores in these two departments were members of production cooperatives and were not individual producers. Production cooperatives joined the stores as a collective.[58] Even if men chose to leave active participation in the stores to the female membership, the cooperative as a whole with all its members remained affiliated with the store. Therefore, membership statistics were not affected by decreased male participation. My observation of store meetings at the end of 1989 indicated, however, that female participation in meetings held in Matagalpa and Jinotega was indeed stronger than one would have expected based on official membership numbers. Thus, all available evidence shows that, under conditions of political conflict, women tended to be more active in the stores than men.

Even after the change in government, the peasant stores continued to be affected by rural violence. As a result, the departments of Matagalpa and Jinotega experienced a drastic decline in the number of stores and their membership from 1990 to 1991 (see tables 6.7 and 6.8). The male-female distribution remained fairly stable in Matagalpa, while women's participation increased somewhat in Jinotega. Because of the overall dramatic decline of the peasant stores in the two departments—thirty-five out of fifty stores closed—it is difficult to interpret the meaning of female participation rates in 1991.

Apart from the Chontales phenomenon, women were highly visible in one other role. They constituted the overwhelming majority of the store

Table 6.7. Development of peasant stores in Matagalpa, 1988–1991

Year	Men	%	Women	%	No. of stores
1988	7,000[a]	87.5	1,000[a]	12.5	48
1989	6,865	87.6	970	12.4	47
1990	7,020	87.9	965	12.1	43
1991	2,115	84.3	395	15.7	13

Source: Cooperative Enterprise of Agricultural Producers (ECODEPA).
[a]Figures for 1988 are rounded off to the nearest thousand.

Table 6.8. Development of peasant stores in Jinotega, 1988–1991

Year	Men	%	Women	%	No. of stores
1988	7,000[a]	87.5	1,000[a]	12.5	10
1989	6,568	88.9	818	11.1	7
1990	6,592	87.4	948	12.6	7
1991	1,092	72.6	412	27.4	2

Source: Cooperative Enterprise of Agricultural Producers (ECODEPA).
[a]Figures for 1988 are rounded off to the nearest thousand.

administrators. This position did not entail considerable influence over the affairs of the stores, since the executive committee was in charge of all important decisions. The administrators were generally young females of peasant background who received low salaries. Further, their administrative duties corresponded to the traditional division of labor prevailing in the rural sector. Nevertheless, participation in this function gave women some control over the operation of the stores, since the administrator proposed to the executive committee the store's purchasing plans.[59] This presented an important opportunity for the needs of female producers to be taken into consideration. Also, it integrated these store employees into the public sphere. Their presence in the store, in turn, facilitated a social climate that female producers felt comfortable with. Unfortunately, women's participation in an administrative capacity was limited to the store level. Among the department and national management, whose decisions greatly affected the lives of female producers, no women were to be found.

The quality of female participation in the peasant stores was not affected by the change in government. Female producers continued to experience the same difficulties. Although active as members, they played hardly any role in the peasant stores' management. Participation in executive positions, albeit limited, was basically a phenomenon at the store level. In 1992, less than 1 percent of the department leaders were female, and not a single woman could be found at the national level.

Conclusion

The struggle for women's emancipation continued with the revolutionary government out of power. Although the fight for women's rights entered a new, difficult stage, few observers maintained that the feminist agenda was dead. On the contrary, preliminary evidence indicated that women were becoming more militant in fighting for their emancipation. AMNLAE, deprived of funding from the Sandinista party, was no longer the main organizational expression of the women's movement. Several AMNLAE officials abandoned the Sandinista organization and assumed leading roles in an emerging autonomous women's movement. In their view, the revolutionary movement in Nicaragua was *machista* and opposed a feminist agenda that challenged male privileges.[60] In March 1992, 800 Nicaraguan women met to discuss the status of women's emancipation. They represented diverse social and political sectors. Azucena Ferrey, a conservative member of the National Assembly, participated, together with Dora María Téllez, a recognized Sandinista leader. In light of AMNLAE's dependent relations with the FSLN, the women rejected the creation of any formal structures in the hope that this would facilitate their independence from both the new government and the Sandinista party.[61] Instead, they decided to proceed with a series of informal "encounters."

The Chamorro government could not change the constitutional provisions of 1987, which protected important rights.[62] Nevertheless, ATC organizers maintained that many constitutional provisions—the one guaranteeing maternity benefits, for example—became meaningless. Employers ignored them on a regular basis, since they were frequently not enforced by the courts. Thus, women were facing serious difficulties under the new government. A concerted attempt was under way to restore and maintain traditional gender relations. The struggle in the ideological sphere was particularly visible in the educational system: new textbooks, financed by USAID, "present images and discussions of correct gender and generational relations."[63] The removal of material on sex education was part of this effort.[64]

At the economic level, women suffered disproportionately from the introduction of neoliberal economic policies. In fact, it has been argued that it is the "feminization of poverty" that allows the successful introduction of these programs.[65] Structural adjustment policies resulted in high unemployment (over 50 percent officially) and restricted social services. The survival of poor households demanded that "women seek new sources of income, stretch household budgets, and take úp the slack of social services that are no longer available."[66] In light of these economic difficulties it is not surprising that female participation in grassroots movements declined. Women complained that these movements lacked the capacity to address their needs. Also, they did not have the time for active participation, and their husbands strongly discouraged them from joining.[67]

The difficulties encountered by rural women were indicative of the general status of women's emancipation in Nicaragua. Although women's rights were advanced during the period of revolutionary rule, the most important changes were confined to the legal sphere. The significant formal gains frequently did not translate into changed practices at the grassroots level. The Sandinista legacy was strongest in the sphere of practical gender interests. Women benefited from improved access to education, health care, and land. Strategic gender interests, i.e., a feminist agenda, were not vigorously pursued by a revolutionary government under attack, whose policy goal of national unity led to the subordination of the struggle for women's rights. Most analysts agree that little was accomplished in the private (domestic) sphere, where the traditional division of labor remained intact. Ironically, as women's progress in the area of practical gender interests was being eroded under the Chamorro government, the women's movement, freed from the fetters imposed by the Sandinista party in the name of "the survival of the revolution," became more successful in addressing strategic gender interests.

Chapter 7

Conclusion: The Sandinista Legacy

[T]he big victor, the big winner of these elections is the Sandinista Front, which brought democracy to Nicaragua. Without the Sandinista Front the Nicaraguan people would never have dreamed of elections such as those which occurred on February 25, 1990.[1]

Many observers have argued that the Nicaraguan revolution failed, since the Sandinista Front was voted out of power. I, on the other hand, would maintain the opposite. The fact that the revolutionary regime was prepared to accept the verdict of the people in an electoral process legitimizes the Sandinista project. Adam Przeworski has emphasized that "the central question concerning transitions is whether they lead to consolidated democracy, that is, a system in which the politically relevant forces subject their interests to the uncertain interplay of democratic institutions and comply with the outcomes of the democratic process. Democracy is consolidated when most conflicts are processed through democratic institutions, when nobody can control the outcomes ex post and the results are not predetermined ex ante, they matter within some predictable limits, and they evoke the compliance of the relevant political forces."[2] By this standard, the change in government from the Sandinistas to Violeta Chamorro constituted a key event in the consolidation of democracy in Nicaragua. Without doubt, the credit for institutionalizing electoral democracy in Nicaragua belongs to the Sandinistas. From a traditional Western perspective, which focuses on political democracy, the Sandinista experiment has to be considered successful. Yet the revolutionary project also has to be evaluated on its own terms. The Sandinistas came to power with the promise to establish social and economic democracy. It was their pronounced goal to fundamentally change the prevailing relations of production in benefit of the poor majority. Did the revolution fulfill its promise to the Nicaraguan people?

During its eleven years in power, the Sandinista government established an impressive record, benefiting the worker and peasant classes. These achievements were recognized internationally. For example, UNESCO honored the 1980 literacy campaign with a prize for the best campaign ever conducted, and the World Health Organization chose to study Nicaragua as a model country for primary health care. Further, there was strong consensus that the agrarian reform had fundamentally changed the relations of production in the Nicaraguan countryside. Thus, the socioeconomic conditions for the popular classes did improve under Sandinista governance. By 1990, however, progress had been halted and in many instances reversed. Many factors, foremost the U.S.-sponsored military aggression and economic boycott, contributed to this situation.

In the political sphere, the Sandinista attempt to give the rural proletariat and the small and medium farmers a voice in the political system was largely successful. Grassroots participation was an effective mechanism for these previously marginalized sectors to gain control over their lives. As I demonstrated, however, relations between the grassroots movements and the Sandinista Front were characterized by the inherent contradiction of a vanguard seeking to strengthen participatory democracy. Dora María Téllez, an eminent leader of the revolutionary movement, affirmed in 1991 that FSLN had been part of the problem rather than the solution: "The mass organizations were too 'party line,' the largest ones did not emerge from the base but were built from the top down. . . . It's true that the people were very anxious to have their own organizations, but instead of building them from the ground up, a whole contingent of party cadre was sent out to form them."[3] Tomás Borge also recognized that relations between the party and the mass organizations were characterized by a tradition of verticalism that "asphyxiate[d] criticism."[4] The Sandinista leadership addressed this problem in the new party program, approved by the 1991 Sandinista Congress. The program expressly "establishes respect for the autonomy of the mass organizations."[5] The evolution of the rural grassroots movements demonstrates that it was indeed the lack of internal democracy and autonomy from the party that limited their development.

Under the Sandinistas, UNAG's militancy in representing the interests of the agricultural producers was a key factor in establishing the farmers' movement as the most important rural grassroots organization in Nicaragua. The strength of UNAG attracted agricultural producers, regardless of their ideological views. The organization's pragmatism allowed it to adjust successfully to the new rules of the game as they emerged under Chamorro. For example, UNAG came to play a key role in the reintegration into society of members of the Nicaraguan resistance.[6] The contras, mostly of peasant origin, were accepted into UNAG with no questions asked. At the grassroots level one did not always find support for the leadership's attempts at reconciliation. In general, however, Sandinista and contra supporters recognized that they had something fundamental in common: they were the primary victims of the conflict that ravaged the country during the 1980s. This insight helped the Nicaraguan peasantry to overcome the legacy of the fratricidal war. It also constituted the foundation for emerging alliances across ideological boundaries. The former enemies joined forces to confront the ruling elites.

It is encouraging that the Sandinista party itself embarked on a process of democratization. In the historic 1991 National Congress, the members of the Sandinista Assembly and the National Directorate were, for the first time, elected in a secret ballot by 581 delegates, who represented all departments of the country. Although the National Directorate elections were controversial since current and proposed future members ran on a single unopposed slate[7] (thus avoiding the possibility that any individual Sandinista leader could be voted out), the process ushered in a new era of openness and accountability. During the Congress, Daniel Núñez and Edgardo García, the leaders of UNAG and ATC, were reelected to the Sandinista Assembly. Whereas almost two-thirds of the former assembly members were voted out, Núñez and García were among the top ten vote-getters. Núñez received the most votes (508 out of 581) and García was supported by 492 delegates.[8] This solid mandate by the party establishment was a mixed blessing. On the one hand, it should strengthen their position in the effort to democratize fully their respective organizations over the anticipated resistance of some members of the Sandinista hierarchy. On the other hand, there is the possibility that farmers and agricultural workers will reject leaders who are that closely identified with the party.

When comparing the UNAG and ATC records under the Sandinistas, it is essential to evaluate their performances within the context of Nicaragua's political economy. The two organizations served constituents with different, sometimes conflicting, class interests and therefore fulfilled distinct functions. ATC, representing the rural proletariat, was primarily a guarantor of popular hegemony, whereas UNAG also constituted the embodiment of national unity. The fortune of both movements was closely linked to the dialectic of the revolutionary project. ATC blossomed during 1979–1980 with the policy of popular hegemony in full force and broke apart in 1981 over the difficult requirements of national unity. UNAG seemed better prepared to serve the objectives of national unity and became a main factor in the successful integration of sectors of the agrarian bourgeoisie into the revolutionary project. Yet the farmers' movement proved in turn incapable of simultaneously focusing on the needs of the marginalized peasant producers, until it redefined its policies in 1986 and sought a new balance in serving its complex social base. The redirection of UNAG's policies coincided—not accidentally—with the renewed emphasis of the Sandinista government to meet the needs of the poor peasantry. Further, the success of programs such as the agrarian reform and the consolidation of the state sector caused problems for ATC, whereas the same policies benefited the development of UNAG. Therefore, the two organizations' strengths and weaknesses were frequently the reflection of policy decisions taken by the government.

The different relations of the two movements with regard to the revolutionary authorities were also functions of their roles during the revolution. ATC, serving the interests of a core support group of the Sandinista project, was successful in raising the consciousness of the rural proletariat and defended the overall goals of the revolution. Although the policies of the ATC leadership at times resulted in discontent among its social base, they strengthened the revolutionary project. UNAG represented a complex class alliance and chose another path. Strongly supportive of the Sandinista government, the movement focused on the revitalization of the productive sector, an absolute necessity for the economic recovery of the country. Since this effort was carried out under the policy of national unity, UNAG needed to assume a more independent profile. Thus, both grassroots movements, each in its own way, contributed to the evolution of a new, revolutionary society. UNAG was without doubt the most effective and significant grassroots movement in the countryside, while the ATC recovered in the late 1980s from its earlier decline. The future development of the two organizations depends on their militancy, as well

as on the willingness of the FSLN and the Chamorro government to provide space for grassroots movements.

The relations of production in the Nicaraguan countryside were indeed restructured during the revolutionary period. The peasant stores
constituted one of the most interesting experiments in this transformation. The stores demonstrated the viability of a democratic, participatory
development strategy. Particularly during the first years of the project, a
large sector of the farming community benefited economically. Most significantly, the stores strengthened grassroots democracy, although their
development suffered from the top-down fashion in which they were initiated. Further, the evolution of the peasant stores was marked by the difficulties of implementing such an ambitious project under conditions of
war. Sadly enough, by 1992 the ECODEPA project had been completely
restructured. Those that had warned early on of the dangers inherent in
neglecting internal democracy and organizational autonomy were
proven right. Economic considerations were given precedence over questions of democratic structure and control. Once again the poor peasants
were relegated to being observers in the economic game controlled by
large and medium producers.

The struggle for women's emancipation was limited by the FSLN's
decision to subordinate the fight for women's rights to other priorities of
the revolution. Women benefited most as members of the peasant and
worker classes, that is, in the area of practical gender interests. Some fem-
inists have argued that the revolutionary government's failure to address
fully women's issues contributed to its defeat. Margaret Randall, who for
many years experienced the reality of socialist revolution firsthand,
makes this point in a broader context: "I now wonder if socialism's failure to make room for a feminist agenda—indeed, to embrace that agenda
as it indigenously surfaces in each history and culture—is one of the reasons why socialism as a system could not survive."[9] Whereas the revolutionary government can be criticized for not having advocated strategic
gender issues more forcefully, one needs to recognize the constraints
under which it operated. One can make an argument that the political
cost of pursuing the essence of any feminist agenda—for example, reproductive freedom—would have been great indeed. Such an agenda was
simply not supported by the majority of Nicaraguan citizens. Carlos
Vilas affirmed that the "struggle against gender subordination and the
multiple expressions of sexism as a specific form of social oppression still
occupies a smaller space, mainly urban and professional women."[10]

Thus, the Sandinista leadership's decision to put the fight for women's rights on the back burner was an easy one. The pursuit of a feminist agenda could be dismissed as violating the national unity policy.

During the 1980s, important sectors of the bourgeoisie tried to sabotage the Sandinista revolution and rejected all efforts by the revolutionary authorities to reach accommodation. Jeffery Paige has argued that "the economic and political power of the agrarian elite [which] had been a significant factor in the success of the revolutionary coalition . . . also exert[ed] a decisive influence on the failure of the Sandinista experiment."[11] The intransigence of the agrarian bourgeoisie made the national unity policy a precarious undertaking.

Once in power, the Chamorro government faced a similar challenge. The broad coalition that had defeated the Sandinistas in the 1990 elections soon fell apart under mutual recriminations. Ironically, the result was a pact between the new government and the Sandinistas, which constituted in essence a national unity policy. Under its terms, the Sandinista Front accepted the role of loyal opposition, while Chamorro gave security guarantees (Sandinista control of the armed forces) and promised to protect important achievements of the revolutionary period, such as the agrarian reform. As a highly visible manifestation of this pact, Chamorro kept Humberto Ortega as head of the Nicaraguan military. In fact, Chamorro had little choice, since the armed forces were not fully under civilian control. According to a law passed by the National Assembly in the weeks leading up to the 1990 elections, the military enjoyed autonomy from civilian control. For example, the army chief of staff was not nominated by the civilian authorities but by a military council.[12] The Sandinistas were justified in their security concerns, considering the highly charged political climate of Nicaragua, which was characterized by military challenges from demobilized contra forces and former Sandinista army and police personnel. Nevertheless, this situation represented a potential threat to the future of Nicaraguan democracy.

Although the Chamorro government controlled an absolute majority in the Nicaraguan legislature, it fell short of the 60 percent of votes needed to implement partial changes in the constitution. This situation, to some measure, protected the social and political framework instituted over eleven years of Sandinista rule. Thus, any fundamental restructuring of Nicaragua's political system required the votes of Sandinista legislators. Even more significant, Sandinista cooperation was essential in light of the serious threat that right-wing sectors within the new government posed to its survival. Chamorro faced a challenge from reactionary forces led by a triumvirate, consisting of Virgilio Godoy, her own vice-president; Arnoldo Aleman, the mayor of Managua; and Alfredo César, the National Assembly's president until 1993. In their view, the president and her closest advisors were traitors, since they were not willing to restore the status quo ante and eliminate the Sandinistas from Nicaragua's social, economic, and political scene. Their position was supported by conservative forces in the United States, led by senator Jesse Helms. This challenge from the right forced the new government to seek Sandinista support in order to remain in power. Therefore, the FSLN entered the postrevolutionary phase in a position of considerable influence. The Chamorro regime could effectively govern only if the Sandinistas would be prepared to play the role of loyal opposition.

The Sandinista Front early on declared its willingness to cooperate with the new government, albeit within clearly defined boundaries. Daniel Ortega expressed the Sandinista Front's support for a "national project" in a speech to the July 1991 National Congress of the FSLN: "We defend a national project that unites Nicaraguans in moving the country forward and better distributing its wealth, and we cannot accept one that seeks stability at the expense of impoverishing the great majority and enriching a minority."[13] Unfortunately, the FSLN proved to be an ineffective advocate of the poor majority's rights. During the first years of the Chamorro government, the popular classes suffered greatly under the austerity policies that were implemented. Nevertheless, the Sandinistas and Chamorro took a step toward cogovernment in January 1993 when the thirty-nine Sandinista delegates joined forces with the nine members of the Center Group (moderate Chamorro supporters) to wrest control from the right, which had dominated the legislature up to this point.[14] The new alliance was based on mutual need. Both sides had misgivings but considered the alternative of a takeover by the extreme right unacceptable.

The revolutionary government was not the only one to lose power at the end of the 1980s because it no longer enjoyed the support of the people it claimed to represent. From Ethiopia to Eastern Europe and the Soviet Union, regimes crumbled under the weight of popular dissent. In October 1991 Daniel Ortega emphasized a central reason for the revolutionary government's February 1990 electoral defeat. He affirmed: "It's not true that [FSLN] lost the peasants; we never had them."[15] Despite its efforts to transform the socioeconomic conditions in the Nicaraguan countryside, the Sandinista movement lost the struggle for "the hearts and minds" of the peasantry. Opposition to the revolution ranged from everyday forms of resistance to peasant participation in the counterrevolutionary war. The agrarian bourgeoisie engaged in capital flight and other forms of "decapitalization," agricultural workers took their "historic vacation," and small farmers decreased production.

This is, however, only half the picture. Thousands of farmers and agricultural workers, organized in UNAG and ATC, would vehemently disagree with Ortega's statement. They strongly supported the Sandinista revolution for most of the 1980s. Yet even their loyalty eventually eroded under the combined weight of counterrevolutionary aggression, a faltering economy, and flawed policies instituted by a government that became increasingly detached from the people. The peasantry's support will be a key factor if the Sandinistas are to return to power in the 1996 elections. The FSLN faces a difficult time ahead. Presently, "Sandinismo has not regained its status as a hegemonic force, and a large part of the peasantry remains disaffiliated from political society."[16]

The Sandinistas' loss at the polls was a blessing in disguise. After eleven years in power, the revolutionary movement needed time to rejuvenate itself and return to its popular roots. So far, the postrevolutionary period has seen a number of interesting developments: (1) the beginning democratization of the Sandinista party; (2) increased autonomy and the institutionalization of formal democratic procedures in the case of the grassroots organizations; and, most surprisingly, (3) the emergence of truly socialist relations of production, in the form of worker-controlled enterprises on former state farms.

In my view, the most important criticism of the Sandinista revolution comes from the left. Critics of the Nicaraguan experiment have argued that the innovative model of Sandinista democracy had been stripped of its participatory content, leaving it a traditional Western-style political system. These voices do have a point. The Sandinistas were ultimately more successful in institutionalizing liberal constitutionalism than fostering effective grassroots participation. Sandinista democracy evolved from a system with an emphasis on economic justice and direct democracy, based on grassroots participation, to one favoring indirect representative democracy.[17]

One cannot judge the Sandinista record without emphasizing the destructive role played by the U.S. government. Nicaragua is a textbook case of U.S. aggression, unleashed because the Reagan and Bush administrations considered U.S. hegemony in the "backyard" as threatened by the Sandinista democratic vision. We will never know how the Sandinista experiment would have evolved had the country enjoyed peace. Whereas history will judge the events of the 1980s, the Nicaraguan people base their views on today's predicament. Nicaragua competes currently with Haiti for the position of poorest country in the hemisphere. Living standards have fallen to the level of the 1930s, and economic deprivation has reached unprecedented heights. Indeed, with its dream of social justice shattered, the poor majority has paid an exceedingly high price for the consolidation of formal democracy.

Methodological Appendix _____

The methodology employed in this study is based on a participant-observer strategy. The difficulties in conducting research in a revolutionary society under conditions of civil strife did not permit some of the more standard methods of data collection. Because of conflicting views and data, every effort was made to use multiple data sources in order to overcome problems of reliability. In order to collect information systematically, I conducted more than eighty formal, in-depth interviews and approximately one hundred open-ended interviews.

I chose respondents from among those in leadership positions in the Sandinista and Chamorro governments, the Sandinista party, the Nicaraguan legislature, the Marxist-Leninist party, the Superior Council for Private Enterprise, and the grassroots movements. I interviewed two members of the National Directorate of the Sandinista Front, Nicaragua's vice-president, the president, the third secretary and several members of the legislature, the vice-presidents of MAP-ML and COSEP, and several other high-ranking officials. I analyzed the role of the rural mass organizations by interviewing the presidents of the Association of Rural Workers, the National Union of Farmers and Ranchers, and the Union of Nicaraguan Agricultural Producers. In addition, I conducted formal interviews with officials at all organizational levels and approximately one hundred open-ended interviews with rural workers and agricultural producers.

Apart from the above interviews, the information used in this study came from the following sources:

1. Published information ranging from academic studies and government documents to the work of nongovernmental institutions

such as the Nicaraguan Institute for Economic and Social Research (INIES), the United Nations Economic Commission for Latin America (ECLA), and the Inter-American Development Bank (I-ADB).

2. Internal documents and reports of the Association of Rural Workers, the National Union of Farmers and Ranchers, and the Union of Nicaraguan Agricultural Producers.

3. Unpublished government documents from the Ministry of Agriculture and Agrarian Reform, the Center for the Study of the Agrarian Reform, the Ministry of Planning, the Ministry of Health, and the Ministry of Education.

4. A systematic clipping and content analysis of all coverage of the Sandinista grassroots organizations in the newspapers *Barricada, El Nuevo Diario,* and *La Prensa* for the full research period. For the period up to 1984, the clipping files of the Central American Historical Institute were consulted.

5. Open-ended interviews and conversations with foreign diplomats and officials of nongovernmental agencies.

I chose to focus on the rural mass organizations because of the neglect and repression the Nicaraguan peasantry has traditionally suffered from the national elite. I intended for my analysis to determine the extent to which the Sandinista Front has been successful in redistributing economic and political power to the peasantry. For each of the two organizations, I arranged interviews with the national leadership. Although I visited all of Nicaragua's six regions and two of the three special zones of the Atlantic coast, my data collection was focused on three areas: region I (Estelí), region V (Boaco and Chontales), and region VI (Matagalpa and Jinotega). I selected these regions because the majority of UNAG's members came from this part of the country and because of the strong representation of local ATC chapters. The three regions were representative of Nicaragua's rural sector. All important rural groups could be found in the area, and agricultural production ranged from Nicaragua's major crops to cattle farming. Also, this part of the country, bordering on Honduras, experienced substantial counterrevolutionary activity, which made it possible to study the grassroots movements under warlike conditions.

By traveling with members of the regional offices to base meetings, I observed the work of the two organizations. On these occasions I interviewed rural workers, agricultural producers, and attending government officials. The base meetings served to provide information on controversial issues, which I then investigated. In order to avoid being identified with the two organizations in the eyes of the peasantry, I frequently carried out field research without logistical support from the Sandinista grassroots movements. Further, interviews with representatives of the rural bourgeoisie, such as the Union of Nicaraguan Agricultural Producers, helped me to obtain a balanced view.

In the case of chapter 5, field research was limited to the departments of Matagalpa and Jinotega in region VI, as well as Boaco and Chontales in region V. These four departments represented 81 of a total of 191 peasant stores in 1989 (42 percent) with 26,100 of the 64,000 members nationwide. The two regions, considered priority areas under the ECODEPA project because of their location in the war zone, had been chosen for the initiation of the rural supply network. Whereas the membership composition of the stores in region V was characterized by a predominance of medium to large private cattle ranchers, region VI showed a high incidence of cooperatives engaged in coffee farming. Also, the agrarian reform was more extensive in region VI than in region V. The general characteristics of the stores in the two regions made them representative of Nicaragua's rural sector. Therefore, one can reasonably assume that the development of the ECODEPA project in these regions reflected the project's success throughout Nicaragua. It is significant to point out, however, that regions V and VI were likely to show higher levels of development than the rest of the country because the stores in those regions were the first to be established and had priority in the project's resource allocation. Finally, they differed from zones of Nicaragua that had not been affected by the war.

Within the two regions, I attempted to obtain a representative sample of stores, since time constraints did not allow the study of all eighty-one stores. Store selection was based on size, age, rural-urban distribution, and level of relative success. In order to obtain a complete picture of the situation in at least one department, I included all stores in the department of Boaco in the study. Overall, I visited a total of twenty stores and interviewed twenty-six store coordinators. In accordance with the focus of the study on the quality of grassroots participation and the formal organization of the project, I observed fourteen general assembly and executive committee meetings at the base level. At the departmental level,

I attended the monthly meetings of the executive committees in all four departments. In the case of Boaco and Chontales, I observed several such reunions, and in the case of Jinotega, I attended a meeting of the departmental general assembly. At the national level, I observed a meeting of the managers of the fifteen departmental ECODEPAs and interviewed the national leadership.

Notes

Preface

1. Gould, *To Lead as Equals*, 16.
2. Sherman, *Foundations of Radical Political Economy*, ix.
3. Democracy is defined here simply as "a system in which parties lose elections." See Przeworski, *Democracy and the Market*, 10.
4. For discussions of the policies of popular hegemony and national unity, see Vilas, *Sandinista Revolution*, and Harris and Vilas, *Nicaragua*.

Chapter 1. The Political Economy of Transition

1. Several important studies have examined the question of transition. See O'Donnell, Schmitter, and Whitehead, *Transitions from Authoritarian Rule*; Fagen, Deere, and Coraggio, *Transition and Development*; Malloy and Seligson, *Authoritarians and Democrats*; Eckstein, *Back from the Future*; Vilas, *Transición desde el subdesarrollo*; Harnecker, *Reflexiones acerca del problema de la transición al socialismo*; and Brown, *Surge to Freedom*.
2. For an excellent study that discusses regime transitions in Latin America and Eastern Europe, see Przeworski, *Democracy and the Market*.
3. Harnecker, *Reflexiones acerca del problema de la transición al socialismo*, 77.
4. Marx, "Critique of the Gotha Program," in Tucker, *Marx-Engels Reader*, 529. Emphasis in original.
5. Vilas, *Transición desde el subdesarrollo*, 50.
6. Núñez Soto, *Transición y lucha de clases en Nicaragua*, 11.
7. Habermas, *Communication and the Evolution of Society*, 150.
8. Sherman, *Foundations of Radical Political Economy*, 42.
9. Laclau and Mouffe, *Hegemony and Socialist Struggle*, 105. Although the

authors discuss the notion of articulation in a different context, their definition is useful for this discussion.

10. Chilcote, *Theories of Development and Underdevelopment,* 126.

11. Sherman, *Foundations of Radical Political Economy,* 80, 260.

12. Fonseca, quoted in Lozano, *De Sandino al triunfo de la revolución,* 58.

13. A number of good studies have examined Nicaraguan-U.S. relations during the 1980s. See, for example, Walker, *Reagan versus the Sandinistas;* Kornbluh, *Nicaragua;* and Pastor, *Condemned to Repetition.*

14. Laclau, "Feudalism and Capitalism in Latin America," 182.

15. See Enríquez, *Harvesting Change.*

16. Gramsci, *Selections from the Prison Notebooks,* 161.

17. Chilcote, *Theories of Development and Underdevelopment,* 126.

18. Poulantzas, *State-Power Socialism.*

19. See Hoffman, *Gramscian Challenge,* for a discussion of the politics of consent in Marxism.

20. Boggs, *Two Revolutions,* 159.

21. Laclau and Mouffe, *Hegemony and Socialist Struggle,* 69. Emphasis in original.

22. Gramsci, *Selections from the Prison Notebooks,* 57; see footnote 5 for this passage.

23. Vilas, *Transición desde el subdesarrollo,* 67. Emphasis in original.

24. Eckstein, *Power and Popular Protest,* 15–16.

25. Laclau and Mouffe, *Hegemony and Socialist Struggle,* 56.

26. Coraggio, "Economics and Politics in the Transition to Socialism," 160.

27. Ibid.

28. See Scott, *Moral Economy of the Peasant;* Migdal, *Peasants, Politics and Revolution;* Popkin, *Rational Peasant;* Paige, *Agrarian Revolution;* and Wolf, *Peasant Wars of the Twentieth Century.*

29. Goodwin and Skocpol, "Explaining Revolutions," 491.

30. Wickham-Crowley, *Guerrillas and Revolution in Latin America,* 299.

31. Goodwin and Skocpol, "Explaining Revolutions," 503.

32. Núñez Soto, *Transición y lucha de clases en Nicaragua,* 15.

33. Ibid., 80.

34. Williams, "Dual Transitions from Authoritarian Rule," 171.

Chapter 2. The Sandinista Hegemonic Vision: Democracy and Revolution

1. Stepan, "Paths toward Redemocratization," 84.

2. *Barricada,* July 20, 1988.

3. One of the first discussions of the policies of popular hegemony and national unity can be found in Vilas, *Sandinista Revolution.* See also Harris and Vilas, *Nicaragua.* This section is informed by their analysis.

4. Harris and Vilas, *Nicaragua,* 4.

5. Vilas, *Sandinista Revolution*, 21.

6. Invernizzi, Pisani, and Ceberio, *Sandinistas*, 50.

7. Guevara, *Guerrilla Warfare*.

8. Ruchwarger, *People in Power*, 19.

9. Harnecker, *Nicaragua*, 84–88.

10. Invernizzi et al., *Sandinistas*, 52–53.

11. Quoted in Marcus, *Sandinistas Speak*, 63. Emphasis added.

12. González Casanova, *El poder al pueblo*, 44. See also FSLN, *Del FSLN a los pueblos del mundo*.

13. Booth, *End and the Beginning*, 146.

14. For an excellent discussion of the ideological roots of the Sandinista movement, see Hodges, *Intellectual Foundations of the Nicaraguan Revolution*.

15. Because the last official census was conducted in 1971, there is considerable debate on the country's class structure. See Vilas, *Sandinista Revolution*, 60–69; Deere and Marchetti, "Worker-Peasant Alliance," 41–43; Ruchwarger, *People in Power*, 246; and Porras, "El movimiento cooperativo en Nicaragua," 14–15.

16. Deere and Marchetti, "Worker-Peasant Alliance," 42.

17. Harsmar, "Centralamerikanska Demokratiuppfattningar," 4.

18. Barber, *Strong Democracy*, xi.

19. Herman and Brodhead, *Demonstration Elections*.

20. Harris and Vilas, *Nicaragua*, 231.

21. Ibid.

22. Quoted in Bruce, *Sandinistas Speak*, 130.

23. I am indebted to Michael Fruehling, first secretary of the Swedish embassy in Nicaragua during the mid-1980s, for sharing his views on this subject. He also helped me to clarify my thoughts on the central issue of mass participation versus mobilization.

24. Harsmar, "Centralamerikanska Demokratiuppfattningar," 26.

25. Quoted in Weber, *Nicaragua*, 145.

26. Humberto Ortega, quoted in Black, *Triumph of the People*, 256. Emphasis in original.

27. For a discussion of the role of the bourgeoisie during the period of the consolidation of Sandinista power, see Gilbert, *Sandinistas*, chapter 5.

28. Booth, *End and Beginning*, 186.

29. Quoted in Vilas, *Sandinista Revolution*, 45.

30. FSLN, "Declaración del FSLN sobre la democracia." See the translation of this text in Black, *Triumph of the People*, 255–56.

31. The section on formal state power draws on Black, *Triumph of the People*, 223–63; Booth, *End and Beginning*, 185–202; and Gilbert, *Sandinistas*, 108–14.

32. Gilbert, *Sandinistas*, 42.

33. Booth, *End and Beginning*, 187.

34. Ibid., 188.

35. Ibid., 191.

36. Black, *Triumph of the People,* 245.

37. Ibid.

38. This section on the grassroots movements is based on interviews with officials of these movements and draws on two chapters by Serra, "Sandinista Mass Organizations," 95–113; and "Grass-Roots Organizations," 65–89.

39. Serra, "Grass-Roots Organizations," 76.

40. Ruchwarger, *People in Power,* 246.

41. Serra, "Grass-Roots Organizations," 66.

42. For a discussion of the evolution of the rural grassroots movements, see chapters 3 and 4.

43. AMNLAE, *Plan de Lucha;* see chapter 6.

44. Serra, "Grass-Roots Organizations," 66.

45. Carlos Núñez, *El papel de las organizaciones de masas en el proceso revolucionario,* 20–21.

46. FSLN, "Declaración del FSLN sobre la democracia."

47. Pérez-Stable, "Pluralism and Popular Power," 170.

48. Walker, *Nicaragua,* 27.

49. Lowy, "La democracia no es un lujo," 12.

50. Coraggio, *Nicaragua,* 75.

51. See interview with Comandante Bayardo Arce in Invernizzi et al., *Sandinistas,* 63–78.

52. Serra, "Grass-Roots Organizations," 76.

53. Invernizzi et al., *Sandinistas,* 69.

54. Aguilar et al., "Orígenes y situación actual de los CDS."

55. Coraggio, *Nicaragua,* 78.

56. Ibid., 19.

57. Lozano, *De Sandino al triunfo de la revolución,* 322.

58. See Arce, "Secret Speech before the Nicaraguan Socialist Party."

59. "Ley Electoral," 69–91.

60. CAHI, "Ante el avance del proceso electoral," 5a.

61. Ibid.

62. Harris and Vilas, *Nicaragua,* 231. See also LASA, "Report of the Latin American Studies Delegation."

63. CAHI, "Ante el avance del proceso electoral," 6a.

64. Booth, *End and Beginning,* 216.

65. Gilbert, *Sandinistas,* 122.

66. Booth, *End and Beginning,* 217.

67. LASA, "Report of the LASA Delegation to Observe the Nicaragua General Election."

68. I am grateful to José Luís Coraggio for pointing this out.

69. Carlos Núñez, "Un parlamento nuevo que sea reflejo del poder del pueblo."

70. Harnecker, *Cuba,* 376.

71. Quoted in Pérez-Stable, "Pluralism and Popular Power," 169.

72. Luxemburg, *Russian Revolution and Leninism or Marxism?*

73. The analysis of the relationship between the Sandinista government and the bourgeoisie draws on Gilbert, *Sandinistas,* 105–27.

74. Ibid., 109.

75. Ibid., 122.

76. Black, *Triumph of the People,* 64.

77. *Constitución política de Nicaragua,* 33.

78. Quoted in Vilas, *Sandinista Revolution,* 157.

79. Gilbert, *Sandinistas,* 111–12.

80. Ruchwarger, *People in Power,* 261.

81. Ibid., 265.

82. Gilbert, *Sandinistas,* 113.

83. Gilbert, "Bourgeoisie," 174; The discussion of this incident is based on the account in Gilbert, COSEP documents, and interviews with COSEP leaders.

84. COSEP, "Carta a Daniel Ortega."

85. Ibid.

86. Gilbert, "Bourgeoisie," 174.

87. CAHI, "Breakthrough for Peace," 7.

88. Ibid.

89. Black, *Triumph of the People,* 335; this section is also based on discussions with Marvin Ortega.

90. FSLN, "Analysis de la coyuntura y tareas de la revolución popular sandinista," 231.

91. *Barricada,* July 20, 1988.

92. Laclau and Mouffe, *Hegemony and Socialist Struggle,* 71.

93. For an analysis of this problem, see Coleman, et al., "Urban Informal Economy in Nicaragua."

94. Bayardo Arce in Invernizzi et al., *Sandinistas,* 63–78.

95. Invernizzi et al., *Sandinistas,* 66; for an excellent discussion of the structure of the Sandinista party, see Gilbert, *Sandinistas,* 41–58.

96. CAHI, "Revolution and Democracy," 44.

97. Ibid., 48.

98. Vilas, "What Went Wrong," 12.

99. CAHI, "Revolution and Democracy," 48.

100. CAHI, "Governing from Below," 40.

Chapter 3. The Rural Proletariat: Beneficiary of Popular Hegemony?

1. Fauné, "Organización y participación popular en el campo," 106–7.

2. Ibid., 107.

3. See Enriquez, *Harvesting Change,* for an excellent account of the dynamics of agro-export production, labor supply, and agrarian reform during the Sandinista revolution.

4. Material on the historical background of ATC is drawn from García, "La

historia de la Asociación de Trabajadores del Campo (ATC)"; Deere and Marchetti, "Worker-Peasant Alliance," 40–73; Deere, Marchetti, and Reinhardt, "Agrarian Reform and the Transition in Nicaragua"; Deere et al., "Peasantry and the Development of Sandinista Agrarian Reform Policy"; Collins et al., *What Difference Could a Revolution Make?*; Ruchwarger, *Struggling for Survival;* various ATC documents; and interviews with officials of ATC and UNAG.

5. Baumeister, cited in Spalding, "State-Private Sector Relations in Nicaragua."

6. Deere and Marchetti, "Worker-Peasant Alliance," 44.

7. Ibid., 45.

8. Ruchwarger, *Struggling for Survival,* 12. For an excellent discussion of the importance of cotton production see Paige, "Cotton and Revolution in Nicaragua."

9. Black, *Triumph of the People,* 275.

10. Blokland, *Participación campesina en el desarrollo económico,* 149.

11. Serra, *El movimiento campesino,* 52–55.

12. Ibid, 53; Blokland, *Participación campesina en el desarrollo económico,* 149.

13. Ortega and Marchetti, "Campesinado, democracia y revolución sandinista," 15.

14. This concept has been developed by James C. Scott. See in particular Scott, *Weapons of the Weak.*

15. Ortega and Marchetti, "Campesinado, democracia y revolución sandinista," 22.

16. For excellent discussions of Nicaragua's history, see Walker, *Nicaragua;* Booth, *End and Beginning;* and Lozano, *De Sandino al triunfo de la revolución.* This section draws on their analysis.

17. Wheelock, *Nicaragua,* 119–20.

18. Blomstrom and Hettne, *Development Theory in Transition,* 30.

19. Lozano, *De Sandino al triunfo de la revolución,* 37. For a much lower estimate of the size of Sandino's forces, see Booth, *End and Beginning,* 44.

20. Selser, *Sandino, general de hombres libres,* 292–97.

21. Lozano, *De Sandino al triunfo de la revolución,* 40; Booth, *End and Beginning,* 51–52.

22. Lozano, *De Sandino al triunfo de la revolución,* 57.

23. Tirado, "El pensamiento político de Carlos Fonseca," 25.

24. Invernizzi et al., *Sandinistas,* 70.

25. Sandino et al., *Nicaragua,* 12.

26. FSLN, *Programa histórico del FSLN,* 13–14.

27. Carlos Fonseca, quoted in Lozano, *De Sandino al triúnfo de la revolucion,* 58.

28. Lozano, *De Sandino el triunfo de la revolución,* 59.

29. Collins et al., *What Difference Could a Revolution Make?* 21–29.

30. García, "La historia de la Asociación de Trabajadores del Campo (ATC)," 85.

31. Deere and Marchetti, "Worker-Peasant Alliance," 49; Molina, "Entrevista a Edgardo García," 108.

32. Ibid.; Collins et al., *What Difference Could a Revolution Make?* 24–26.

33. Ortega and Marchetti, "Campesinado, democracia y revolución sandinista," 17.

34. Deere and Marchetti, "Worker-Peasant Alliance," 50; Collins et al., *What Difference Could a Revolution Make?* 26.

35. *El Machete* no. 25, March 1983, 7; García, "La historia de la Asociación de Trabajadores del Campo," 88.

36. Molina, "Entrevista a Edgardo García," 108.

37. Gould, *To Lead As Equals,* 287.

38. Ibid., 287–88.

39. García, "La historia de la Asociación de Trabajadores del Campo," 84.

40. Deere and Marchetti, "Worker-Peasant Alliance," 48.

41. Gould, *To Lead As Equals,* 296.

42. Ortega and Marchetti, "Campesinado, democracia y revolución sandinista," 17–18.

43. Ibid., 16.

44. Gould, *To Lead As Equals,* 296.

45. The Sandinista experience in the mountains, witnessing and sharing the suffering of Nicaragua's peasantry, has been captured in a number of outstanding biographies and novels. See Cabezas, *La montaña es algo mas que una immensa estepa verde;* Borge, *La paciente impaciencia;* Ramírez, *La marca del Zorro.*

46. Gould, *To Lead As Equals,* 275.

47. Ibid.

48. Molina, "Entrevista a Edgardo García," 108.

49. *Barricada,* March 25, 1983.

50. Internal ATC document, June 1988.

51. See also Collins et al., *What Difference Could a Revolution Make?* 27–28.

52. ATC, "Cual es la lucha de los trabajadores del campo?" 7–9.

53. Ibid., 9.

54. ATC, *ATC Asamblea Nacional Constitutiva,* 43.

55. García, "La historia de la Asociación de los Trabajadores del Campo," 91; Deere and Marchetti, "Worker-Peasant Alliance," 51.

56. Deere and Marchetti, "Worker-Peasant Alliance," 53–57.

57. Deere et al., "Peasantry and the Development of Sandinista Agrarian Reform Policy," 81.

58. Ehlers, "La organización de los trabajadores," 10.

59. CIERA, *La reforma agraria en Nicaragua, 1979–1989: Organización y participación popular en el campo,* 113.

60. Black, *Triumph of the People,* 272.

61. Ehlers, "La organización de los trabajadores," 11; Fauné, "Organización y participación popular en el campo," 117.

62. CIERA, *La reforma agraria en Nicaragua: Cifras y referencias documentales* 39.

63. Black, *Triumph of the People,* 272.

64. Tables 3.2 and 3.3 report different membership figures for 1989 because the data in the two tables were compiled on different dates in that year.

65. CIERA, *La reforma agraria en Nicaragua, 1979–1989: Organizacion y participación popular en el campo,* 169.

66. This number represented 25 percent of the economically active population in the rural sector. See Porras, "El movimiento cooperativo en Nicaragua," 15, and Blokland, *Participación campesina en el desarrollo económico,* 143–47. Estimates on the size of the rural proletariat vary. For a good discussion of this problem, see Vilas, *Sandinista Revolution,* 63–66.

67. Several publications report a total ATC membership of about 70,000 in the late 1980s. According to ATC sources, however, this figure did not represent the actual strength of the union. It included about 20,000 sugar workers who ceased to belong to ATC in 1983–1984 and became part of CST.

68. Ruchwarger, *Struggling for Survival,* 35, footnote 30.

69. ATC, *ATC Asamblea Nacional Constitutiva,* 54.

70. ATC, "Declaración de principios," 54.

71. Fauné, "Organización y participación popular en el campo," 118.

72. Invernizzi, et al., *Sandinistas,* 69.

73. ATC, "Estatutos de la Confederación General de Trabajadores Agropecuarios," 6.

74. Ehlers, "La organización de los trabajadores," 11.

75. Ruchwarger, *Struggling for Survival,* 21–22.

76. The discussion of ATC's organizational structure draws on Fauné, "Organización y participación popular en el campo," 105–29; Ruchwarger, *Struggling for Survival;* a June 1988 internal ATC document; and interviews with union officials.

77. Fauné, "Organización y participación popular en el campo," 121.

78. Ibid.; Ruchwarger, *People in Power,* 267.

79. See Ruchwarger, *People in Power,* 259–61, for a discussion of the meaning of this "participation."

80. Ferrari, "Del combate antisomocista," 5.

81. *El Machete* no. 17, July 1982, 11.

82. ATC, *ATC Asamblea Nacional Constitutiva,* 44.

83. Wedin, *Nicaragua,* 41.

84. Kaimowitz and Havens, "Nicaragua in Transition," 20.

85. CAHI, "Making the Economy," 41.

86. Ibid., 42.

87. ATC, *ATC Asamblea Nacional Constitutiva,* 51. Emphasis mine.

88. Ibid., 54.

89. ATC, "Ponencia sobre la constitución política," 9.

90. See Collins et al., *What Difference Could a Revolution Make?* 79–85, and Deere et al., "Peasantry and the Development of Sandinista Agrarian Reform Policy," 82, for a discussion of these events.

91. Collins et al., *What Difference Could a Revolution Make?* 82; Deere et al., "Peasantry and the Development of Sandinista Agrarian Reform Policy," 82.

92. Ortega, "Discurso pronunciado," 26.

93. Wheelock, "Discurso pronunciado," 38.

94. Serra, "Participación política y organizaciones populares en la revolución sandinista," 19.

95. *El Nuevo Diario,* March 19, 1983.

96. *Barricada,* January 27, 1983.

97. Fauné, "Organización y participación popular en el campo," 118.

98. Serra, "Participación política y organizaciones populares en la revolución sandinista," 18.

99. Fauné, "Organización y participación popular en el campo," 118.

100. CAHI, "Rural Workers Fight to Become Owners," 16–17.

101. CAHI, "Privatization," 31.

102. Ibid.

103. ATC, "Informe central 1991–1992," 5.

104. Ibid., 4.

105. Ibid.

106. CAHI, "Year of UNO Economic Policies," 38–39.

Chapter 4. Agricultural Producers: The Dialectics of Popular Hegemony and National Unity

1. Daniel Núñez, "If the Peasantry Did Not Trust the Revolution We Would Be Through," 368.

2. Spalding, "State-Private Sector Relations in Nicaragua," 25.

3. Ibid., 28.

4. Daniel Núñez, "Producers of This Country Support Our Revolutionary Government," 360.

5. Spalding, "State-Private Sector Relations in Nicaragua," 29–30.

6. Ibid., 30.

7. Baumeister and Neira Cuadra, "Making of a Mixed Economy," 180.

8. Spalding, "State-Private Sector Relations in Nicaragua," 52.

9. Spalding, "Capitalists and Revolution," 18.

10. Ibid., 4.

11. Luciak, "National Unity and Popular Hegemony," 136.

12. Ruchwarger, *People in Power,* 222.

13. Coraggio, Nicaragua, 81; CIERA, *La reforma agraria en Nicaragua, 1979–1989: Organización y participación popular en el campo*, 300.

14. Ruchwarger, "Sandinista Mass Organizations and the Revolutionary Process," 105.

15. Interview with Tirado, December 16, 1989.

16. Baumeister, "Estado y campesinado en el gobierno sandinista."

17. Coraggio, *Nicaragua*, 81.

18. Baumeister and Neira Cuadra, "Making of a Mixed Economy," 189.

19. Ibid., 177.

20. Luciak, "Participatory Development in Sandinista Nicaragua," 29–53.

21. Ruchwarger, *People in Power*, 230.

22. Ibid.

23. Ruchwarger, "Sandinista Mass Organizations and the Revolutionary Process," 102.

24. Baumeister, "Structure of Nicaraguan Agriculture and the Sandinista Agrarian Reform," 24.

25. Ibid.

26. Baumeister, "Estado y campesinado en el gobierno sandinista," 8.

27. Baumeister and Neira Cuadra, "Making of a Mixed Economy," 184.

28. CAHI, "Making the Economy," 36.

29. UNAG, *La Unión Nacional de Agricultores y Ganaderos de Nicaragua*. Emphasis added.

30. CAHI, "Making the Economy," 42.

31. Ibid., 37.

32. Blokland, *Participación campesina en el desarrollo económico*, 152.

33. Gould, *To Lead As Equals*, 250.

34. Baumeister, "Estado y campesinado en el gobierno sandinista," 13.

35. Daniel Núñez, "A 8 años," 98. See also Paige, "Agrarian Policy and the Agrarian Bourgeoisie in Revolutionary Nicaragua," 3.

36. *El Nuevo Diario*, November 20, 1984.

37. Ortega and Marchetti, "Campesinado, democracia y revolución sandinista," 18, 26.

38. Ibid., 21.

39. Daniel Núñez, "If the Peasantry Did Not Trust the Revolution We Would Be Through," 367.

40. Ortega and Marchetti, "Campesinado, democracia y revolución sandinista," 38.

41. Serra, *El movimiento campesino*, 122, 184.

42. Ibid., 122.

43. Ortega and Marchetti, "Campesinado, democracia y revolución sandinista," 39.

44. For an excellent analysis of class relations during the Somoza period, see Gould, *To Lead As Equals*, part 2.

45. Marvin Ortega, "Cooperativas y democracia en la revolución sandinista," 9.

46. UNAG, *Main Report*, 9. Emphasis added.

47. Serra, *El movimiento campesino*, 111.

48. Ortega and Marchetti, "Campesinado, democracia y revolución sandinista," 40.

49. This section draws from Luciak, "National Unity and Popular Hegemony," 123–27.

50. Ibid., 125–27.

51. CIERA, *La reforma agraria en Nicaragua, 1979–1989: Organizacion y participación popular en el campo*, 52–53.

52. Spalding, "Capitalists and Revolution," 34.

53. Ibid., 2.

54. For an excellent discussion of the evolution of the cooperative movement under the Sandinistas, see Serra, *El movimiento campesino*.

55. UNAG Nacional, "Somos una fuerza," 1, 8; see also Serra, *El movimiento campesino*, 122.

56. Deere, Marchetti, and Reinhardt, "Peasantry and the Development of Sandinista Agrarian Policy," 83; Deere and Marchetti, "Worker-Peasant Alliance," 56.

57. Ibid.

58. Baumeister and Neira Cuadra, "Making of a Mixed Economy," 181.

59. Marvin Ortega, "Cooperativas y democracia en la revolución sandinista," 8.

60. Serra, *El movimiento campesino*, 226.

61. This discussion is based on Serra, *El movimiento campesino*, 149, and conversations with UNAG leaders.

62. Ibid.

63. Ibid., 112, 122.

64. The CIA's *Nicaragua Manual*.

65. Daniel Núñez, "A 8 años," 99; UNAG, "Somos una fuerza," 6–7.

66. Serra, "Participación política y organizaciones populares en la revolución sandinista," 20.

67. Interview with Daniel Núñez, July 9, 1985.

68. Blokland, *Participación campesina en el desarrollo económico*, 153.

69. Serra, *El movimiento campesino*, 234.

70. Ibid.

71. Colburn, "Foot Dragging and Other Peasant Responses to the Nicaraguan Revolution," 192.

72. Ortega and Marchetti, "Campesinado, democracia y revolución sandinista," 40.

73. Marvin Ortega, "Cooperativas y democracia en la revolución sandinista," 5.

74. Colburn, *Post-Revolutionary Nicaragua*, 97.

75. Blokland, *Participación campesina en el desarrollo económico,* 146, 154. Blokland uses the number of peasant families instead of the economically active population to derive his totals.

76. Ibid., 153 and table 4.5.

77. Ibid., 3.

78. Daniel Núñez, "If the Peasantry Did Not Trust the Revolution We Would Be Through," 373.

79. For an excellent discussion of the relations between the revolutionary government and the rural bourgeoisie, see Spalding, "Capitalists and Revolution."

80. Spalding, "Capitalists and Revolution," 15; Paige, "Agrarian Policy and the Agrarian Bourgeoisie in Revolutionary Nicaragua," 17.

81. Luciak, "National Unity and Popular Hegemony," 136–37.

82. *Barricada,* November 25, 1989.

83. *Barricada,* November 27, 1989; Spalding, "Capitalists and Revolution," 24.

84. Interviews with Sandinista sources, November 1989. See also Spalding, "Capitalists and Revolution," 37.

85. Spalding, "Capitalists and Revolution," 26.

86. Luciak, "National Unity and Popular Hegemony," 137.

87. Paige, "Agrarian Policy and the Agrarian Bourgeoisie in Revolutionary Nicaragua," 3; Rosendo Díaz, "Las relaciones han mejorado pero," 16.

88. Interview with Gúrdian, July 22, 1988.

89. Spalding, "Capitalists and Revolution," 38.

90. Ibid., 20; Luciak, "National Unity and Popular Hegemony," 136; and Blokland, *Participación Campesina en el Desarrollo Económico,* 3.

91. Baumeister, "Estado y campesinado en el gobierno sandinista," 13.

92. Interview with Tijerino, July 27, 1988.

93. UNAG, *La organización de los productores del campo,* 24. Emphasis added.

94. Blokland, *Participación campesina en el desarrollo económico,* 328, footnote 14.

95. Ibid., 156.

96. Interview with Daniel Núñez, November 14, 1989.

97. Blokland, *Participación campesina en el desarrollo económico,* 157–58.

98. Ibid., 158.

99. Ibid.

100. Interview with Tirado, December 16, 1989.

101. See Blokland et al., "Participación popular y organización campesina," for an interesting case study illustrating this point.

102. Serra, "Participación política y organizaciones populares en la revolución sandinista," 14.

103. Ibid., 12.

104. Interview with Tirado, August 9, 1989.

105. *Barricada,* November 27, 1989.

106. Consejo Supremo Electoral, "Listas de ciudadanos."

107. *Barricada,* November 25, 1989.

108. Daniel Núñez, "A 8 anos," 98.

109. Tirado, "Movimiento sindical y organizaciones de masas en la revolución popular sandinista," 91.

110. Daniel Núñez, "Intervención de Daniel Núñez," 46.

111. Deere et al., "Peasantry and the Development of Sandinista Agrarian Policy," 91.

112. Wheelock, *Entre la crisis y la agresion,* 29.

113. Deere et al., "Peasantry and the Development of Sandinista Agrarian Policy," 102.

114. Baumeister, "Estado y campesinado en el gobierno sandinista," 3.

115. Ortega, "Cooperativas y democracia en la revolución sandinista," 3.

116. Interview with Laguna, January 31, 1986.

117. Daniel Núñez, "A 8 anos," 96.

118. UNAG, "Informe evaluativo," 37.

119. SIDA, "Information om det Svenska Utvecklingssamarbetet med Nicaragua."

120. UNAG, "Convocatoria y normas del proceso de base."

121. UNAG, "Estatutos de la Unión Nacional de Agricultores y Ganaderos U.N.A.G.," 4. Emphasis in original.

122. Ibid., 6.

123. Blokland, *Participación campesina en el desarrollo económico,* 4.

124. Ibid., 8.

125. "Un carnet, una organización," *Productores* no. 4, 32.

126. See Luciak, "Challenge of Peace," for an analysis of UNAG's role in the reconciliation process.

127. UNAG, "Informe evaluativo," 6.

128. Ibid., 15.

Chapter 5. New Relations of Production: Cooperative Peasant Stores

1. CAHI, "Making the Economy," 38.

2. Blokland, *Participación campesina en el desarrollo económico,* 167.

3. Ibid., 152.

4. ECODEPA-UNAG, "Reglamento de ECODEPA," 2; UNAG/SCC, "Convenio general de cooperación," 1–2.

5. I use the term project to refer to the peasant stores and the departmental and national ECODEPAs.

6. Interview with Kjeller, August 2, 1988.

7. Blokland, *Participación campesina en el desarrollo económico,* 169.

8. Serra and Frenkel, "Peasantry and Development in Nicaragua," 23.

9. Ibid.

10. This section is based on ECODEPA-UNAG, "Reglamento de ECODEPA," 1–10, and Jackson et al., "Project Evaluation," 26–27.

11. Jackson et al., "Project Evaluation," 39.

12. ECODEPA-UNAG, "Reglamento de ECODEPA," 15.

13. Ibid., 4.

14. Ockerman, "Impacto económico."

15. Blokland, *Participación campesina en el desarrollo económico,* 171; Jackson et al., "Project Evaluation," 13.

16. Blokland, *Participación campesina en el desarrollo económico,* 171.

17. Barrios, "Que la rentabilidad sea la base," 21.

18. Ortega, "Cooperativas y democracia en la revolución sandinista," 17.

19. Ibid.

20. See the methodological appendix for an elaboration of the focus of this study.

21. ECODEPA-UNAG, "Reglamento de ECODEPA," 7.

22. Jackson et al., "Project Evaluation," 29.

23. UNAG-ECODEPA NACIONAL, "Autodiagnostico de las empresas cooperativas de productores agropecuarios," statistical annex.

24. Jackson et al., "Project Evaluation," 28.

25. ECODEPA-UNAG, "Reglamento de ECODEPA," 8.

26. Jackson et al., "Project Evaluation," 28.

27. Ibid., 28.

28. Internal ECODEPA documents.

29. UNAG/SCC, "Convenio general de cooperación," 1.

30. ECODEPA-UNAG, "Reglamento de ECODEPA," 4.

31. Small producers are defined as owning fewer than 35 hectares of land, medium producers hold from 35 to 350 hectares, and large producers own more than 350 hectares. Although farm size alone is not a very good indicator for distinguishing between social sectors (type of production and quality of land need to be taken into account), these categories are generally accepted for analysis of Nicaragua's rural sector.

32. Jackson et al., "Project Evaluation," 6.

33. DGRA MIDINRA et al., "Evaluación del ordenamiento de la red de distribución en el campo," 17.

34. ECODEPA-UNAG, "Reglamento de ECODEPA," 8.

35. Ibid., 4.

36. Thirty percent was a high estimate. Blokland (1992) reports that only 13 percent of the members were not affiliated with UNAG.

37. CAHI, "Two Voices of the Private Sector," 31.

38. Hemisphere Institute, "Election Results."

39. Ibid.

40. Interview with Calero, November 24, 1989.

41. Marvin Ortega, "Estudio de base de las tiendas campesinas."

42. UNAG/SCC, "Convenio general de cooperacion," 2.

43. ECODEPA-UNAG, "Reglamento de ECODEPA," 1.

44. Jackson et al., "Project Evaluation," 44.

45. Ibid., 48.

46. Internal UNAG/ECODEPA documents.

47. ECODEPA Boaco, *Libro de actas,* Boaco, February 25, 1989.

48. Daniel Núñez, "A 8 anos," 96.

49. Baumeister and de Vylder, "Appraisal," 2.

50. Wiggins, "Informe preliminar," 27.

51. UNAG, "Recomendaciones para la reestructuración del sistema cooperativo de acopio y comercialización campesina."

52. Jackson et al., "Project Evaluation," 34.

53. Barrios, "Que la rentabilidad sea la base," 19.

54. Serra and Frenkel, "Peasantry and Development in Nicaragua," 26.

55. DGRA MIDINRA et al., "Evaluación del ordenamiento de la red de distribución en el campo," 24.

56. Ibid., 5.

57. Serra, *El movimiento campesino,* 119.

58. Interview with Vargas, December 13, 1989.

59. Wiggins, "Informe preliminar," 13.

60. Interview with Daniel Núñez, November 14, 1989.

61. Ruíz, quoted in Jackson et al., "Project Report," 1.

62. Vilas, "Family Affairs," 309–41.

63. Baumeister and de Vylder, Appraisal," 19.

64. Interview with Daniel Núñez, November 14, 1989.

65. Daniel Núñez, "Farmers' View," 20.

Chapter 6. The Struggle Goes On: Rural Women in the Nicaraguan Transition

1. Harris, *Marxism, Socialism, and Democracy in Latin America,* 181–82. See also, Randall, *Gathering Rage.*

2. Molyneux, "Mobilization Without Emancipation?" 282–83.

3. Ibid., 284.

4. For an excellent analysis of Sandinista policies, see Chamorro, "La mujer," 117–43. The section on the historical background draws on her analysis.

5. FSLN, *Programa histórico del FSLN,* 32.

6. Ibid., 32–33.

7. Chamorro, "La mujer," 119.

8. In the case of this point and many others, I am indebted to four anonymous reviewers who reviewed a version of this chapter in article form. They made many excellent suggestions that helped me to clarify my arguments.

9. Mason, "Women's Participation in Central American Revolutions," 64.

10. Ramírez-Horton, "Role of Women in the Nicaraguan Revolution," 150–52.

11. For excellent accounts of this phase of the revolution, see Molyneux, "Women," 145–62; Chamorro, "La mujer"; and Chuchryk, "Women in the Revolution," 143–65.

12. Chamorro, "La mujer," 121.

13. Molineux, "Women," 152.

14. Ibid.

15. Benería and Roldan, *Crossroads of Class and Gender,* 9.

16. Serra, "Grass-Roots Organizations," 49–75.

17. Chamorro, "La mujer," 13

18. FSLN, "El FSLN y la mujer," 145–50.

19. Chamorro, "La mujer," 132–33.

20. FSLN, "Proclama del FSLN," 135.

21. Mason, "Women in Central American Revolutions," 74.

22. Pérez and Siu, "La mujer en la economía nicaragüense," cited in Chamorro, "La mujer," 127.

23. CIERA, *La reforma agraria en Nicaragua: Mujer y transformación de la vida rural,* 14.

24. Vargas, "La mujer en la crisis económica."

25. The ATC data presented in this and other tables are not as complete as one would like them to be. Reliable ATC data are very difficult to obtain and are not consistent over years, since ATC officials frequently change the way in which they are calculated.

26. CIERA, *La reforma agraria en Nicaragua: Mujer y transformación de la vida rural,* 81.

27. Molina, "Entrevista a Edgardo García," 114.

28. ATC, "Informe central 1991–1992," 4.

29. ATC—Secretaría de la Mujer, "Informe central: V Asamblea de Obreras Agrícolas," statistical annex.

30. CAHI, "Privatization," 31.

31. These figures are my calculations based on data obtained from ATC.

32. Ruchwarger, *Struggling for Survival,* 80.

33. CIERA, *La reforma agraria en Nicaragua: Mujer y transformación de la vida rural,* 82.

34. Ibid.

35. Ruchwarger, *Struggling for Survival,* 80.

36. Pérez-Aleman, "Economic Crisis and Women in Nicaragua," 250.

37. Ibid.

38. See the seven "Informes" published by ATC's women's secretariat.

39. ATC—Secretaría de la Mujer, "Informe central: V Asamblea de Obreras Agrícolas," 14.

40. ATC, "Informe central 1991–1992," 6.

41. ATC—Secretaría de la Mujer, "Informe central: VII Asamblea Nacional de Trabajadoras Agropecuarias," 10.

42. See for example, ATC—Secretaría Nacional de la Mujer, *En nuestra defensa*.

43. See Jaquette, *Women's Movement in Latin America*.

44. For an evaluation of the Women's Section, see CENZONTLE, "Evaluacion: La sección de la mujer de la UNAG."

45. Pérez-Aleman, "Economic Crisis and Women in Nicaragua," 247.

46. Paola Pérez et al., "Sintesis de resultados de investigación mujer campesina y organización," 12.

47. Ibid., 1.

48. Ibid., 4.

49. "La mujer ha socado"; interview with Benigna Mendiola in Productores n.7, October 1991, 12.

50. UNAG—Sección de la Mujer, "Plan de lucha," 7–9.

51. UNAG, "Memorias."

52. UNAG, "Informe evaluativo de la Junta Directiva Nacional al II Congreso de UNAG," 28.

53. Ibid.

54. ECODEPA, "Reglamento de tiendas campesinas y ECODEPA," 2.

55. Jackson et al., "Project Evaluation," 30.

56. Pérez et al., "Síntesis de resultados de investigación mujer campesina y organización," 9.

57. Ibid.

58. ECODEPA, "Reglamento de tiendas campesinas y ECODEPA," 4.

59. Ibid., 13.

60. Lomba, "Futuro, en femenino," 39.

61. This account is based on interviews with three participants of the "encuentro," Managua, July 1992; see also O'Kane, "A su propio ritmo," 35–36.

62. *Constitución política de Nicaragua*, 25–27.

63. Kampwirth, "Mother of the Nicaraguans," 11–12.

64. I am indebted to one of the four anonymous reviewers for pointing this out.

65. CAHI, "Women in Nicaragua," 40.

66. Babb, "From Coops to Kitchens," 3.

67. Fonseca, "Labor and Politics are a Man's Concern, Women Say."

Chapter 7. Conclusion: The Sandinista Legacy

1. CAHI, "Governing from Below," 40.

2. Przeworski, *Democracy and the Market*, 51.

3. CAHI, "Interview with Dora María Téllez," 32.

4. CAHI, "Revolution and Democracy," 44.

5. CAHI, "Sandinista Congress," 10.

6. See Luciak, "Political Economy of Reconciliation in Nicaragua."

7. Prevost, "FSLN in Opposition," 161.

8. CAHI, "FSLN National Congress," 14.

9. Randall, *Gathering Rage,* 37.

10. Vilas, "After the Revolution," 97.

11. Paige, "Agrarian Policy and the Agrarian Bourgeoisie in Revolutionary Nicaragua," 1.

12. See O'Kane and Marin, "Militarismo," 22.

13. Daniel Ortega, quoted in CAHI, Volume 10, Number 122, (1991), p. 41.

14. CAHI, "New Year, New US President, New Look in Nicaragua," 4.

15. Daniel Ortega quoted in CAHI, "Behind the Birth of the Recontras," 20.

16. CAHI, "Rural Violence and the Right Wing's Try for Chaos," 4.

17. See Vanden and Prevost, *Democracy and Socialism in Sandinista Nicaragua,* 129, for a similar assessment.

Bibliography

Author's Interviews

Aburto, Manuel. Director of Cooperative Services, ECODEPA Nacional. Managua, July 6, 1992.

Aguilar, Marcia. ATC secretary of international relations in Matagalpa. Matagalpa, July 13, 1992.

Aragon, Juan Ramon. Member of UNAG's national directorate. Teustepe, November 22, 1989.

Asplund, Daniel. Member of the Nicaraguan mission of the Swedish International Development Agency (SIDA). Managua, August 2, 1988.

Barrios, Miguel. General manager of ECODEPA. Managua, July 6, 1992.

Baumeister, Eduardo. Argentine sociologist. Managua, November 15, 1989; July 10, 1992.

Berrios, Francisco. ECODEPA Jinotega manager. Jinotega, December 20, 1989.

Blanco, Alberto. Vice-director of organization and cooperative development, UNAG national office. Managua, July 25–26, 1988.

Bolt, Gladys. Member of UNAG executive committee. Matagalpa, October 26, 1986; July 29–30, 1988; August 1, 1989; December 1, 1989; July 12, 1992.

Bonilla, Horacio. President of UNAG in region V. Juigalpa, November 28, 1989.

Briones, José María. President of the Association of Ranchers of Estelí (ASOGAES), a private producer organization affiliated with UPANIC in region I. Estelí, January 31, 1986.

Bucardo, Ariel. Vice-president of UNAG. Managua, May 21, 1985; August 5, 1988; November 27, 1989; and July 8, 1992.

Cabezas, Omar. Coordinator of the Sandinista Defense Committees. Managua, July 27, 1989.

Cajina, Fabricio. Coordinator of San José de los Remates peasant store. San José de los Remates, December 9, 1989.

Calero, Juan. Coordinator of Muelle de los Bueyes peasant store. Muelle de los Bueyes, November 24, 1989.

Camas, Francisco. ATC secretary of international relations. Managua, August 4, 1988.

Chavarría, Denis. ATC secretary for organization. Managua, August 2, 1988.

Cuadra, Carlos. Vice-president of MAPML. Managua, July 10, 1985.

Dávila, Francisco. Manager of Matagalpa ECOPEDA. Matagalpa, November 23, 1989.

Díaz, Rosendo. Secretary-general of the Union of Nicaraguan Agricultural Producers. Managua, February 17, 1986.

Escoto, Geronimo. Vice-coordinator of Wasaca Abajo and coordinator of ECODEPA Matagalpa. Wasaca Abajo, December 13, 1989.

Falla, Rafael. Official in charge of finance, UNAG national office. Managua, February 13, 1986.

Fauné, Angelica. Consultant to UNAG. Managua, July 2, 1992.

García, Edgardo. Secretary-general of the Association of Rural Workers. Managua, July 5, 1985; July 27, 1989; July 22, 1992.

Gomez, Domingo. ATC secretary for education and propaganda. Managua, January 19, 1985.

González, Marco. Member of UNAG national executive committee and general manager of the Cooperative Enterprise for Agricultural Producers. Managua, February 20, 1986; August 1, 1988; August 3, 1989; December 4, 1989.

González, Oscar. MIDINRA official in charge of cooperative development. Matagalpa, December 18, 1989.

Guerrero, Aaron. ECODEPA Juigalpa manager. Juigalpa, November 21, 1989.

Gúrdian, Ramiro. President of the Union of Nicaraguan Agricultural Producers and vice-president of the Superior Council of Private Enterprise. Managua, June 28, 1985; July 22, 1988; July 27, 1989.

Gutierrez, Francisco ("Chico"). President of Boaco UNAG. Boaco, November 30, 1989.

Hassan, Moisés. Member of Sandinista Nicaragua's first governing junta in 1979. Managua, August 15, 1988.

Haugstveit, Nils. Representative of NORAD. Managua, December 14, 1989.

Herrera, Dora. Secretary of ATC women's section, Managua, July 21, 1992.

Herrera, Manuel. Vice-president of UNAG in region VI. Matagalpa, November 24, 1989.

Jiménez, Lucío. Secretary-general of the Sandinista Workers' Federation. Managua, August 3, 1989.

Johansen, Karl Inge. Norwegian adviser to UNAG. Managua, December 14, 1989.

Kjeller, Bengt. Main representative of the Swedish Cooperative Center (SCC) and principal adviser to ECODEPA. Managua, August 2, 1988; and Muelle de los Bueyes, November 25–26, 1989.

Laguna, Roberto. President of UNAG in region I. Estelí, January 31, 1986.

Lara, Wilberto. Cofounder of ATC and second president of UNAG. Managua, April 21, 1985.

López, Herrera Carina. President of the Credit and Service Cooperative "Antonio Gutierrez." Matagalpa, November 23, 1989.

López, Sergio. Member of Matagalpa training section. Wasaca Abajo, December 13, 1989.

Lovo, Joaquín. Vice-minister of government. Managua, July 20, 1992.

Maletin, Fernando. Secretary-general of the Workers' Front. Managua, July 5, 1985.

Marin, Matilde. Former vice-manager of ECODEPA Juigalpa. Nueva Guinea, November 25–26, 1989.

Mejia, Apollonio. President of the CAS "Felix Pedro González." Teustepe, November 22, 1989.

Mendoza, Esmeralda. Head of ATC women's secretaríat in Matagalpa. Matagalpa, July 13, 1992.

Mendoza, Neris. In charge of CDC in Teustepe. Teustepe, November 22, 1989.

Morales, Luís Felipe. UNAG representative on the National Cattle Commission. Juigalpa, November 21, 1989.

Núñez, Carlos. President of the National Assembly and member of FSLN national directorate. Managua, February 18, 1986.

Núñez, Daniel. President of the National Union of Farmers and Ranchers. Managua, July 9, 1985; July 22, 1989; November 14, 1989; July 22, 1992.

Ockerman, Torbjorn. Swedish adviser to ECODEPA Matagalpa. Matagalpa, November 11, 1989.

Pastor, Justo. Founder of the peasant store of San Buenaventura. Boaco, December 4, 1989.

Pérez, Mario. Adviser to the president of UNAG. Managua, June 19, 1985; February 17, 1986.

Pérez, Pedro. Coordinator of the Tierra Azul peasant store. Tierra Azul, November 30, 1989.

Ramírez, Sergio. Vice-president of the Sandinista government. Managua, July 24, 1989.

Rivera, Arquímedes. Director-general of ECODEPA (1985–1990). Managua, December 4, 1989.

Rodriguez, Alcides. Member of UNAG executive committee in region VI. Matagalpa, July 31, 1988.

Rusmore, Cathy. Adviser to the women's section of UNAG. Managua, November 16, 1989.

Saenz, "Chico" Javier. Cofounder of UNAG and president in region VI. Matagalpa, June 21, 1985; February 15, 1986; July 30, 1988.

Sequeira, Fabio. Head of MIDINRA in region V. Juigalpa, November 28, 1989.

Siles, Oren. Coordinator of Matiguas and member of the executive committee of ECODEPA. Matagalpa, December 5, 1989; Matiguas, December 12, 1989.

Solórzano, Mauricio. Manager of ECODEPA Boaco. Boaco, December 4, 1989.

Tijerino, Juan. Cofounder of the Association of Cattlemen (FAGANIC), third secretary of Nicaraguan National Assembly (1984–1990), and a senior UNAG official. Managua, January 27, 1986; July 27, 1988.

Tirado, Víctor. Member of the national directorate of FSLN. Managua, July 3, 1985; August 9, 1989; December 16, 1989. In the case of the August 9 and December 16, 1989, interviews, Tirado supplied written replies to questions.

Valle, Martha Heriberta. Member of UNAG national executive committee and head of the women's section in Matagalpa. Managua, July 10, 1992.

Vargas, Carmelo. Coordinator of Wasaca Abajo and member of the executive committee of ECODEPA Matagalpa. Wasaca Abajo, December 13, 1989.

Published and Unpublished Sources

Aguilar, Lourdes, et al. "Orígenes y situación actual en los CDS." Classified report. Managua: INIES, 1985.

Arce, Bayardo. "En Nicaragua se juega el destino de America Latina." Speech by Comandante Bayardo Arce delivered at the First Anti-Imperialist Congress, February 20, 1985. *Pensamiento Propio* no. 21 (March 1985): 2–11.

———. "Secret Speech before the Nicaraguan Socialist Party (PSN)." U.S. Department of State Publication no. 9422, 1985.

Association of Nicaraguan Women, Luisa Amanda Espinosa (AMNLAE). *Plan de Lucha.* Managua, 1984.

Association of Rural Workers (ATC). *ATC Asamblea Nacional Constitutiva: Memorias.* Managua: DAP-SENAPEP, 1979.

———. *Ayer y Hoy.* Pamphlet. Managua: ATC, 1984.

———. "Cual es la lucha de los trabajadores del campo?" *El Machete* (February 1979).

———. "Declaración de principios." In *ATC Asamblea Nacional Constitutiva: Memorias.* Managua: DAP-SENAPEP, 1979.

———. "Estatutos de la Confederación General de Trabajadores Agropecuarios: Asociación de Trabajadores del Campo (ATC)." Managua, 1992.

———. "Informe Central 1991–1992." Managua, 1992.

———. "Ponencia sobre la constitución política." Mimeograph. Managua, 1985.

———. *Revolución y mujeres del campo.* Managua, 1985.

Association of Rural Workers (ATC)—Secretaría de la Mujer. "Informe Central: V Asamblea de Obreras Agrícolas." Managua, 1989.

———. "Informe Central: VII Asamblea Nacional de Trabajadoras Agropecuarias." Managua, 1992.

———. *En nuestra defensa: No a la violencia.* Managua, 1992.

Babb, Florence. "From Coop to Kitchen: Nicaraguan Women in and out of the Labor Force." Paper presented at the Seventeenth International Congress of the Latin American Studies Association, Los Angeles, 1992.

Barber, Benjamin. *Strong Democracy: Participatory Politics for a New Age.* Berkeley: University of California Press, 1984.

Baumeister, Eduardo. "Estado y campesinado en el gobierno sandinista." A paper presented at the International Latin American Studies Meeting, Washington, D.C., April 4–6, 1991.

———. "The Structure of Nicaraguan Agriculture and the Sandinista Agrarian Reform." In *Nicaragua: A Revolution under Siege,* edited by Richard Harris and Carlos Vilas. London: Zed, 1985.

Baumeister, Eduardo, and Neira Cuadra. "The Making of a Mixed Economy: Class Struggle and State Policy in the Nicaragua Transition." In *Transition and Development: Problems of Third World Socialism,* edited by Richard R. Fagen, Carmen Diana Deere, and José Luís Coraggio. New York: Monthly Review Press/Center for the Study of the Americas, 1986.

Baumeister, Eduardo, and Stefan de Vylder. "Appraisal: Nicaragua—Tiendas Campesinas—Proyecto ECODEPA/Centro Cooperativo Sueco." Stockholm, 1991.

Benería, Lourdes, and Martha Roldan. *The Crossroads of Class and Gender: Industrial Homework, Subcontracting, and Household Dynamics in Mexico City.* Chicago: University of Chicago Press, 1987.

Black, George. *Triumph of the People: The Sandinista Revolution in Nicaragua.* London: Zed, 1981.

Blokland, Kees. *Participación campesina en el desarrollo económico: La Unión Nacional de Agricultores y Ganaderos de Nicaragua durante la revolución sandinista.* Doetinchem, Neth.: Paulo Freire Stichting, 1992.

Blokland, Kees, et al. "Participación popular y organización campesina: Experiencia de la UNAG en Teustepe." Managua, n.d.

Blomstrom, Magnus, and Bjorn Hettne. *Development Theory In Transition: The Dependency Debate and Beyond—Third World Responses.* London: Zed, 1984.

Boggs, Carl. *The Two Revolutions: Gramsci and the Dilemmas of Western Marxism.* Boston: South End, 1984.

Booth, John. *The End and the Beginning: The Nicaraguan Revolution.* Boulder: Westview, 1985.

Borge, Tomás. *La paciente impaciencia.* Managua: Editorial Vanguardia, 1989.

Bossert, Thomas. "The Promise of Theory." In *Promise of Development,* edited by Peter Klaren and Thomas Bossert. Boulder: Westview, 1986.

Brown, J. F. *Surge to Freedom: End of Communist Rule in Eastern Europe.* Durham: Duke University Press, 1991.

Bynke, Kalle, et al. "Evaluación del Proyecto UNAG/ECODEPA/Centro Cooperative Sueco." Managua, December 1986.

Cabezas, Omar. *La montaña es algo mas que una immensa estepa verde.* Managua: Editorial Nueva Nicaragua, 1982.

Castro, Vanessa, and Gary Prevost, eds. *The 1990 Elections in Nicaragua and Their Aftermath.* Lanham, Md.: Rowman and Littlefield, 1992.

Center for the Study of the Agrarian Reform (CIERA). *La democracia participativa en Nicaragua.* Managua: CIERA, 1984.

——. *La reforma agraria en Nicaragua, 1979–1989: Cifras y referencias documentales.* Managua: CIERA, 1989.

——. *La reforma agraria en Nicaragua, 1979–1989: Mujer y transformación de la vida rural.* Managua: CIERA. 1989.

——. *La reforma agraria en Nicaragua, 1979–1989: Organización y participación popular en el campo.* Managua: CIERA, 1989.

——. *Mujer y agroexportación en Nicaragua.* Managua: Editorial Union, 1987.

Central American Historical Institute (CAHI). "Ante el avance del proceso electoral, la abstención estimula la intervención." *Envío* 4, no. 8 (August 1984): 1a–12a.

——. "Breakthrough for Peace." *Envío* 8, no. 92 (March 1989): 3–9.

——. "The FSLN National Congress." *Envío* 10, no.122 (September 1991): 14.

——. "Governing from Below: Speech by President Daniel Ortega Saavedra, February 27, 1990, Nonaligned Plaza." *Envío* 9, no. 104 (March–April 1990): 40–42.

——. "Interview with Dora María Téllez: The Revolution Is Not Lost." *Envío* 10, no.122 (September 1991):28–37.

——. "Making the Economy: Our Own Interviews with UNAG Leaders." *Envío* 8, no. 95 (June 1989): 35–44.

——. "New Year, New U.S. President, New Look in Nicaragua." *Envío* 12, no. 138 (January–March 1993): 3–14.

——. "Privatization: Left, Right and Center." *Envio* 10, no. 124 (November 1991): 20–34.

——. "Revolution and Democracy: Excerpts from a Speech by Tomás Borge." *Envío* 9, no. 107 (June 1990): 44–48.

——. "Rural Violence and the Right Wing's Try for Chaos." *Envío* 12, nos. 139–41 (April 1993): 3–10.

——. "Rural Workers Fight to Become Owners." *Envío* 10, no. 118 (May 1991): 16–19.

——. "The Sandinista Congress: Rich, Controversial, Inconclusive." *Envío* 10, no. 122 (September 1991): 3–13.

——. "Two Voices of the Private Sector: Interviews with Gilberto Cuadra and Gladys Bolt." *Envío* 8, no. 99 (October 1989): 30–39.

——. "A Year of UNO Economic Policies: The Rich Get Richer . . ." *Envío* 10, no. 116 (March 1991): 30–49.

——. "Women in Nicaragua: The Revolution on Hold." *Envío* 10, no. 119 (June 1991): 30–41.

Centro para la Participación Democratica y el Desarrollo (CENZONTLE). "Evaluacion: La Sección de la Mujer de la UNAG." Managua, 1990.

Chamorro, Amalia. "La mujer: Logros y límites en 10 anos de revolucion." *Cuadernos de Sociologia* 9–10 (January–June 1989): 117–43.

Chilcote, Ronald H. *Theories of Development and Underdevelopment.* Boulder: Westview, 1984.

Chuchryk, Patricia M. "Women in the Revolution." In *Revolution and Counter-revolution in Nicaragua,* edited by Thomas W. Walker. Boulder: Westview, 1991.

The CIA's Nicaragua Manual: Psychological Operations in Guerrilla Warfare. New York: Vintage, 1985.

Colburn, Forrest D. *Post-Revolutionary Nicaragua: State, Class, and the Dilemmas of Agrarian Policy.* Berkeley: University of California Press, 1986.

———. "Foot Dragging and Other Peasant Responses to the Nicaraguan Revolution." In *Everyday Forms of Peasant Resistance,* edited by Forrest D. Colburn. Armonk, N.Y.: M. E. Sharpe, 1989.

Coleman, Kenneth M., et al. "The Urban Informal Economy in Nicaragua: Preliminary Observations." Paper presented at the World Congress of the Latin American Studies Association, Miami, Florida, December 4–6, 1989.

Collins, Joséph, with Frances Moore Lappe and Nick Allen. *What Difference Could a Revolution Make? Food and Farming in the New Nicaragua.* San Francisco: Institute for Food and Development Policy, 1982.

Consejo Supremo Electoral. "Listas de ciudadanos presentados como candidatos a consejales municipales por ocho partidos políticos y dos alianzas." Managua, November 17, 1989.

Constitución Política de Nicaragua. Managua: Editorial El Amanecer, 1987.

Coraggio, José Luis. "Economics and Politics in the Transition to Socialism." In *Transition and Development: Problems in Third World Socialism,* edited by Richard R. Fagen, Carmen Diana Deere, and José Luís Coraggio. New York: Monthly Review Press, 1986.

———. *Nicaragua: Revolución y democracia.* Mexico City: Editorial Linea, 1985.

Deere, Carmen Diana, and Peter Marchetti. "The Worker-Peasant Alliance in the First Year of the Nicaraguan Agrarian Reform." *Latin American Perspectives* 8, no. 2 (Spring 1981): 40–73.

Deere, Carmen Diana, Peter Marchetti, S. J. Reinhardt, and Nola Reinhardt. "Agrarian Reform and the Transition in Nicaragua." Unpublished manuscript. Managua, 1983.

———. "The Peasantry and the Development of Sandinista Agrarian Policy, 1979–1984." *Latin American Research Review* 20, no. 3 (1985): 75–109.

Dixon, Marlene, ed. *Nicaragua under Siege.* San Francisco: Synthesis, 1985.

Eckstein, Susan, ed. *Back from the Future: Cuba under Castro.* Princeton: Princeton University Press, 1994.

———. *Power and Popular Protest: Latin American Social Movements.* Berkeley: University of California Press, 1989.

Economic Commission for Latin America (ECLA). *Statistical Yearbook for Latin America 1975*. New York: ECLA, 1976.

Ehlers, Heliette. "La organización de los trabajadores, un proceso no acabado." *El Machete* no. 82 (February 1988).

Empresa Cooperativa de Productores Agropecuarios (ECODEPA). "Autodiag-nostico de las empresas cooperativas de productores agropecuarios." September 1989.

———. *Estatutos de ECODEPA y tiendas campesinas: Lineas de trabajo*. Managua: Editorial Productores, 1991.

———. *Libro de actas*. Boaco, Nicaragua, September 8, 1989.

———. "Reglamento de tiendas campesinas y ECODEPA." April 1989.

Engels, Friedrich. "Socialism: Utopian and Scientific." In *The Marx-Engels Reader*, edited by Robert C. Tucker. New York: Norton, 1978.

Enríquez, Laura J. *Harvesting Change: Labor and Agrarian Reform in Nicaragua, 1979–1990*. Chapel Hill: University of North Carolina Press, 1991.

Fagen, Richard F. "Studying Latin American Politics: Some Implications of a Dependencia Approach." *Latin American Research Review* 12, no. 2 (Summer 1977): 3–26.

Fagen, Richard F., Carmen Diana Deere, and José Luís Coraggio. *Transition and Development: Problems in Third World Socialism*. New York: Monthly Review Press/Center for the Study of the Americas, 1986.

Fauné, María Angelica. "Organización y participación popular en el campo." *Revolución y Desarrollo* no. 5 (July 1989): 105–29.

Ferrari, Sergio. "Del combate antisomocista . . . a la gestion obrera: Entrevista con Edgardo García." *Trinchera* 1, no. 12 (August 1989).

Fonseca, Carlos. *Ideario politico de Augusto César Sandino*. Managua: DEPEP, 1984.

Fonseca, Robert. "Labor and Politics are a Man's Concern, Women Say." *Interpress Service*, November 13, 1992.

Frente Sandinista de Liberación Nacional (FSLN). "Analysis de la coyuntura y tareas de la revolucion popular sandinista (documento de las 72 horas)." In *Nicaragua: Diagnostico De Una Traicion*, edited by Octavio Sanabria and Elvyra Sanabria. Barcelona: Plaza and Janes Editores, 1986.

———. "Declaración del FSLN sobre la democracia." *Barricada*, August 24, 1980.

———. "El FSLN y la mujer en la revolución popular sandinista." *Revolución y Desarrollo* no. 5 (July 1989): 144–50.

———. "Proclama del FSLN: La mujer y la revolucion." *Cuadernos de Sociologia* (May–December 1987).

———. *Programa histórico del FSLN*. Managua: DEPEP, 1984.

García, Edgardo. *La historia de la Asociación de Trabajadores del Campo (ATC)*. Managua: ATC, 1979.

Gilbert, Dennis. *Sandinistas: The Party and the Revolution.* New York: Blackwell, 1988.

González Casanova, Pablo. *El poder al pueblo.* Mexico City: Ediciones Oceano, 1985.

———. *La democracia en Mexico.* Mexico City: Serie Popular Era, 1983.

Goodwin, Jeff, and Theda Skocpol. "Explaining Revolutions in the Contemporary Third World." *Politics and Society* 17, no. 4 (1989): 489–509.

Gould, Jeffey L. *To Lead as Equals: Rural Protest and Political Consciousness in Chinandega, Nicaragua, 1912–1979.* Chapel Hill: University of North Carolina Press, 1990.

Gramsci, Antonio. *Selections from the Prison Notebooks.* Edited and translated by Quintin Hoare and Geoffrey Nowell Smith. London: Lawrence and Wishart, 1971.

Guevara, Ernesto "Che." *Guerrilla Warfare.* Introduction and case studies by Brian Loveman and Thomas M. Davies, Jr. Lincoln: University of Nebraska Press, 1985.

Habermas, Juergen. *Communication and the Evolution of Society.* London: Heinemann, 1979.

Handal, Shafik Jorge, and Carlos M. Vilas. *The Socialist Option in Central America: Two Reassessments.* New York: Monthly Review Press, 1993.

Harnecker, Martha. *Cuba: Dictadura o Democracia.* Mexico City: Siglo 21 editores, 1984.

———. *Los conceptos elementales del materialismo historico.* Mexico City: Siglo 21 editores, 1985.

———. *Nicaragua: El papel de la vanguardia: Entrevista al comandante de la revolución Jaime Wheelock sobre la historia del frente sandinista.* Panama City: Centro de Capacitacion Social, 1986.

———. *Reflexiones acerca del problema de la transición al socialismo.* Managua: Editorial Nueva Nicaragua, 1986.

Harris, Richard. *Marxism, Socialism, and Democracy in Latin America.* Boulder: Westview, 1992.

Harris, Richard, and Carlos Vilas, eds. *Nicaragua: A Revolution under Siege.* London: Zed, 1985.

———. *La revolución en nicaragua: Liberación nacional, democracia popular y transformación economica.* Mexico City: ERA, 1985.

Harsmar, Mats. "Centralamerikanska Demokratiuppfattningar: En analys av demokratisynen hos PLN i Costa Rica, FSLN i Nicaragua och Nicaraguas vapnande opposition." Unpublished manuscript, Uppsala University (Sweden), 1988.

Hemisphere Institute. "Election Results." March 1990.

Herman, Edward S., and Frank Brodhead. *Demonstration Elections: U.S.-Staged Elections in the Dominican Republic, Vietnam, and El Salvador.* Boston: South End, 1984.

Hodges, Donald C. *Intellectual Foundations of the Nicaraguan Revolution.* Austin: University of Texas Press, 1986.

Hoffman, John. *The Gramscian Challenge: Coercion and Consent in Marxist Political Theory.* New York: Blackwell, 1986.

Hyden, Goran. *Beyond Ujamaa: Underdevelopment and an Uncaptured Peasantry.* Berkeley: University of California Press, 1979.

Invernizzi, Gabriele, Francis Pisani, and Jesús Ceberio. *Sandinistas: Entrevistas a Humberto Ortega Saavedra, Jaime Wheelock Román y Bayardo Arce Castano.* Managua: Editorial Vanguardia, 1986.

Jackson, Donald R., et al. "Project Evaluation: UNAG/ECODEPA/SCC." November 1989.

Jaquette, Jane S., ed. *The Women's Movement in Latin America: Feminism and the Transition to Democracy.* Boulder: Westview, 1991.

Kaimowitz, David, and Eugene Havens. "Nicaragua in Transition: Agriculture and the State." Paper presented at the Annual Meeting of the Latin American Studies Association, Washington, D.C., March 4–7, 1982.

Kampwirth, Karen. "The Mother of the Nicaraguans: Doña Violeta and the UNO's Gender Agenda." Paper presented at the Seventeenth International Congress of the Latin American Studies Association, Los Angeles, 1992.

Kornbluh, Peter. *Nicaragua: The Price of Intervention.* Washington, D.C.: Institute for Policy Studies, 1987.

Laclau, Ernesto. "Feudalism and Capitalism in Latin America." In *Promise of Development: Theories of Change in Latin America,* edited by Peter Klaren and Thomas Bossert. London: Thetford, 1985.

Laclau, Ernesto, and Chantal Mouffe. *Hegemony and Socialist Struggle: Towards a Radical Democratic Politics.* London: Verso, 1985.

Latin American Studies Association (LASA). "Report of the Latin American Studies Delegation to Observe the Nicaragua General Election of November 4, 1984." *LASA Forum* 15, no. 4 (Winter 1985).

"Ley Electoral." *Cuadernos de Pensamiento Propio* no. 7 (May 1984).

Lomba, Mariuca. "Futuro en femenino: Entrevista con Sofia Montenegro." *Pensamiento Propio* 7, no. 73 (1990).

Lowy, Michael. "La democracia no es un lujo." *Pensamiento Propio* no. 18 (1984).

———. "Las organizaciones de masas, el partido y el estado: La democracia en la transición al socialismo." Paper presented at the seminar "Los Problemas de la Transición en Pequenas Economias Perifericas." Managua, September 1984.

———. "Mass Organization, Party, and State: Democracy in the Transition to Socialism." In *Transition and Development: Problems in Third World Socialism,* edited by Richard R. Fagen, Carmen Diana Deere, and José Luís Coraggio. New York: Monthly Review Press/Center for the Study of the Americas, 1986.

Lozano, Lucrecia. *De Sandino al triunfo de la revolución.* Mexico City: Siglo 21 editores, 1985.

Luciak, Ilja A. "National Unity and Popular Hegemony: The Dialectics of Sandinista Agrarian Reform Policies, 1979–1986." *Journal of Latin American Studies* 19 (May 1987): 113–40.

———. "Participatory Development in Sandinista Nicaragua: Grass-roots Movements and Basic Needs." *Scandinavian Journal of Development Alternatives* 7, no. 4 (December 1988): 29–53.

———. "The Political Economy of Reconciliation in Nicaragua: Contras and Compas in a Quest for Peace and Land." Paper presented at the Seventeenth International Congress of the Latin American Studies Association, Los Angeles, 1992.

Luxemburg, Rosa. *The Russian Revolution and Leninism or Marxism?* Ann Arbor: University of Michigan Press, 1982.

Malloy, James M., and Mitchell A. Seligson, eds. *Authoritarians and Democrats: Regime Transition in Latin America.* Pittsburgh: University of Pittsburgh Press, 1987.

Marcus, Bruce, ed. *Nicaragua: The Sandinista People's Revolution.* New York: Pathfinder, 1985.

———, ed. *Sandinistas Speak: Speeches, Writings, and Interviews with the Leaders of Nicaragua's Revolution.* New York: Pathfinder, 1982.

Marx, Karl. "Critique of the Gotha Program." In *The Marx-Engels Reader,* edited by Robert C. Tucker. New York: Norton, 1978.

———. "Introduction to a Contribution to the Critique of Political Economy." In *The Marx-Engels Reader,* edited by Robert C. Tucker. New York: Norton, 1978.

Mason, T. David. "Women's Participation in Central American Revolutions: A Theoretical Perspective." *Comparative Political Studies* 25, no. 1 (April 1992): 63–89.

Migdal, Joel S. *Peasants, Politics, and Revolution.* Princeton: Princeton University Press, 1974.

Ministry of Agricultural Development and Agrarian Reform (MIDINRA). "Avance y perspectivas de la reforma agraria." Managua, 1986.

———. ECODEPA, MICOIN, MIPRES, PROAGRO. "Evaluación del ordenamiento de la red de distribución en el campo." Managua, 1987.

———. *Marco jurídico de la reforma agraria Nicaragüense.* Managua: MIDINRA, 1982.

Ministry of Planification (MIPLAN). *Plan de reactivación economica en beneficio del pueblo, 1980.* Managua: MIPLAN, 1980.

Molina, Javier. "Entrevista a Edgardo García, secretario general de la ATC, La Asociación de Trabajadores del Campo: A diez años de revolución." *Cuadernos de Sociología* nos. 9–10 (January–June 1989): 107–15.

Molyneux, Maxine. "Mobilization without Emancipation? Women's Interests,

State, and Revolution." In *Transition and Development: Problems in Third World Socialism,* edited by Richard R. Fagen, Carmen Diana Deere, and José Luis Coraggio. New York: Monthly Review Press, 1986.

———. "Women." In *Nicaragua: The First Five Years,* edited by Thomas W. Walker. New York: Praeger, 1985.

National Union of Farmers and Ranchers (UNAG). "Convocatoria y normas del proceso de base y propuesta de estrategia y lineas del II Congreso de UNAG." Managua, 1992.

———. "Estatutos de la Unión Nacional de Agricultores y Ganaderos U.N.A.G." Managua, 1992.

———. "Informe evaluativo." Managua, 1988.

———. "Informe evaluativo de la Junta Directiva al II Congreso de UNAG (1986–1992)." Managua, 1992.

———. "Informe trimestral para ASDI." Matagalpa, March 1989.

———. "Informe trimestral para ASDI." Matagalpa, August 1989.

———. *La Unión Nacional de Agricultores y Ganaderos de Nicaragua: La organización de los productores del campo Nicaragüense.* Managua: UNAG, 1984.

———. *Los pequeños y medianos productores.* Managua: UNAG, 1982.

———. "Main Report: First National Congress. Mimeograph." Managua, 1986.

———. "Recommendaciones para la reestructuración del sistema cooperativo de acopio y comercialización campesina (ECODEPA-T.C.)." Internal UNAG document. November 1989.

———. "Resolución final: Primera asamblea nacional." Mimeograph. Managua, 1982.

———. "Somos una fuerza: Consolidados de los resultados estadísticos del autodiagnostico cooperativo." Managua: UNAG, September 1989.

National Union of Farmers and Ranchers (UNAG)—Centro Cooperative Sueco (SCC). "Convenio general de cooperación entre la Unión National de Agricultores y Ganaderos (UNAG) y el Centro Cooperativo Sueco." Estocolmo, October 1987.

———. "Minutas de acuerdo de la revisión anual de apoyo del SCC a UNAG/ECODEPA." Managua, 1989.

National Union of Farmers and Ranchers (UNAG)—ECODEPA NACIONAL, Equipo de Capacitación. "Autodiagnostico de las empresas cooperativas de productores agropecuarios—Unidad V—organización cooperativa." Managua, September 1989.

National Union of Farmers and Ranchers (UNAG)—Sección de la Mujer. "Memorias: III Encuentro Nacional de Mujeres Campesinas." Managua, 1991.

———. "Plan de lucha de las mujeres organizadas en la UNAG." Managua, 1989.

Nicaraguan Institute of Social Security and Welfare (INSSBI). *Forty-Eight Months of Foreign Aggression.* Managua: INSSBI, 1984.

Núñez, Carlos. *El papel de las organizaciones de masas en el proceso revolucionario.* Managua: Secretaría Nacional de Propaganda y Educación Política (SENAPEP), 1980.

———. "Informe de la primera legislatura de la asamblea nacional." Mimeograph. Managua, 1985.

———. "Un parlamento nuevo que sea reflejo del poder del pueblo." *Barricada,* October 27, 1984.

Núñez, Daniel. "A 8 años: La Unión Nacional de Agricultores y Ganaderos." *Cuadernos de Sociología* 9–10 (January–June 1989): 95–105.

———. "The Farmers' View." *Envío* 10, no. 116 (January-February 1991): 18–22.

———. "If the Peasantry Did Not Trust the Revolution We Would Be Through." In *The Sandinista People's Revolution,* edited by Bruce Marcus. New York: Pathfinder, 1985.

———. "Intervención de Daniel Núñez." *Economía y Revolución* no. 1 (October 1987): 42–46.

———. "The Producers of This Country Support Our Revolutionary Government." In *The Sandinista People's Revolution,* edited by Bruce Marcus. New York: Pathfinder, 1985.

Núñez Soto, Orlando. *Transición y lucha de clases en Nicaragua 1979–1986.* Mexico City: Siglo 21 editores, 1987.

Ockerman, Torbjörn. "Impacto económico del proyecto UNAG-ECODEPA: Julio 1985–Junio 1989." Managua, September 1989.

O'Donnell, Guillermo, Philippe C. Schmitter, and Laurence Whitehead, eds. *Transitions from Authoritarian Rule: Comparative Perspectives.* Baltimore: Johns Hopkins University Press, 1986.

———. *Transitions from Authoritarian Rule: Latin America.* Baltimore: Johns Hopkins University Press, 1986.

O'Kane, Trish, and Raul Marin. "Militarismo: El reverso de la medalla." *Pensamiento Propio* 10, no. 88 (March 1992).

Ortega, Daniel. "Discurso pronunciado por el comandante de la revolución y miembro de la Junta de Gobierno de Reconstrucción Nacional, Daniel Ortega Saavedra." In *Association of Rural Workers (ATC), ATC Asamblea Nacional Constitutiva: Memorias.* Managua: DAP-SENAPEP, 1979.

Ortega, Humberto. *50 años de lucha sandinista.* Managua: Ministerio del Interior, n.d.

Ortega, Marvin. "Cooperativas y democracia en la revolución sandinista." Paper presented at Congreso Americanista, Amsterdam, 1988.

———. "Estudio de base de las tiendas campesinas." Managua, 1988.

Ortega, Marvin, and Peter Marchetti. "Campesinado, democracia y revolución sandinista: Notas sobre los limites y posibilidades de la democracia en una sociedad rural atrasada." Managua, 1986.

Paige, Jeffery. "Agrarian Policy and Agrarian Bourgeoisie in Revolutionary Nicaragua." University of Michigan, 1992.

———. "Cotton and Revolution in Nicaragua." In *States versus Markets in the World System*, edited by Peter Evans, Dietrich Rueschemeyer, and Evelyn Huber Stephens. Beverly Hills, Calif.: Sage, 1985.

Pastor, Robert. *Condemned to Repetition: The United States and Nicaragua.* Princeton: Princeton University Press, 1987.

Pérez, Paola, and I. Siu. "La mujer en la economía nicaragüense: cambios y desafíos." Paper presented at the Fifth Congress of ANICS, Managua.

Pérez, Paola, et al. "Síntesis de resultados de investigación mujer campesina y organización." *Instituto Nicaragüense de la Mujer.* Managua, 1989.

Pérez-Aleman, Paola. "Economic Crisis and Women in Nicaragua." In *Unequal Burden: Economic Crisis, Persistent Poverty, and Women's Work,* edited by Lourdes Benería and Shelley Feldman. Boulder: Westview, 1992.

Pérez-Stable, Marifeli. "Pluralism and Popular Power: An Interview with Sergio Ramírez Mercado." In *Nicaragua under Siege,* edited by Marlene Dixon. San Francisco: Synthesis, 1985.

Popkin, Samuel. *The Rational Peasant: The Political Economy of Rural Society in Vietnam.* Berkeley: University of California Press, 1979.

Porras, Alonso. "El movimiento cooperativo en Nicaragua." *Economía y Revolución* no. 1 (October 1987): 14–19.

Poulantzas, Nicos. *State-Power Socialism.* London: Verso, 1980.

Prevost, Gary. "The FSLN in Opposition." In *The 1990 Elections in Nicaragua and Their Aftermath,* edited by Vanessa Castro and Gary Prevost. Lanham, Md.: Rowman and Littlefield, 1992.

Przeworski, Adam. *Democracy and the Market: Political and Economic Reforms in Eastern Europe and Latin America.* Cambridge: Cambridge University Press, 1991.

Queiser Morales, Waltraud, and Harry Vanden. "Relations with the Non-aligned Movement." In *Nicaragua: The First Five Years,* edited by Thomas W. Walker. New York: Praeger, 1985.

Ramírez, Sergio. *La marca del Zorro: Hazañas del Comandante Francisco Rivera Quintero Contadas a Sergio Ramírez.* Managua: Editorial Nueva Nicaragua, 1989.

Ramírez-Horton, Susan E. "The Role of Women in the Nicaraguan Revolution." In *Nicaragua in Revolution,* edited by Thomas A. Walker. New York: Praeger, 1982.

Randall, Margaret. *Gathering Rage: The Failure of Twentieth-Century Revolutions to Develop a Feminist Agenda.* New York: Monthly Review Press, 1992.

"Reforma a la ley de la reforma agraria." *La Gaceta: Diario Oficial* no. 8 (January 13, 1986).

Ruchwarger, Gary. "Las organizaciones de masas sandinistas y el proceso revolucionario." In *La revolución en Nicaragua: liberación nacional, democracia
popular y transformación economica,* edited by Richard Harris and Carlos
Vilas. Mexico City: ERA, 1985.

———. *People in Power: Forging a Grassroots Democracy in Nicaragua.* South
Hadley, Mass.: Bergin and Garvey, 1987.

———. "The Sandinista Mass Organizations and the Revolutionary Process." In
Nicaragua: A Revolution under Siege, edited by Richard Harris and Carlos
Vilas. London: Zed, 1985.

———. *Struggling for Survival: Workers, Women, and Class on a Nicaraguan
State Farm.* Boulder: Westview, 1989.

Sanabria, Octavio, and Elvyra Sanabria. *Nicaragua: Diagnostico de una traición.*
Barcelona: Plaza and Janes Editores, 1986.

Sandinista National Liberation Front (FSLN). "Analysis de la coyuntura y tareas
de la revolución popular sandinista (documento de las 72 horas)." In
Nicaragua: Diagnostico de una traición, edited by Octavio Sanabria and
Elvyra Sanabria. Barcelona: Plaza and Janes Editores, 1986.

———. "Declaración del FSLN sobre la democracia." *Barricada,* August 24,
1980.

———. *Del FSLN a los pueblos del mundo: Informe sobre la coyuntura, tenden-
cias guerra popular prolongada, proletaria, insurrecional.* Barcelona: Ediciones Conosur, 1979.

———."El FSLN y la mujer en la revolución popular sandinista." *Revolución y
Desarrollo* no. 5 (July 1989): 144–50.

———. *Nicaragua: La estrategia de la victoria.* Mexico City: Editorial Nuestro
Tiempo, 1983.

———. *Programa histórico del FSLN.* Managua: Departamento de Propaganda
y Educación Política del FSLN, 1984.

"Sandinistas, Foes Seek Remedies for Ailing Economy." *Miami Herald,* February
21, 1989.

Scott, James C. *The Moral Economy of the Peasant: Rebellion and Subsistence in
Southeast Asia.* New Haven: Yale University Press, 1976.

———. *Weapons of the Weak: Everyday Forms of Peasant Resistance.* New
Haven: Yale University Press, 1985.

Selser, Gregorio. *Sandino, general de hombres libres.* Ciudad Universitaria
Rodrigo Facio, Costa Rica: EDUCA, 1979.

Serra, Luis. *El movimiento campesino: Su participación politica durante la revolución sandinista 1979–1989.* Managua: Universidad Centroamericana,
1991.

———. "The Grass-roots Organizations." In *Nicaragua: The First Five Years,*
edited by Thomas W. Walker. New York: Praeger, 1985.

———. "Participación política y organizaciones populares en la revolución sandinista." Managua: ITZTANI, 1989.

————. "The Sandinista Mass Organizations." In *Nicaragua in Revolution*, edited by Thomas W. Walker. New York: Praeger, 1982.

Serra, Luis, and Veronica Frenkel. "The Peasantry and Development in Nicaragua." Managua, 1988.

Sherman, Howard J. *Foundations of Radical Political Economy*. Armonk, N.Y.: Sharpe, 1987.

Spalding, Rose J. "Capitalists and Revolution: State-Private Sector Relations in Revolutionary Nicaragua (1979–1990)." Paper presented at the Sixteenth International Congress of the Latin American Studies Association, Washington, D.C., April 4–6, 1991.

————. "State-Private Sector Relations in Nicaragua: The Somoza Era." Paper presented at the Midwest Latin American Studies Association Meeting, Chicago, November 6–7, 1987.

————, ed. *The Political Economy of Revolutionary Nicaragua*. Winchester, Mass.: Allen and Unwin, 1987.

Stepan, Alfred. "Paths toward Redemocratization: Theoretical and Comparative Considerations." In *Transitions from Authoritarian Rule: Comparative Perspectives*, edited by Guillermo O'Donnell, Philippe C. Schmitter, and Laurence Whitehead. Baltimore: Johns Hopkins University Press, 1986.

Stoltenberg, Thorvald. "Report to Willy Brandt, President of the Socialist International, on the Nicaraguan Election, November 4, 1984." Mimeograph. London, 1984.

Superior Council of Private Enterprise (COSEP). "Carta a Daniel Ortega, coordinador de la Junta de Gobierno de Reconstrucción Nacional, 19 de Octubre, 1981." Mimeograph. Managua, 1981.

Swedish Cooperative Center (SCC). "Nicaragua: Programa de apoyo a UNAG y ECODEPA." Managua, 1987.

Swedish International Development Authority (SIDA). "Information om det Svenska Utvecklingssamarbetet med Nicaragua." Managua, 1987.

Thome, Joseph, and Kaimowitz, David. "Agrarian Reform." In *Nicaragua: The First Five Years*, edited by Thomas W. Walker. New York: Praeger, 1985.

Tirado, Víctor. "El pensamiento político de Carlos Fonseca." In Departamento de Propaganda y Educación Política del FSLN (DEPEP), *Carlos Fonseca: Siempre*. Managua: Centro de Publicaciones Sílvio Mayorga, 1982.

————. "Movimiento sindical y organizaciones de masas en la revolución popular sandinista." *Cuadernos de Sociología* no. 9–10 (January–June 1989).

Tucker, Robert C., ed. *The Marx-Engels Reader*. New York: Norton, 1978.

Vanden, Harry E., and Gary Prevost. *Democracy and Socialism in Sandinista Nicaragua*. Boulder: Rienner, 1993.

Vargas, Oscar R. "La mujer en la crisis economica." *Barricada*, July 1992.

Vilas, Carlos M. "After the Revolution: Democratization and Social Change in Central America." In *The Socialist Option in Central America: Two Reassess-*

ments, edited by Shafik Jorge Handal and Carlos M. Vilas. New York: Monthly Review Press, 1993.

———. "Family Affairs: Class, Lineage, and Politics in Contemporary Nicaragua." *Journal of Latin American Studies* 24, no. 2 (May 1992): 309–41.

———. *The Sandinista Revolution: National Liberation and Social Transformation in Central America.* New York: Monthly Review Press, 1986.

———. *Transición desde el subdesarrollo: Revolución y reforma en la periferia.* Caracas: Editorial Nueva Sociedad, 1989.

———. "What Went Wrong." *NACLA* 24, no. 1 (June 1990): 10–18.

Walker, Thomas. *Nicaragua: The Land of Sandino.* Boulder: Westview, 1981.

———, ed. *Reagan versus the Sandinistas.* Boulder: Westview, 1987.

———, ed. *Revolution and Counterrevolution in Nicaragua.* Boulder: Westview, 1991.

———, ed. *Nicaragua in Revolution.* New York: Praeger, 1982.

———, ed. *Nicaragua: The First Five Years.* New York: Praeger, 1985.

Weber, Henri. *Nicaragua: Den Sandinistiska Revolutionen.* Stockholm: Bokforlaget Roda Rummet, 1983.

Wedin, Ake. *Nicaragua: Cambio de viento.* Stockholm: Institute for Latin American Studies, 1983.

Weeks, John. *The Economies of Central America.* New York: Holmes and Meier, 1985.

Wheelock, Jaime. "Discurso pronunciado por el comandante de la revolución y vice-ministro de la reforma agraria, Jaime Wheelock." In *Association of Rural Workers (ATC), ATC Asamblea Nacional Constitutiva: Memorias.* Managua: DAP-SENAPEP, 1979.

———. *Entre la crisis y la agresión: La reforma agraria sandinista.* Managua: Editorial Nueva Nicaragua, 1985.

———. *Imperialismo y dictadura.* Havana: Editorial de Ciencias Sociales, 1980.

Wickham-Crowley, Timothy P. *Guerrillas and Revolution in Latin America: A Comparative Study of Insurgents and Regimes since 1956.* Princeton: Princeton University Press, 1992.

Wiggins, Steve. "Informe preliminar: La ECODEPA—su organización, administración y rentabilidad." Managua, September 1989.

Williams, Philip. "Dual Transitions from Authoritarian Rule: Popular and Electoral Democracy in Nicaragua." *Comparative Politics* 26, no. 2 (January 1994): 169–85.

Wolf, Eric R. *Peasant Wars of the Twentieth Century.* New York: Harper and Row, 1969.

Index